Revisiting the European Union as Empire

The European Union's stalled expansion, the Euro deficit and emerging crises of economic and political sovereignty in Greece, Italy and Spain have significantly altered the image of the EU as a model of progressive civilization. However, despite recent events the EU maintains its international image as the paragon of European politics and global governance.

This book unites leading scholars on Europe and empire to revisit the view of the European Union as an 'imperial' power. It offers a reappraisal of the EU as empire in response to geopolitical and economic developments since 2007 and asks if the policies, practices and priorities of the Union exhibit characteristics of a modern empire.

This text will be of key interest to students and scholars of the EU, European studies, history, sociology, international relations and economics.

Hartmut Behr is professor of international politics at Newcastle University, UK.

Yannis A. Stivachtis is associate professor of political science at Virginia Polytechnic Institute and State University, USA.

Critical European Studies
Edited by Hartmut Behr, *University of Newcastle, UK* and Yannis A. Stivachtis, *Virginia Tech, USA*

1 **Mapping European Empire**
Tabulae Imperii Europaei
Russell Foster

2 **Revisiting the European Union as Empire**
Edited by Hartmut Behr and Yannis A. Stivachtis

Revisiting the European Union as Empire

Edited by Hartmut Behr and
Yannis A. Stivachtis

Routledge
Taylor & Francis Group
LONDON AND NEW YORK

First published 2016 by Routledge

2 Park Square, Milton Park, Abingdon, Oxon OX14 4RN
711 Third Avenue, New York, NY 10017

Routledge is an imprint of the Taylor & Francis Group, an informa business

First issued in paperback 2017

British Library Cataloguing in Publication Data
A catalogue record for this book is available from the British Library

Library of Congress Cataloging-in-Publication Data
A catalog record for this book has been requested

ISBN: 978-1-138-81819-4 (hbk)
ISBN: 978-1-138-71676-6 (pbk)

Typeset in Times New Roman
by Apex CoVantage, LLC

Contents

Notes on contributors

Editors

Hartmut Behr is Professor of International Politics at Newcastle University (UK). His work includes studies in political theory, international relations theory and sociology of knowledge of the discipline, difference and "otherness", and critical European studies. His most recent books include: *A History of International Political Theory: Ontologies of the International* (2010): *Hans J. Morgenthau: The Concept of the Political* (2012, together with Felix Roesch); and *Politics of Difference* (2014). He is currently working on a new monograph called *Conditions of Critique: On humane and responsible politics*. He is Principal Investigator of the Leverhulme-funded research network on "Critical Theory Meets Classical Realism."

Yannis A. Stivachtis is Associate Professor of Political Science at Virginia Tech. His most recent publications include: *Human and State (In)Security in a Globalized World* (2011); *Europe after Enlargement* (2014, with Mark Webber); *The European Union and Peace-building* (2013, with Max Stephenson and Laura Zanotti); *EUrope and the World* (2012); and *The Road to EU Membership: The Economic Transformation of Turkey* (2011, with Selen Sarisoy Guerin). He is currently working on a monograph entitled *European Union and Global Order*. He serves as Chair of the English School section of the International Studies Association (ISA); Chair of the Social Sciences Research Division and Head of the Politics & International Affairs Research Unit of ATINER (Athens Institute of Education and Research); and Senior Advisor of RIEAS (Research Institute for European & American Studies).

Contributors

József Böröcz is Professor of Sociology at Rutgers, The State University of New Jersey. He was founding director (1995–2007) of the Institute for Hungarian Studies at Rutgers. He is author of the award-winning book *The European Union and Global Social Change: A Critical Geopolitical Economic Analysis* (Routledge 2009), and co-editor of *Empire's New Clothes: Unveiling EU-Enlargement* (Central Europe Review e-book 2000). His areas of research interest include the historical sociology of supra-state formation, (post-)state-socialisms and the new economic and moral geopolitics of the global power shift.

Nora Fisher Onar, a Transatlantic Academy Fellow of the German Marshall Fund in Washington, DC, is a research associate of the Centre for International Studies at the University of Oxford. She has published numerous articles and book chapters in academic and policy fora. She received her doctorate in international relations from the University of Oxford and holds master's and undergraduate degrees from Johns Hopkins SAIS and Georgetown University, respectively. Her monograph, *Acts of State: Politics, Performance, and the Eastern Questions(s)* proposes a novel theoretical prism onto the relationship between history, memory and politics via the drama of Turkey and its region's past and present quandaries.

Russell Foster read History at Corpus Christi College, Cambridge, and both International Relations and Human Geography at Newcastle University. His PhD, awarded in 2013, investigates the EU as symbolic empire. In 2012 he was elected a Fellow of the Royal Geographical Society and in 2013 was ESRC Visting Scholar at Virginia Tech. Recent publications include *Tabulae Imperii Europeai: Mapping European Empire* (2015); *The Crisis of the Twenty-First Century: Empire in the Age of Austerity* (with Matthew Johnson, 2014); and 'Tabula Imperii Europae: A Cartographic Approach to the Current Debate on the European Union as Empire,' *Geopolitics* 18(2), 2013. He is currently Marie-Curie Fellow in the Department of European Studies, University of Amsterdam, working on an EU-funded project to redesign the Union's symbols.

Aylin Güney is Professor of International Relations at Yasar University (Izmir, Turkey) and holds the Jean Monnet Chair for International Relations and European Studies granted by the European Commission. She currently serves as the Head of the Department of International Relations and Vice-Dean of the Faculty of Economics and Administrative Sciences. She has published articles in journals such as *Turkish Studies, Armed Forces and Society, Journal of Balkan and Near Eastern Studies, South European Society and Politics*, and *Middle Eastern Studies* as well as several book chapters. Her main areas of interest are European Integration, EU Enlargement, civil–military relations in Turkey, the Cyprus issue and Turkish–American Relations.

Kalypso Nicolaidis is Professor of International Relations and Director of the Center for International Studies at the University of Oxford. She was previously associate professor at Harvard University's Kennedy School of Government. She is chair of Southeastern European Studies at Oxford and Council member of the European Council of Foreign Relations. In 2008–2010, she was a member of the Gonzales reflection group on the future of Europe 2030, set up by the European Council. She also served as advisor on European affairs to the Greek, Dutch and UK governments; the European Parliament; the European Commission; OECD and UNCTAD. Her work has been published in numerous journals, including *Foreign Affairs, Foreign Policy, The Journal of Common Market Studies, Journal of European Public Policy* and *International Organization*. Her last works are: 'Special Issue on Normative Power Europe' (in the journal *Conflict and Cooperation*) and *European Stories: Intellectual Debates on Europe in National Context* (OUP 2010). She received her PhD from Harvard in 1993.

Robert Phillipson is Professor Emeritus (formerly Research Professor) at Copenhagen Business School's Department of English. He is perhaps best known for writing *Linguistic Imperialism and English-Only Europe?: Challenging Language Policy*. He received his undergraduate degree from Cambridge University and his PhD from the University of Amsterdam. His interests include language pedagogy, language policy and linguistic human rights. On 21 February 2010, Phillipson was awarded the UNESCO Linguapax Prize along with Miquel Siguan i Soler.

Georgeta Pourchot, a former member of the Romanian Parliament, is the Director the Online MA in Political Science (OLMA) at Virginia Tech as well as of Two Capitals, Two Masters (a dual degree in partnership with the University of Kent, Brussels). She is an Adjunct Fellow with the Center for Strategic and International Studies (CSIS). She has worked as deputy director for the International Action Commissions Program at the Center for Strategic and International Studies in Washington, DC. She earned an MA in political science from Virginia Tech and a PhD in international studies from Old Dominion University. Her research interests include Central Europe, Russia and Central Asia, US foreign policy, security and democratization studies, and the English School of International Relations. She is the author of *Eurasia Rising: Democracy and Independence in the Post-Soviet Space* (Praeger 2008).

Jan Zielonka is Professor of European Politics at the University of Oxford and Ralf Dahrendorf Professorial Fellow at St Antony's College. His book publications include *Europe as Empire: The Nature of the Enlarged European Union* (OUP 2006); *Europe Unbound: Enlarging and Reshaping the Boundaries of the European Union* (Routledge 2002); *Democratic Consolidation in Eastern Europe, Vol. 1 & 2* (OUP 2001); *Explaining Euro-Paralysis: Why Europe Is Unable to Act in International Politics* (Macmillan 1998); and *Political Ideas in Contemporary Poland* (Avebury 1989). He studied law at the University of Wroclaw, Poland, and Political Science at the University of Warsaw, where he received his PhD in 1981. In January 1996 he was appointed professor of political science at the European University Institute in Florence (Joint Chair in European Studies at the Robert Schuman Centre for Advanced Studies and the Department of Political and Social Sciences).

European Union

An empire in new clothes?

Hartmut Behr and Yannis A. Stivachtis

Introduction

The political and academic discourse(s) of whether or not the European Union (EU) can be understood as a form of empire are, first, controversial and, second, encounter widely indignant disapproval by those who 'like' the EU as well as by orthodox EU scholarship. From such perspectives, the EU is understood as a 'normative', that is, good, power that spreads and conducts politics guided by human rights, democracy, and free markets, while 'empire' is understood as something evil, martial, and aggressive (amongst others, Manners, 2002; Telo, 2006; Whitman, 1998). This somewhat simplified dichotomy is in desperate need of clarification, and in this clarification exists the approach of this book and its attempt to assemble some of the most important contributors to the first wave of the 'EU-as-empire-discourse' to revisit their arguments after some 10 years.

In order to summarize the main features of this discourse, now and then: in the context of the 2004 Eastern enlargement, the question arose among some political scientists, historians, and sociologists of whether the EU is indeed something sui generis as the orthodox political and academic discourse widely held (see for the first, the first wave of 'EU-as-empire-discourse', for instance: Behr, 2007; Boeroecz, 2001; Diez, 1999; Engelbrekt, 2002; Hansen, 2002; Kovacs, 2001; Waever, 1997; Beck/Grande, 2007; Zielonka, 2006, Philipson, 2002; for the latter, see, for example: Phelan, 2012; Eichengreen, 2008). This questioning of the sui generis argument initiated comparative perspectives into European and global history that resulted in mainly the three observations of (1) politics of conditionality by the EU (Stivachtis, 2008; Grabbe, 2002; Schimmelpfennig, 2004; Anastasakis and Bechev, 2003); (2) a geopolitical centre–periphery model in the EU characterized by asymmetric relations of wealth, power, and rights (Bartolini, 2005; Tunander et al., 1997; Copus, 2001; Behr, 2007); and (3) a discourse of and on European civilization in relation to the EU as global actor (Mitzen, 2006; European Commission, 2014; Merlingen, 2007). Politics of conditionality, geopolitics of centre–periphery, and civilizational discourse resemble historically, whether one likes or not, features that are likewise evinced by what is noncontroversially termed empire (historically see Benton, 2002; Eisenstadt, 1963; Sinopoli, 1994). Thus, the question seems to be indeed not whether the EU shows indicators that are (historically also) typical for empire, but, first, *what kind of empire* is the EU and, second, what at all *is* empire more fully and conceptually understood. The chapters collected here, approach and provide different perspectives and answers to these two questions. In doing so, and in having done so some 10 years ago in first attempts, these undertakings stem *not* from some dislike of the EU, but rather from disquiet and some dissatisfaction with the Union, carried by the wish to guard and rescue a worthwhile idea of supranational order. The 'EU-as-empire-discourse' was thus born from empathy (but concern) with the Union and was looking *beyond* approaches as they are established in orthodox EU scholarship but well established in other social sciences (such as discourse analysis, iconographic analysis, historiographical analysis, linguistic analysis, etc.).

One more observation may be added here that is, too, addressed in some of the following chapters: as this book and its chapters are written in the context and under the influences of modern, present-day language structures and semantics (in this case, English), they all suffer from one particular shortcoming in relation to their epistemologies as epistemology is influenced by language and by semantically generated and (re)inforced perceptions (on the relation between language and epistemology, see Shapiro, 1992; Marcuse, 1964; Chomsky, 1968; Danto, 1969; Nagel, 1969). This epistemological limitation determines the above mentioned disapproval of the 'EU-as-empire-discourse' by orthodox EU scholarship and politics. To be more precise: there was some igniting thought in José Manuel Baroso when he labeled the EU a 'non-imperial empire', but unfortunately he backpedaled very quickly. However, the idea he came from was correct. What we are talking about here, relates to a widely held and linguistically reasoned incapability to think of 'empire' other than as something aggressive, evil, and martial. This limitation is due to an age-long process of narrowing down the width that was comprised by the Latin '*imperium*' that stands at the roots of our English 'empire'. This process of narrowing-down has resulted in that we nowadays do not even have an adjective of 'empire' other than 'imperial' which inevitably sounds like, and is historically linked with, Chinese, Ottoman, British, Spanish, etc. expansion and 18th and 19th century warfare. 'Empire' thus appears as a political order that we cannot talk about other than dismissively. One aspect of the 'EU-as-empire-discourse' is hence to (re)open our imagination and to (re)gain a language that is more appropriate to empirical features and political experience rather than normatively pejorative (however, probably without being aware of it).

Such a more appropriate language, and subsequently political imagination and approaches, have not only to take into account the width of Latin '*imperium*' (see Champion, 2004; Erskine, 2010; Folz, 1969; Foster, 2015), but further to this the Ciceronian twin concept of '*patrocinium*' (see for Cicero his *De re publica, De officiis*, and *De legibus*). Without delving here on linguistic nuances and genealogies, it might suffice to briefly mention the breadth of both '*imperium*' and '*patrocinium*' (for the latter we even have no noun in modern English) in order to see what we as moderns have lost in terms of political imagination (why most of us are inclined to construe 'empire' – as the word we are left with – inevitably as something 'bad'). Both the Latin nouns of '*imperium*' and '*patrocinium*' encompass meanings such as 'order', 'power', 'authority', 'government', 'rule', 'mandate', 'tenure', 'patronage', 'responsibility', and 'protectorate'. Mentioning this, does not necessarily intend to promote the argument that 'empire' would be something 'good', but rather that it is a valuable *analytical* concept for the study of contemporary politics that is not to be dismissed due to normative likes and dislikes that appear indeed to be caused by language/epistemological limitations.

The empire discourse

The empire discourse is primarily related to the role of the United States in post–World War II international affairs and especially the U.S.'s international status following the end of the Cold War. However, the EU's eastward enlargement and its efforts to play a more active role in world affairs in the post–Cold War era have brought the empire discourse into EU studies. In this respect, the debate has been about the nature of EU power and its strategy to achieve its foreign and security policy objectives.

The United States as 'Empire'

The modern, 20th- and 21st-century discourse on empire initially gained prominence in relation to the U.S. involvement in world politics. Specifically, the idea of the U.S. as an empire emerged after the end of WWII as the United States and the Soviet Union quickly became superpowers. After the fall of the Soviet Union, the U.S. became the world's only superpower, with its military posts around the world declaring to provide security for allies and operating as it wished without constraints of other powers. Its hegemony encouraged the U.S. to act like an empire, imposing its views and constituting security cordons around the world (Craig, 2004). In addition, it has been claimed that the U.S. engaged in new imperialist ventures not only militarily but also economically. Consequently, it has been argued that the U.S. is the sole example of geopolitical hegemony since the fall of the Roman Empire in that it can set conditions for peace and security of the world, has predominance in world economy, and manages security organizations, such as NATO (O'Brien and Clesse, 2002).

Characterizing some aspects of U.S. foreign policy and international behavior as 'American empire' is controversial but not uncommon. Chalmers Johnson (2000) posits that the idea of American exceptionalism impairs popular recognition of American imperial conduct since it has governed other countries via surrogates. These surrogates were domestically weak, right-wing governments that would collapse without American support. Sidney Lens and Howard Zinn (2003) have argued that from its inception, the U.S. has used every means available to dominate other nations. Niall Ferguson (2004; 2005) argues that in both military and economic terms, the U.S. is nothing short of the most powerful empire in history. Indeed, as Christopher Gray points out, the U.S. has about 5 per cent of the world's population but spends almost 50 per cent of all military budgets (Gray, 2003, 7). For the moment, there is no credible counterbalancing power or combination of powers that can match it. The U.S. military divides the world into geographical commands that extend across various world regions and the U.S. military circles the globe with permanent military bases and weapons caches. It is worth noting that even before the occupation of Iraq, the U.S. had over 750 military bases in more than 130 countries and this number may be greater today (Gray, 2003, 7).

However, as Robert Jackson and Philip Towle (2006, 22) indicate, Americans tend to regard themselves as reluctant imperialists. Although their presidents have not hesitated to pronounce global ambitions and enact policies of extraterritorial significance, the fact remains that for the Americans the U.S. is not an empire and if by some chance it is, then, it is one of a kind. Some contend that empire status is vital to prevent evil (terrorism and tyranny) in the world (Simes, 2003). As such they contend that the American empire is benevolent and their only fear is that it may become weak, overstretched or collapse. For example, Ferguson believes that the U.S. has an unparalleled ability and opportunity to take the role of positive global leadership and shape the world around its values of free markets, the rule of law, and representative government (Ferguson, 2004). He argues that the U.S. is a 'liberal' form of empire, which can benefit all peoples by enhancing prosperity and democracy, and by creating a kind of benevolent, negotiated global order upholding the rules of international law and coercing deviants with military power. In other words, Ferguson believes that the current international order needs America's enlightened leadership. Robert Kaplan (2005) also adopts the positive empire thesis and emphasizes the role that the U.S. troops play in carrying American foreign policy on almost every continent. Michael Mandelbaum does not utilize the concept of 'empire', but he argues that he contends that the U.S. is indispensable as a benign world government (Mandelbaum, 2005). For Mandelbaum, the U.S. provides world government through world-wide military deployments and rules for the global economy.

Some critical scholars, such as Michael Mann and Benjamin Barber take these arguments about the U.S. as empire further. They share the view that any empire built on military domination will eventually fail (Mann, 2003; Barber, 2003). Andrew Bacevich has also argued that the U.S. constitutes an 'informal' empire, not colonial in policy, but still richly equipped with imperial paraphernalia such as troops, ships, planes, bases, proconsuls, and local collaborators (Bacevich, 2002) and has attacked the seduction of America into military adventures (Bacevich, 2005). Following the same line of argumentation, Chalmers Johnson (2000 and 2004) suggests that the American empire is not liberal but military. In his 2000 book, Johnson predicted that U.S. interventionism abroad would create the climate for catastrophic terrorist attacks at home, while in his 2004 book he warned that the rampant militarism could spell the end of American constitutional democracy. His argument stems from the notion that U.S. foreign policy revolves around a seemingly endless quest to accumulate military bases overseas. Military power has consolidated these bases in a new form of global and imperial rule. Johnson claims that because threats to homeland security are usually exaggerated, not only the U.S. becomes more and more militarized but also the Department of Defense far exceeds the Department of State in terms of influence. Consequently, regional military commanders have more power than ambassadors and their influence is growing as they oversee private military companies whom the U.S. both arms and trains to defend the interests of the American empire. Johnson holds that the large defense budget and the massive troop deployments overseas starve domestic needs in order to feed the colonial machine. Johnson concludes that 9/11 provided the U.S. with an excuse to expand the U.S. military, to abandon its alliance partners, treaties and laws, and to launch its imperial rule.

David Harvey (2003) argues that although the U.S. does not fit the old model of an imperial nation, it nonetheless has shown such predilections for some time. Harvey cites the U.S.'s ruthlessness in pressing global hegemony since the 1800s, including the internment of Japanese in World War II and the recent Patriot and Homeland Security Acts. He examines the symbiotic and parasitic relationship between Wall Street, the U.S. Treasury, and the International Monetary Fund as he explores how the U.S. has used an array of tactics, from trade embargoes to military force, to gain geopolitical influence. Finally, critics of the U.S. as empire focus on the negative aspects of a colossus determined and able to get its way in the world (Simes, 2003; Todd, 2003).

The European Union as 'Empire'

There is a general consensus that the EU represents a new kind of power in international politics (Diez, 2005; Manners, 2002; Whitman, 1998) and that it plays an ever increasing role in world affairs (Elgstrom and Smith, 2006; Orbie, 2008). The increasingly important role of the EU in world affairs is reflected in the development of the European Foreign and Security Policy (EFSP) (Kirchner and Sperling, 2007). The range of instruments at the EU's disposal continues to increase in size and scope. The use of these instruments is guided by the ambitious objectives set out in the European Security Strategy (ESS) that was adopted in December of 2003 and which for the first time established principles and set clear objectives for advancing the EU's security interests based on the EU's core values. The *Report on the Implementation of the European Security Strategy* that was presented in December of 2008 reinforced the 2003 European Security Strategy (EC, 2008, 1).

European Union's conceptualization of global order

On 12 October 2012, the EU was awarded the Nobel Peace Prize. José Manuel Barroso, President of the European Commission, and Herman Van Rompuy, President of the European Council, jointly offered a press release following acceptance of the award, asserting that "over the last sixty years, the European Union has reunified a continent split by the Cold War around values of respect for human dignity, freedom, democracy, equality, the rule of law and respect for human rights." The presidents explicitly illustrated the EU's conceptualization of global order as they elaborated:

> These are also the values that the European Union promotes to make the world a better place for all. The European Union will continue to promote peace and security in the countries close to us and the world at large.
>
> (EC, 2012b)

In other words, the EU has sought to conceptualize global order in terms of the spread and adoption of its own values and norms.

However, it has not been until the Maastricht Treaty in 1991 that the EU specified its foreign policy objectives, which included, among other things the promotion of democracy and the rule of law and human rights (European Commission, 2012a). The Draft Constitutional Treaty proclaimed that the EU's policies should aim at "preserving peace, preventing conflicts and strengthening international security" and that in doing so, the EU would be guided by the principles that inspired its own creation and evolution and which are rooted in traditions of "democracy, human rights, fundamental freedoms and the rule of law" (Tocci, 2007, 7). These principles were reaffirmed in the Lisbon Treaty.

In 2003 then, the EU published its Security Strategy, which was slightly revised and updated in 2008 (European Commission, 2003). In these documents, the EU identified threats to international peace and security and indicated the ways in which it sought to address these threats. Examining the ESS, one can easily observe that the EU has taken a comprehensive approach to security where "the internal and external aspects of security are indissolubly linked" (European Commission, 2003, 2) and where security is regarded as a precondition of development (European Commission, 2003, 2). According to the ESS, the EU perceives non-domestic threats in two overarching forms. Menaces stemming from states in the EU's immediate and nearby neighborhood are seen as peripheral threats, while the second class of threats is much broader, emerging from states outside of the EU's neighborhood area.

One of the most significant security threats identified in the ESS is bad governance – reflected in corruption, abuse of power, weak or collapsed institutions and lack of accountability (European Commission, 2003, 4). Therefore, spreading good governance, supporting social and political reform, dealing with corruption and the abuse of power, establishing rule of law and protecting human rights are viewed by the EU as the best means for increasing European security. Because state failure is assumed to lead to organized crime and/or terrorism, the EU uses a variety of tools, including political and economic conditionality, to ensure the establishment of well-governed democratic states.

The two fundamental pillars of the ESS are: building security in the EU's neighborhood and promoting an international order based on effective multilateralism (European Commission, 2003, 9). The EU's security strategy is rather explicit in defining the neighborhood "as a key geographical priority of EU external action . . ." (European Commission, 2003, 9). Nathalie Tocci draws attention to the fact that the European Neighborhood Policy (ENP) is unequivocally directed at promoting the EU's values "as a means to spread stability, security and prosperity in the southern and eastern neighbourhoods . . . and to strengthen the EU's contribution to the solution of regional conflicts" (Tocci, 2007, 7).

The development of well-functioning international institutions and a rule-based international order are identified as fundamental EU objectives. However, 'effective multilateralism' is to be based on a set of principles, values and norms that reflect those of the European Union. For example, the ESS notes that "the quality of international society depends on the quality of the governments that are its foundation" (European Commission, 2003, 10). As a result, the best protection for EU's security is a world of well-governed democratic states. Trade and development policies are seen as powerful tools for promoting democratic reforms. Contributing to better governance through assistance programs, conditionality and targeted trade measures remains an important feature in EU's policy.

But what kind of capabilities are available to the EU to achieve these objectives? This discussion is associated with the question of the EU's identity as a 'civilian', 'military', and 'normative power'.

The idea that the EU could become a power that does not rely primarily on military but on civilian means was first formulated by Francois Duchene (1973). 'Civilian power' has been defined as involving three key features: the centrality of economic power to achieve political goals; the primacy of diplomatic cooperation to solve international problems; and the willingness to use legally binding supranational institutions to achieve international progress (Twitchett, 1976, 1–2). However, the linkage between the EU as 'empire' and EU as a 'civilian power' is better reflected in Hans Maull's definition of a civilian power as a state "whose conception of its foreign policy role and behavior is bound to particular aims, values, principles, as well as forms of influence and instruments of power in the name of a civilization of international relations" (Maull, 1990, 92–3).

On 9 May 2000, to celebrate the 50th anniversary of the Schuman Declaration, the EU distributed publicity material entitled '50 Years of Solidarity, Prosperity and Peace' (European Commission, n.d.). According to this material, the EU saw itself as representing a 'civilian power'. The status of the EU as a global civilian power was also pronounced by Romano Prodi (2000, 3) who stated that "we must aim to become a global civil power at the service of sustainable global development. After all, only by ensuring sustainable global development can Europe guarantee its own strategic security." However, the inability of the EU to deal with the Yugoslav crisis made several scholars and practitioners argue about the need of the EU to develop and deploy its military power to achieve its foreign and security policy goals.

The Treaty on European Union (TEU), signed in 1991, signaled the intent of the EU Member States to move beyond a 'civilian power Europe' and to develop a defense dimension to the international identity of the Union (Whitman, 1998, 135–6). According to Ian Manners (2002, 237), the move from the single structure of the EC to the three-pillar structure of the EU was part of a "fundamental shift from civilian to military power, assuming that the development of a common foreign and security policy was eventually to include defense policy".

The trend towards 'military power Europe' can most clearly be found in the European Security and Defense Policy (ESDP) agreed upon at the June 1999 Cologne European Council which committed the EU to having a 60,000-person rapid reaction force (RRF) (Stivachtis, 2004 and 2005). With the Treaty of Lisbon, ESDP came under the auspices of EFSP. This militarization of the EU that has been highlighted by the Union's involvement in a number of international military operations is not without criticism. For example, it has been argued that it weakens the EU's 'distinct profile' of having a civilian international identity (Zielonka, 1998, 229) or that it promotes an image of the EU as a potential hegemonic and imperial power.

Richard Rosecrance (1998, 22) has argued that "Europe's attainment is normative rather than empirical" and that "it is perhaps a paradox to note that the continent which once ruled the world through the physical impositions of imperialism is now coming to set world standards in normative terms." Elements of this normative power can also be found in the critical perspective of Johann Galtung, who argues that ideological power is "powerful because the power sender's ideas penetrate and shape the will of the power recipient's will through the media of culture" (Galtung, 1973, 33).

Manners sought to illustrate that the EU should be best conceived as a 'normative power Europe'. His effort begins by briefly surveying the conceptual history of 'civilian power' and 'military power Europe' since the early 1980s in order to locate these traditional conceptions of the EU's international role. He then introduces the idea of 'normative power Europe', discussing the EU's normative difference and normative basis and explaining how EU norms are diffused. He concludes that the concept of 'normative power' represents a valuable addition to one's own understanding of the EU's civilian and military power in world politics.

Manners' empirical evidence that the EU is a normative power relies largely on the policies it pursues. Specifically, investigating the EU's normative basis, Manners argues that unlike what happened with historical empires and contemporary global powers, the EU's normative difference comes from its historical context, hybrid polity and political–legal constitution (Manners, 2002, 240). In the post–Cold War period, this combination has accelerated a commitment to placing universal norms and principles at the center of its relations with its Member States (Merlingen et al., 2001) and the world (Clapham, 1999). Manners argues that the EU has gone further towards making its external relations informed by, and conditional on, a catalogue of norms which come closer to those of the European Convention on Human Rights and Fundamental Freedoms (ECHR) and the Universal Declaration of Human rights (UDHR) than most other actors in world politics (Manners, 2002, 241).

The discursive construction of the EU as a normative power is one that most EU politicians and technocrats engage. As Thomas Diez puts it,

> there may well be disagreement about the development of the EU's military capacities between Council and Commission, and between different member

> states and different directorate-generals, yet the representation of Europe as a force for peace and well-being is nearly consensual.
>
> (Diez 2005, 619)

According to Diez (2005, 314) debates about the character of EU's identity as a global actor ignore or underestimate the 'power' that lies in the representation of the EU as a 'normative power'. He notes that not only is the success of this representation a precondition for other actors to agree to the norms set out by the EU, but it also constructs an identity of the EU against an image of 'Others' in the 'outside world'. Diez argues that this has important implications for the way EU policies treat those 'Others', and the degree to which its adherence to its own norms is scrutinized within the European Union. In this sense, the discourse of the EU as a normative power constructs a particular self of the EU, while it attempts to change others through the spread of its own particular norms.

Diez suggests that normative power connotes the characteristic of a Weberian type of power relationship (as A being able to make B do what s/he would otherwise not have done). This relationship, according to Diez, takes on a 'Lukesian twist in the form of a kind of hegemonic power', namely the power to shape the values of others (Diez, 2005, 614). In addition, normative power refers to particular 'means'. In other words, it is not a power that relies on military force, but a power in which norms in themselves achieve what otherwise is done by military arsenals or economic incentives (Diez, 2005, 614).

This does not mean that normative power cannot go alongside other forms of power in international relations, notably military and economic forms (Diez, 2005, 615). Indeed, the latter two may underpin normative power, although normative power must not be reduced to economic or military power if it is to make sense as a separate category. For instance, as Diez has put it, the EU is most likely to 'shape conceptions of the normal' in the context of EU membership candidacies, when the interest to join the EU can be assumed to be an important factor determining the impact of EU norms (Diez, 2005, 615).

Diez correctly points out that normative power is not the opposite of military power (Diez, 2005, 620). Helene Sjursen has also emphasized that it is entirely conceivable that military force is used to back up the spread of civilian values, partly because the application of civilian means would imply the pre-existing institutionalization of civilian values in order to be effective (Sjursen, 1998, 122). Yet the more normative power builds on military force, the less it becomes distinguishable from traditional forms of power, because it no longer relies on the power of norms itself. Indeed, the imposition of norms through military force cannot be equated with successfully changing others, which relies primarily on socialization processes.

It is in this context that a comparison is drawn between the U.S. and the EU as 'empires'. According to Diez (2005, 621), it is necessary to consider the long-established assessment of U.S. foreign policy as strongly influenced by the frontier-myth, resulting in the "Godgiven duty to spread the dream and promise of America beyond its own shores"; a predisposition that, as Michael Cox notes, "inevitably infused American foreign policy with a particularly moralistic and idealistic tone" (Cox 2003, 238). The U.S.'s normative power was, for example, very visible during Woodrow Wilson's presidency and in his 'Fourteen Points'. Also after World War II, when one could already see the dominance of military power and American hegemony in play, the U.S. helped to create a series of international institutions that would 'civilize' international politics.

Diez rightly points out that even the invasion of Iraq cannot easily be dismissed as mere power politics as it was driven by a particular worldview with strong ideas of how democracy should work within a particular liberal governmental frame (Diez, 2005, 622). Yet, interests and norms cannot easily be separated (Cox, 2003, 239). Building up institutions after the World War II was a projection of American norms, just as much as it safeguarded American interests. This was due to the fact that those norms were supposed to spread a conception of life that would match that of the U.S. to build a 'community of ideals, interests and purposes' (Diez, 2005, 622).

However, there is an important difference between the EU and the United States. Unlike the EU, the U.S. has sought to project, and sometimes impose, its own norms while refusing to bind itself to international treaties. This difference should be understood not as a distinction between a normative and a military power, but rather an indication of a normative power in which military power is becoming increasingly important.

Today, the EU faces a situation similar to the one that the U.S. was facing during the first part of the 20th century. Back then, the U.S. was not at all eager to intervene in conflicts outside its own hemisphere. President Wilson's aim was to spread his version of liberal peace throughout the world so that interventions would no longer be necessary. The idea was to do so not with military means, but with binding normative commitments. Yet over time, the military back up of this normative power came to be of ever-increasing importance. And even though the U.S.' reluctance to entertain imperial ambitions should not be overestimated this supplementation of norms with force was not solely due to imperial ambitions on the part of the United States. It was partly a response to international calls for U.S. involvement and engagement.

Currently, the EU is facing similar calls both for acquiring more military power and for using military force to achieve certain goals. In the case of the U.S., the entanglement of normative and military power is underpinned by a belief in the universal validity of its own norms and a missionary zeal to spread these norms to other places. But similar discourses have now been adopted by European politicians and EU officials. The ESS makes it clear that a peaceful and stable global order requires the creation of democratic states and the spread of European values and norms across the globe.

Book structure

The present volume begins with Georgeta Pourchot's chapter challenging the basic premises of the argument advanced in this book. According to Pourchot,

'EU-as-empire-scholarship' insufficiently addresses traditional conceptual elements of empires such as conquest, coercion, pillaging, and hierarchy. As a result, a partial – and negative – image of the state of the EU as empire would emerge from such scholarship which would, according to Pourchot, benefit from more historically contextualized accounts of the drivers of enlargement, the sustainability elements of enlargement, and the modern types of hierarchy arising from post-communist states' accession to the European Union.

In response to traditional conceptualizations of 'empire', such as the one advanced by Pourchot, Hartmut Behr's chapter engages a relation between two contested and complex concepts, those of 'empire' and 'governing from the distance'. In his chapter, Behr first goes back to the Latin term of '*imperium*' and explores its manifold meanings of which the English 'empire' appears to be a narrowed-down imagination over centuries of linguistic and political controversies. He then employs a historiographical approach that suggests a feature of '*imperium*' which appears to have survived in contemporary politics and which serves as a tool to identify 'empire'/'*imperium*' in our times. This feature can be captured by the imaginary for – what Behr calls – 'governing from a distance' and thus draws on Edward Said and Michel Foucault, at the same time linking them back to the Latin richness of '*imperium*' and the question of instruments of governing. It is within this context that the EU, according to Behr, can be seen as representing a contemporary form of empire.

Another feature of contemporary empire is suggested by Jan Zielonka. According to Zielonka, empire represents a type of political organization in which the metropolis exercises control over diverse peripheral actors through formal annexations and/or various forms of informal domination. Although at first sight it seems that the EU cannot be classified as empire, Zielonka argues that the EU represents a vast territorial unit with sizeable power and resources and which often imposes severe domestic constraints on formally sovereign actors, including its own member states. Like all empires, the EU would also have a civilizing narrative, if not a civilizing mission since it claims to be an indispensable agent of modernity and peace in Europe and beyond. Zielonka's chapter not only demonstrates how the EU looks, walks, and talks as empires do, but, too, examines the implications of this phenomenon for the evolving nature of European politics.

In his chapter on the EU as empire in the 21st century, József Böröcz adopts a historical–sociological approach and argues that West European societies have played a central, and exceptionally privileged, part in the history of global capitalism. According to Böröcz's analysis, some of the geopolitical and economic foundations of that centrality and privilege have recently begun to show powerful signs of erosion. His contribution regards the supra-state and the public authority of the European Union as an instrument of a strategic coalition among west and central European capital, state apparatuses and populations, aiming to optimize their geopolitical position under present-day conditions. The key instrument of this new global adjustment would bear a clear resemblance to the asymmetrical linkages that constituted the geopolitics of power of empires throughout much of global history. In light of this framework, Böröcz further examines how membership and association agreements work as 'enforcement chains'.

Aligning with the logic of Böröcz's chapter, Yannis Stivachtis seeks to reexamine the concept of 'empire' and demonstrates its application to the case of the European Union. It begins with the acknowledgement that the majority of scholars and practitioners have been very reluctant to consider the EU as an empire mainly due to the lack of aggressive imperial and expansionist tendencies that are historically associated with empires. However, the chapter argues that the process of the creation and expansion of an empire has not been historically uniform and that the establishment of an empire can take different forms in the presence of 'international anarchy'. Stivachtis claims that sometimes empires may represent the end result of aggressive imperial tendencies and, at other times, be 'just' the outcome of a more peaceful process of international cooperation. To this end, he focuses on the EU's policy of conditionality and its application to the Union's enlargement, neighborhood, and development policies to demonstrate how they have all served to create a 'non-imperial empire'.

Resonating with important aspects raised by Stivachtis, Aylin Güney's study analyzes competing and converging geopolitical imaginations of Europe and their impact on European Union enlargement politics. Güney's chapter first presents the analytical tools of critical geopolitics to understand how geopolitical identities may eventually be translated into EU's enlargement policies, especially towards Central and Eastern European countries and Turkey. The study then explains two different geopolitical identifications that stand behind the conceptualizations of Europe of 'Europe as neo-Westphalian state' and 'Europe as neo-Medieval Empire'. The chapter then continues to analyse the effect of these competing and/or converging geopolitical identifications on the formation of Europe's geopolitical discourses and examines how this imagination has been translated into policies of inclusion and exclusion within European Union enlargement schemes.

Portraying the EU as torn between imperial and non-imperial features, Kalypso Nicolaidis and Nora Fisher Onar argue in their chapter that the EU suffers from a 'post-imperial' condition that has problematic consequences for its internal and external policies. They point out that different and multiple meanings of the 'imperial past' prevail in countries in East and Central Europe, Southern or Northern Europe, as well as in former European colonies which see the EU through the lens of their postcolonial status. It is the confrontation between these imperial legacies and the difficulty to transcend them by recognizing then and now the critical role of 'others' in the constitution of the EU project which forge Europe's imperial condition. They suggest that while the EU has made much formal and indeed substantial progress toward confronting echoes of imperialism, imperial patterns die hard. Moreover, they claim that many of the symbolic and effective types of oppression, which they unveiled and fought, still exist. But the echoes are fainter and more confusing than in immediately postcolonial times; for example, power is more diffuse and hybridity more pervasive. This would result in policies that are counterproductive to the EU's interests, not least in its relations with Turkey and its Eastern neighbors.

Robert Phillipson's chapter examines the relationship between language and global order. The myth of '*terra nullius*', Philipson contends, has been succeeded by an expansion of the cultural universe of the USA (as a '*cultura nullius*') and English. He argues that English is fraudulently marketed as a '*lingua nullius*' although it serves all equally well. Nevertheless, this would constitute a linguistic imperialism that, too, permeates EU institutional activities. In this context, globalization and global English are seen as interlocking projects. Philipson points to the role of the European Court of Justice in advancing European integration and neoliberalism, demonstrating how European Commission initiatives, like the Bologna process, strengthen English in continental Europe. Philipson arrives at two main conclusions: first, that this authoritarian executive managerialism is undemocratic, and second, loose reference to English as a '*lingua franca*' in political and academic discourse conceals the role of English as the neo-imperial language of the transnational global corporate class made up by the power complex of the US–NATO–EU.

Another historiographical and genealogical perspective is offered by Russell Foster, who points out that 'empire' as a political term would not refer to a taxonomy of state power, but to a *claim* of a political unit as the solely legitimate and superior order of the world. Therefore, Foster argues, 'empire' is a normative and exclusionary discourse of sovereignty, legitimacy, duty, and manifest destiny. This would be most effectively conveyed through the coded language of symbols. Foster considers symbols to be the most powerful form of communication acting as a social solvent, encoding everyday life with the presence of a political ideology. However, Foster's chapter demonstrates that the EU's symbols express not only what the Union *is*, but most importantly what it *should be*, namely a political order which blurs the EU and Europe into a single, imperial synecdoche.

References

Anastasakis, Othon and Dimitar Betchev. 2003. EU Conditionality in South East Europe: Bringing Commitment to the Process. *South East European Studies Programme, European Studies Centre*, St Antony's College, University of Oxford.

Bacevich, Andrew. (ed.). 2002. *The Imperial Tense: Prospects and Problems of American Empire*. New York: Ivan Dee.

Bacevich, Andrew. 2005. *The New American Militarism*. Oxford: Oxford University Press.

Barber, Benjamin. 2003. *War, Terrorism and Democracy*. New York: Norton.

Bartolini, Stefano. 2005. *Restructuring Europe: Centre Formation, System Building, and Political Structuring between the Nation State and the European Union*. Oxford: Oxford University Press.

Beck, Ulrich and Edgar Grande. 2007. Cosmopolitanism. Europe's Way Out of Crisis. *European Journal of Social Theory* 10(1): 67–85.

Behr, Hartmut. 2007. The European Union in the Legacies of Imperial Rule? EU Accession Politics viewed from an historical comparative perspective. *European Journal of International Relations* 13(2): 239–262.

Benton, Lauren. 2002. *Law and Colonial Cultures: Legal Regimes in World History, 1400–1900*. Cambridge: Cambridge University Press.

Boeroecz, Jozsef. 2001. Empire and Coloniality in the "Eastern Enlargement" of the European Union. In Jozsef Boeroecz and Melinad Kovacs (eds.), *Empire's New Clothes: Unveiling EU Enlargement*, pp. 4–50, www.ce-review.org.

Champion, Craig. (ed.). 2004. *Roman Imperialism: Readings and Sources*. Cambridge, MA: Cambridge University Press.
Chomsky, Noam. 1968. *Language and Mind*. New York: Harcourt Brace Jovanovich.
Clapham, Andrew. 1999. Where is the EU's Human Rights Common Foreign Policy, and How Is It Manifested in Multilateral Fora? In P. Alston (ed.), *The EU and Human Rights*. Oxford: Oxford University Press.
Copus, A. K. 2001. From Core-Periphery to Polycentric Development: Concepts of Spatial and Aspatial Peripherality. *European Planning Studies* 9(4): 539–552.
Cox, Michael. 2003. The Empire's Back in Town. *Millennium: Journal of International Studies* 32(1): 327–336.
Craig, Campbell. 2004. American Realism versus American Imperialism. *World Politics* 57: 141–171.
Danto, Arthur. 1969. Semantical Vehicles, Understanding, and Innate Ideas. *Language and Philosophy*, 122–137. New York: New York University Press.
Diez, Thomas. 1999. Speaking "Europe": The Politics of Integration Discourse. Special Issue, *Journal of European Public Policy* 6(4): 598–613.
Diez, Thomas. 2005. Constructing the Self and Changing Others: Reconsidering "Normative Power Europe." *Millennium: Journal of International Studies* 33(3): 613–636.
Duchene, Francois. 1973. The European Community and the Uncertainties of Interdependence. In M. Kohnstamm and W. Hager (eds.), *A Nation Writ Large? Foreign Policy Problems before the European Community*. Basingstoke: Macmillan.
Eichengreen, Barry. 2008. *Sui Generis EMU*. Brussels: European Commission Directorate-General for Economic and Financial Affairs, Publications
Eisenstadt, Shmuel N. 1963. *The Political System of Empires*. Glencoe, IL: Free Press.
Elgstrom, Ole and Michael Smith. 2006. *The European Union's Roles in International Politics*. London: Routledge.
Engelbrekt, Kjell. 2002. Multiple Asymmetries: The European Union's Neo-Byzantine Approach to Eastern Enlargement. *International Politics* 39(1): 37–51.
Erskine, Andrew. 2010. *Roman Imperialism*. Edinburgh: Edinburgh University Press.
European Commission. n.d. *The Schuman Declaration: 9 May 1950*. http://europa.eu/about-eu/basic-information/symbols/europe-day/schuman-declaration/index_en.htm
European Commission. 2003. *European Security Strategy: A Secure Europe in a Better World*. www.consilium.europa.eu/uedocs/cmsUpload/78367.pdf
European Commission. 2008. *Report on the Implementation of the European Security Strategy: Providing Security In a Changing World*. www.consilium.europa.eu/ueDocs/cms_Data/docs/pressdata/EN/reports/104630.pdf
European Commission. 2012a. *EU Awarded the Nobel Peace Prize*. http://ec.europa.eu/languages/news/20121012-eu-nobel-peace-prize_en.htm
European Commission. 2012b. *Joint statement of José Manuel Barroso, President of the European Commission, and Herman Van Rompuy, President of the European Council on the award of the 2012 Nobel Peace Prize to the EU*. http://europa.eu/rapid/press-release_MEMO-12–779_en.htm#PR_metaPressRelease_bottom
European Commission. 2014. *A Global Actor in Search of a Strategy. European Union Foreign Policy Between Multilateralism and Bilateralism*. http://ec.europa.eu/research/social-sciences/pdf/policy_reviews/kina26572enc.pdf
Ferguson, Niall. 2004. *Empire: The Rise and Demise of the British World Order and the Lessons for Global Power*. New York: Basic Books.
Ferguson, Niall. 2005. *Colossus: The Rise and Fall of the American Empire*. New York: Penguin Books.

Folz, R. 1969. *The Concept of Empire in Western Europe: From the Fifth to the Fourteenth Century*. Frome: Edward Arnold.

Foster, Russell. 2015. *Tabulae Imperii Europaei: Mapping European Empire*. London: Routledge.

Galtung, Johann. 1973. *The European Community: A Superpower in the Making*. London: Allen & Unwin.

Grabbe, Heather. 2002. European Union Conditionality and the Acquis Communautaire. *International Political Science Review* 23(3): 249–268.

Gray, Christopher. 2003. The Costs of Empire. ORBIS, 7: 359–370.

Hansen, Peo. 2002. European Integration, European Identity and the Colonial Connection. *European Journal of Social Theory* 5(4): 483–498.

Harvey, David. 2003. *The New Imperialism*. Oxford: Oxford University Press.

Jackson, Robert and Philip Towle. 2006. *Temptations of Power: The United States in Global Politics after 9/11*. London: Palgrave Macmillan.

Johnson, Chalmers. 2000. *Blowback: The Costs and Consequences of American Empire*. London: Little, Brown.

Johnson, Chalmers. 2004. *The Sorrows of Empire*. New York: Holt.

Kaplan, Robert. 2005. *Imperial Grunts: the American Military on the Ground*. New York: Random House.

Kirchner, Emil and James Sperling. 2007. *EU Security Governance*. Manchester: Manchester University Press.

Kovacs, Melinda. 2001. Putting Down and Putting Off: The EU's Discourse Strategies in the 1998 and 1999 Follow-up Reports. In Jozsef Boeroecz and Melinad Kovacs (eds.) *Empire's New Clothes: Unveiling EU Enlargement*, pp. 196–234, www.ce-review.org.

Lens, Sidney and Howard Zinn. 2003. *The Forging of the American Empire: From the Revolution to Vietnam: A History of American Imperialism*. London: Pluto Press.

Mandelbaum, Michael. 2005. *The Case of Goliath: How America Acts as the World's Government in the 21st Century*. New York: Public Affairs.

Mann, Michael. 2003. *Incoherent Empire*. New York: Verso.

Manners, Ian. 2002. Normative Power Europe. *Journal of Common Market Studies* 40(2): 235–258.

Marcuse, Herbert. 1964. *The One-dimensional Man. Studies in the Ideology of Advanced Industrial Society*. Boston: Beacon Press.

Maull, Hans. 1990. German and Japan: The New Civilian Powers. *Foreign Affairs* 69(5): 91–106.

Merlingen, Michael. 2007. Everything Is Dangerous: A Critique of 'Normative Power Europe. *Security Dialogue* 38(4): 435–453.

Merlingen, Michael, C. Mudde and U. Sedelmeier. 2001. The Right and the Righteous? European Norms, Domestic Politics and Sanctions against Austria. *Journal of Common Market Studies* 39(1): 59–77.

Mitzen, Jennifer. 2006. Ontological Security in World Politics: State Identity and the Security Dilemma. *European Journal of International Relations* 12(3): 341–370.

Nagel, Thomas. 1969. Linguistics and Epistemology. In *Language and Philosophy*, 171–181. New York University Press.

O'Brien, Patrick and Almand Clesse. (eds.). 2002. *Two Hegemonies: Britain 1846–1914 and the United States 1941–2001*. Aldershot: Ashgate.

Orbie, Jan. (ed.). 2008. *Europe's Global Role: External Policies of the European Union*. Aldershot: Ashgate.

Phelan, William. 2012. What Is *Sui Generis* About the European Union? Costly International Cooperation in a Self-Contained Regime. *International Studies Review* 14(3): 367–385.

Phillipson, Robert. 2002. *English-only Europe? Challenging Language Policy*. London: Routledge.

Prodi, Romano. 2000. *2000–2005: Shaping the New Europe*. Speech to the European Parliament, Strasburg, 15 February.

Rosecrance, Richard. 1998). The European Union: A New Type of International Actor. In Jan Zieloka (ed.), *Paradoxes of European Foreign Policy*, 15–23. The Hague: Kluwer Law International.

Schimmelpfennig, Frank and U. Sedelmayer. 2004. Governance by Conditionality: EU rule Transfer to the Candidate Countries of Central and Eastern Europe. *Journal of European Public Policy* 11(4): 669–687.

Shapiro, Michael. 1992. *Reading the Postmodern Polity. Political Theory as Textual Practice*. Minneapolis: University of Minnesota Press.

Simes, Dimitri. 2003. America's Imperial Dilemma. *Foreign Affairs*, November/December, 91–102.

Sinopoli, Carla M. 1994. The Archaeology of Empires. *Annual Review of Anthropology* 23: 159–180.

Sjursen, Helene. 1998. Missed Opportunity or Eternal Fantasy?: The Idea of a European Security and Defense Policy. In J. Peterson and H. Sjursen (eds.), *A Common Foreign Policy for Europe? Competing Visions of the CFSP*. London: Routledge.

Stivachtis, Yannis A. 2004. Common Foreign and Security Policy (CFSP) and European Security and Defense Policy (ESDP) After Iraq. In Yannis A. Stivachtis (ed.), *Current Issues in European Integration*, 117–142. Athens: ATINER.

Stivachtis, Yannis A. 2005. The European Defense and Security Policy: Evolution and Changes.' In Yannis A. Stivachtis (ed.), *Global Governance and International Security*, 267–88. Athens: ATINER.

Stivachtis, Yannis. 2008. The Standard of Civilization in Contemporary International Society: The Case of the European Union. *Contemporary Politics* 14(1): 71–90.

Telo, Marion. 2006. *Europe, a Civilian Power*. New York: Palgrave.

Tocci, Nathalie. 2007. *The EU and Conflict Resolution: Promoting Peace in the Backyard*. London: Routledge.

Todd, Emmanuel. 2003. *After the Empire: The Breakdown of American Order*. New York: Columbia University Press.

Tunander, Ola et al. 1997. *Geopolitics in Post-wall Europe: Security, Territory, and Identity*, London: Sage.

Twitchett, K. (ed.). 1976. *Europe and the World; The External Relations of the European Market*. New York: St. Martin's Press.

Wæver, Ole. 1997. Emerging European Analogies to Pre-Nation State Imperial Systems. In Ola Tunander, Pavel Baev and Victoria Einagel (eds.), *Geopolitics in Post-Wall Europe: Security, Territory, and Identity*, 59–93. London: Sage.

Whitman, Richard. 1998. *From Civilian to Superpower? The International Identity of the European Union*. Basingstoke: Macmillan.

Zielonka, Jan. 1998. *Explaining Euro-paralysis: Why Europe is Unable to Act in International Politics*. Basingstoke: Macmillan.

Zielonka, Jan. 2006. *Europe as Empire: The Nature of the Enlarged European Union*. Oxford: Oxford University Press.

1 EU's eastern 'empire'

Georgeta Pourchot

Introduction

When in July 2007, Jose Manuel Barroso, the president of the EU Commission, referred to the EU as 'a non-imperial empire,' alarm bells went off in European capitals. The British, already nervous about the European project, were told by their tabloids that they should fear this EU empire that 'will rule over Britain,' with Barroso as the 'emperor.' Shadow Europe Minister Mark Francois said that the 'British public will be genuinely surprised to hear the suggestion that we are now part of an EU Empire, which the revived constitution will supposedly help to work better' (Milland 2007).

In an attempt to limit the damage, Mr. Barroso's spokesman clarified that

> No one needs to have imperial nightmares tonight. President Barroso, at his press conference on the new EU Reform Treaty, referred to a quote by the philosopher Peter Sloterdijk to emphasize that the EU is anything but a superstate. EU member states came together peacefully, democratically and voluntarily – the president would not want it any other way.
>
> (Waterfield 2007)

The concept of the EU as empire sparked debate among scholars. Even before 2007, rising scholarship re-conceptualized empire and neo-imperialism, particularly as it reflected on America's rising global power (Harvey 2003; Mooers 2006), and on the seeming effects of (unregulated and pernicious) globalization of capitalism (Becker et al. 1987; Hardt and Negri 2000; Negri 2003; Hardt and Negri 2004; Negri 2006). It is therefore important to reflect on conceptual aspects of empires to better understand the implications arising from such understanding of the European project, particularly with respect to the newest members from Central Europe. The concept of EU as empire was not articulated in 1973, when the United Kingdom, Ireland and Denmark joined; nor in 1981 when Greece joined, nor in 1986 when Spain and Portugal were admitted; it was articulated during, and in the aftermath of enlargement to fifteen Central and Eastern European states. The Eastern dimension seems to drive this line of theoretical argumentation. What is it about enlargement to former communist states that gives the EU an empire dimension?

The scholarship on EU as empire proposes new analytical frameworks. Control over or intrusion in sovereign affairs, soft borders, governance issues, use of 'soft' power to influence sovereign affairs, and the particularity of decision-making procedures and processes are offered in defense of the notion that the EU has become, or is on its way of becoming an empire (Zielonka 2006, 150–156). The EU system of rule, and imposition of its 'standards of civilization' on Central Europeans is seen as reminiscent of nineteenth-century imperial models (Behr 2007). A new form of 'liberal empire' characterized by the forceful extension of free markets, electoral democracies and human rights, championed primarily by the United States and the EU is emerging (Colas 2007, 176–184). A legacy of colonialism and empire is identified in new patterns of inequality, hierarchy, domination and exclusion during the EU accession process and beyond (Böröcz 2001, 14). Central Europe's continued subordination to 'the West' has turned it into a 'colonial object' for EU decision-makers, with Central Europeans having no choice but to yield to EU pressures in order to gain membership (Burgess 1997). Which analytical categories are retained from the traditional conceptualization of empires to justify using empire terminology remains unclear. There is (implicit) recognition that coercion, subjugation by force, pillaging and overpowering, all typical empire analytical tools, are missing from EU policies and procedures (Zielonka 2006, 54–59; Böröcz 2001; Colas 2007). That begs the question as to why we should use empire/imperial language to define the EU, if basic features that define traditional empires are missing.

I argue that recent empire scholarship partially addresses traditional characteristics of empire, what leads to an incomplete, negative and somewhat unfair image of the EU as empire. Traditional empire scholarship incorporates three basic assumptions that differentiates this particular body politic from other types of governance. The coercion assumption implies that empires were created mostly by force, by a power center/core with or without a grand scheme of annexation, with the periphery reacting or submitting itself to the center. The sustainability assumption implies that empires were created to sustain a particular lifestyle of the core, at the expense of the periphery. The hierarchy assumption implies that the core is always in command, dictating the rules of coexistence to the periphery; the periphery has the rights and privileges that the core allows it to have. The traditional empire scholarship goes well beyond these three assumptions to analyze commonalities and differences among the various empires of the past; but for a body politic to meet the definition of empire, it needs to meet these three assumptions. In what follows, I address how recent scholarship reflects on these three assumptions.

The coercion assumption

Who drives the process of empire-formation? The coercion assumption refers to the direction and mechanics of the pressure for enlargement of the body politic.

Traditional empire scholarship is unambiguous about the direction of empire-building. The core, defined as a center of political and military power drives the (violent) conquest of peripheries. Describing the rise and fall of the Roman empire, Gibbon talks about 'conquest' as the critical ingredient in the ambitions of the powerful Rome to 'subdue the whole earth,' via 'prosecution of remote wars' (Gibbon 2000, 9–13). The British Empire is described by Ferguson in terms such as 'governing a quarter of the world population', as well as the negative connotations associated with the slave trade as leading to an empire 'built on oppression and exploitation' (Ferguson 2002, ix–xii). Reviewing empires in world history, Burbank and Cooper refer to 'violence and day-to-day coercion' as main characteristics, with operations designed to 'both exploit and rule' (Burbank and Cooper 2010, 2). For John Hobson, one of the early scholars studying the dynamics of empires, imperialism was 'the disposition of metropolitan society to expand its rule' and empire was 'annexed territory' (Hobson 1965, 15–17). Schumpeter and Lenin shared the view that the root of empire was in imperialism, defined as the tendency of a state to territorial expansion by force (Schumpeter 1955), driven by the capitalist search for overseas resources, markets and profits (Lenin 1939). Michael Doyle defines empires as 'effective control, whether formal or informal, of a subordinated society by an imperial society.' Closely related, imperialism is 'the process of establishing and maintaining an empire' (Doyle 1986, 30). Of note, much of this scholarship was produced as the European project was on its way, and contains no reference to the EC/EU as an 'empire in the making'.

Recent empire scholarship drops the coercion assumption. The 'conquest' clause is inexistent and the assumption of 'by force' is missing, with little to no explanation for the omission. Beck and Grande identify a new type of empire, the 'cosmopolitan empire' whose characteristics relate not to 'national demarcation and conquest, but to overcoming national borders, voluntarism, consensus, transnational interdependence and the political added value accruing from cooperation' (Beck and Grande 2007, 53). Lundestad first uses the concept 'by invitation' in reference to an American post-World War II empire in Western Europe, with the latter seeking a powerful ally to secure itself against the communist threat (Lundestad 1986). Nye refers to 'soft power' and 'unipolarity' to describe the U.S. hegemony (not empire), and differentiates between sources of authority that rely on 'peaceful, consensual exchange' among parties, rather than the 'coercive power' of a core (Nye 2001). Colas, partly in response to Hardt and Negri, partly in an attempt to actualize the concept of empire, calls for a more balanced approach in new empire scholarship, reminding us that historical context is relevant and should be adequately represented in such analyses. To those who accuse the U.S. of imperial ambitions around the world, he offers a reminder that military action in hot spots such as the Balkans or Afghanistan was followed by experiments in nation-building rather than by permanent military occupations, which would indeed justify an empire/imperialism framework of analysis (Colas 2007, 178–179). To those scholars who see 'mere pretext' of imperial flavor in military action in Iraq or Kosovo, he counters with a reminder that human rights abuses, genocide and violent action existed long before US/EU intervention; in fact, intervention was brought about by the realities of unacceptable genocide against Kurds, Kosovars and other ethnic groups. 'To reduce such history to mere "pretext" is not just politically disingenuous . . . it is also analytically disabling' (Colas 2007, 180). Colas favors the concept of 'liberal empire' a 'very different kind of empire' from the traditional ones, to frame recent US/NATO/EU actions in promoting a new world order based on liberal values of self-government, civil liberties and territorial integrity (Colas 2007, 178).

The conquest/coercion clause is further replaced in new empire scholarship by 'influence/control over,' 'interference in sovereign affairs,' and 'domination/pressure.' Zielonka promotes the concept of 'EU as empire' arguing that the EU is the illustration of a new type of empire, a 'neo-medieval empire' with characteristics such as soft borders in flux; persistence of socio-economic and cultural differentiation; disjunction between authoritative allocations, functional competencies and territorial constituencies; and interpenetration of various types of political units and loyalties (Zielonka 2006, 9–20). 'Imperial behavior' or 'attitude' is the ability of a state to 'exert influence' on other states (Zielonka 2008, 474); and to 'promote [. . .] the imperial center's norms and values in various peripheral actors' (Zielonka 2008, 480). In this view, 'the Union looks and acts like an empire because it tries to assert political and economic control over various peripheral actors through formal annexations or various forms of economic and political domination,' although the EU is not seen as an empire in the sense of Britain's nineteenth-century empire (Zielonka 2008, 475).

While in the Signature of Empires that Böröcz creates, conflict/war/subjugation are listed as typical features of traditional empires, these analytical categories disappear in his formulaic articulation of imperial order (Böröcz 2001, 17–18). Instead, 'mechanisms of control' are identified that do not include coercion or use of force. This reduction of the traditional definition allows the 'EU as empire' argument to proceed, framing the EU as the driver of enlargement, without having to justify the absence of EU coercion on Central European states to join.

Behr uses the imposition of Western standards of civilization and practices of 'authoritative knowledge' during the accession process to underscore the EU's imperial tendencies, akin to those of the nineteenth century (Behr 2007, 249). The EU's 'civilizing mission' is said to be reflected in the politics of EU accession. The standard of civilization argument also rests on the logic that the core (EC/EU) drives the assimilation of a periphery (Central and Eastern Europe) that is, in civilizational terms, beneath its standards. Analyzing historical patterns of similar assimilations that Western Europe successfully, or unsuccessfully, led throughout a history of colonization of the world, Behr argues that the EU is currently using the standard of civilization logic to bring former communist countries into its area of political and economic dominance. Implicit in these analyses is that the EU is driving the process of enlargement, and is doing so pressuring other states into EU institutional frames whether the candidates fit the frames or not.

Even if coercion and use of force are largely absent from new empire scholarship, implicit in empire *usage*, however, is that the coercion assumption applies to the EU in principle. The clarification from Barroso's spokesperson makes that point when it refers to Central Europe coming together 'peacefully,' as opposed to being the result of wars of annexation or conquest, and 'voluntarily,' as opposed to being forced into the European Union.

The presentation of the historical context of enlargement could also be improved. Most new empire scholarship presents EU enlargement with a distinct focus on the EU's imposition of rules, laws, and principles of good and acceptable behavior on Central Europe; while the historical context of Central European aspirations, implorations, even informally begging Brussels to open its doors to former communist states is glossed over rapidly. Böröcz, Burgess and Zielonka acknowledge that it was the Central Europeans starting the process of EU enlargement, but Central Europeans' voluntary application to join the EU does not receive nearly as much treatment as EU mechanisms of influence over Central European sovereign decisions. Instead, a strong impression is created that it was the EU championing and (forcefully) initiating eastward enlargement. This interpretation does not do justice to the historical record of post–Cold War EU enlargement.

The record shows that the reason EU enlargement did occur has far more to do with the candidates' determination to become members than with the EU pushing its own agenda of 'expansion by invitation' (Zielonka 2008, 475). To honor Colas's call for contextualization, invitations were issued because there was Central European pressure on Brussels to issue the invitations, rather than because Brussels came up with the idea of enlargement in the first place. Central European pressure on Brussels led to years of internal debate within the EC/EU about the willingness and ability to enlarge to the East, and internal divisions among members about who should be allowed in, and who should be kept out. While Germany seemed keen on enlargement to Central Europe, France and Great Britain were far more reticent. While Nordic states like Denmark, Finland and Sweden proactively supported the membership of the Baltic states, neither France nor Germany were warm to the idea (Fritsch and Uibopuu 2005, 211). These differences, as well as the lack of clarity on what the EC/EU should do about the former communist countries' pressure for enlargement led to prolonged debates within the EC/EU to sort out its priorities in a post-Cold War world. Enlargement to the east was reluctantly agreed, accession negotiations eventually started, and a high bar was set for potential candidates. As such, one can hardly argue that the process of EC/EU enlargement was driven by 'the core,' or that there was coercion involved in extending invitations for opening accession negotiations.

Within six months of the watershed year of 1989, 'turning back to Europe' became a political slogan in Central Europe expressing the 'longing for a fast reintegration into the larger "House of Europe,"' specifically into the European Community (Bayer 2005, 53). Even the Baltic countries, with their history of having been part of the Soviet Union saw themselves as candidates for the House of Europe, where they felt they belonged, and from which they had been unjustly separated (Fritsch and Uibopuu 2005, 209, 211). Ash argued that Central European states saw their membership in the EU as a symbol of the burial of their totalitarian past, a healing of the unnatural separation and forced division of Europe conceived at Yalta in 1944 (Ash 1993, 8). From Brussels, however, they were receiving inconclusive signals about the future ten years after the end of the Cold

War. Until about 1998, Brussels' attitude towards the future of Central Europe remained 'obscure' (Price and Landau 1999, 10).

The European Agreements (EAs) of the early nineties were the first indication that the European Community was ready to consider a stronger relationship with former communist countries, as long as they demonstrated commitment to market economy and democratic reforms (European Commission 1990). EAs, however, did not articulate that the European Community had membership for Central Europeans as their objective (Avery and Cameron 1998, 17). Initially, the European Community considered these EAs *alternatives* to accession, not pre-accession steps (Marasceau and Montaguti 1995, 1328). The scholarship arguing that the EU is incorporating Central Europe 'by invitation' scantly reflects on this historical context.

For Central Europeans, the Preambles of EAs clearly stated that EU membership was their *ultimate objective*. The Preamble to the EC–Hungary stated that 'Having in mind that the final objective of Hungary is to become a member of the Community and that this [agreement] . . . will help to achieve this objective,' (Official Journal L 347, 1993). The Preamble to the EC–Poland similarly articulated that 'Recognizing the fact that the ultimate objective of Poland is to become a member of the Community, and that this association . . . will help to achieve this objective' (Europe Agreement 1993). The preambles of the other Central European countries articulated the same membership aspiration.

A reorientation of relations slowly emerged beginning in the early nineties. In the conclusions of the Presidency of the European Council in Lisbon, 1992, Central European applications for admission into the European Community were seen as a historic opportunity for the promotion of Western European values throughout the continent (Commission of the European Communities 1992, 53). The issue of Euro-Atlantic norm promotion features heavily in the imposition of standards of civilization argument, but one has to ask what came first, the EU imposition of norms, or the Central European request to join an area in which such norms were in place. Such problematization rarely features in new empire scholarship; a more balanced account of the historical context would enrich this argument. Moreover, Central Europeans are seen as (helpless) pawns in a geopolitical game of the new redrawing of the European map, a view which pays little attention to the voluntary nature of these countries' desire to join the EU.

The process of accession was lengthy and for the most part painful for Central Europeans. Some authors have argued that the intrusive accession process with all its requirements and the obligation to join the *acquis* stifled the emergence of a homegrown democracy in Central Europe. Preoccupied to meet Brussels's requirements, Central Europeans did not have choices in how they were to design democratic institutions, Western models were imposed on them that they had to accept (Burgess 1997). While the imposition of Western values and norms during the accession process is well documented, a reminder of the historical context is again needed. Central Europe was emerging from forty-five years of communist rule, with little or no experience in democratic practices, a communist political mentality, centralized economies and bureaucracies, and generally poor. In many of these countries, former communist nomenclatures had a strong influence on political processes, and by mid-nineties, several states elected former communists to power. There was a concern inside and outside Central Europe that large portions of the populace did not understand or were not ready for democratic rule. To argue that they could have identified their own brand of democratic practices ignores the realities on the ground in the early nineties, some of which persist to this day. The EU accession process thus gave leaders in these countries an excuse to implement unpopular reforms in order to move their countries away from old mentalities. Of note, despite having to implement laws and principles that ran counter to sovereign interests and cultures, such as the sale of land to foreigners, or completing neighborhood agreements among states that were not altogether friendly (Romania–Hungary, for example), Central Europeans chose to proceed with reforms demanded by the *acquis*. They could have chosen to limit their new relationship with the EU to EAs; they could have chosen a type of neighborhood agreement that would have been less intrusive in their sovereign affairs (as Ukraine did); or they could have quit the accession process altogether. Yet, they voluntarily continued the process, even in cases where reforms went against long-held domestic values. The EU as empire scholarship argues that Central Europeans had no choice but to agree to reforms demanded by the *acquis*, but it does not address possible available alternatives.

This historical context is scantly discussed by new empire scholarship and when it is, it tends to be explained as the result of a 'subordination' mentality of the Eastern half of Europe to the Western one (Burgess 1997, 107–120). There was certainly a strong degree of socialization into Western, liberal norms imbedded in the enlargement process that Central Europeans were not ready for, but which they accepted and pursued as a trade-off for membership. New empire scholarship highlights this socialization as a negative process, a proof of EU's imperial intention to dominate Central Europe. Other scholars remind us that the socialization process 'plays a crucial role in the quest for legitimate membership of any social group.' Socialization helps candidates become ready to undertake the duties and responsibilities of membership of the group, and helps them show their worth as potential candidates (Kliewer and Stivachtis 2007, 143). As such, the negative overtones of EU as empire scholarship are sometimes difficult to understand.

Interviews taken *ex post facto* by scholars studying the process of NATO and EU enlargements indicate that NATO officials found it challenging to train Central Europeans into liberal norms. 'We had to explain to them that we, in the West, had learned to take very seriously fundamental freedoms of individuals, as well as principles of transparency and accountability to society. We had learned that nothing else would do. The problem was, we did not see the same commitment in [Central Europeans] that we were talking to. *If they were to become like us* [emphasis added], this had to change' (Gheciu 2005, 114). Beyond achieving economic, political, or military interoperability, the goal was to reach 'mental interoperability,' as Central Europeans displayed resistance, and discomfort with the 'new thinking' (Gheciu 2005, 119). Interviews with recipients of socialization into Western norms reveal that they had a level of distrust towards their Western instructors. Participants in PfP courses and Marshall Center graduates referred to one particular analogy, 'that of the poor relative, whose rich, sophisticated relatives invite them to dinner but never let them forget the social and economic gap between them' (Gheciu 2005, 120). Böröcz likens this process to the EU in the role of a 'schoolmaster trying to discipline the rowdy brats under their control,' a 'kindergarten phantasy' reminiscent of imperial power (Böröcz 2001, 30). Yet, the flip side of this image is that of Central Europeans submitting themselves to an uncomfortable process, voluntarily, and continuing in that process despite discomfort, distrust and resentment of their Western counterparts. This is the more balanced image that the new empire scholarship has to come to terms with and explain if the argument of EU as empire is to gain ground.

The sustainability assumption

The sustainability assumption is grounded in the following: who sustains whom in empires? Empires of the past were created to sustain a particular lifestyle of the core at the expense of the periphery; in fact, empires of the past were created with a strong component of pillaging annexed territories. The periphery sustained the core with the taxes it paid, and with natural and human resources. Rulers of empires had 'basic and constant objectives' such as 'to monopolize, or at least insure the possibility of rapidly mobilizing sufficient economic and manpower resources to make it certain that any of their goals and policies would be constantly implemented and that their services would be maintained,' and that they retained the 'continuous control and regulation of economic resources' (Eisenstadt 1963, 121).

In the case of the EU, the core sent technical assistance and modernization resources to the Eastern periphery before and after EU enlargement, to bring it up to speed with the core's market reforms and infrastructure modernization requirements.

EU as empire scholarship sees technical and assistance programs for Central Europe as yet another mechanism of subordination/domination, a way to keep the region dependent on Brussels. Böröcz explains that EU companies constitute the largest investor group in Central Europe while the Central European portion of investment in EU portfolio is minuscule by comparison; this he considers as an example of the siphoning off of 'unprecedented (amounts) of the national product' of applicant states (Böröcz 2001, 18). At the same time, a discussion of the amount of EU technical assistance to Central Europe is missing.

A more balanced analysis of the sustainability assumption would find that through the end of 2000, PHARE acted as the financial pillar for the preparation of Central European membership, assisting fourteen countries. In 1999 in Berlin, the European Council decided to expand financial assistance and two additional instruments were approved: SAPARD, a program for assistance in agriculture, with an annual budget of 520 million euro; and ISPA, a program of assistance for structural policy, with an annual budget of 1.04 billion euro. An additional program, OBNOVA provided assistance to Western Balkan countries (Albania, Bosnia-Herzegovina, Croatia and Former Yugoslav Republic of Macedonia, or FYROM) from 1996 until 2001. Finally, the CARDS regulation (Community Assistance for Reconstruction, Development and Stabilization) was agreed in December 2000, to provide coordination and disbursement of assistance programs to Albania, Bosnia-Herzegovina, Croatia, the Federal Republic of Yugoslavia, and FYROM (Sajdik and Schwarzinger 2008, 91; Europa n.d.-a, n.d.-b).

PHARE evolved from supporting economic transformation throughout the region, to deepening the reform processes via institution building and investments. Institution building was undertaken via programs such as the Twinning Program, where partnerships between administrative units in EU member countries and a candidate country were set up. Between 1997 and 2003, over 800 twinning programs were set up, with technical and administrative assistance offered to candidates. After 2006, the EU provided a Transitory Facility instrument designed to assist new EU members in the build-up of necessary administrative capacities in the areas in which structural funds could not be applied. Investments in the infrastructure of the candidate countries was also necessary in order for candidates to meet the requirements of the *acquis*; seventy percent of PHARE's budget was earmarked for that purpose, to assist with the development of the transport sector, and environmental protection projects such as supplies of drinking water, waste water management, treatment of waste and improvement in air quality. Programs were bilateral, with the EU and a candidate identifying the areas of most pressing need for development (Sajdik and Schwarzinger 2008, 88–95).

The financial value of the PHARE program was re-evaluated periodically, and adjusted based on identified priorities. Between 1990 and 1994, the portfolio of PHARE was 4.2 billion euros; that jumped to 6.693 billion euros between 1995 and 1999. Between 2000 and 2006, the budget was 1.56 billion euros per year. SAPARD received an additional 520 billion euros per year, with another 1.04 billion per year in institution-building funds (Sajdik and Schwarzinger 2008; Tatham 2009, 293–302). By setting up and funding the PHARE program, the EU 'core' contributed to helping the candidate countries get ready for EU membership. Pillaging of 'annexed' territory is thus hard to defend in support of the EU as empire argument. Incorporating such statistics into the discussion of EU's dominance over Central Europe would clarify where the scholarship stands on the issue.

Euro-skeptics and realists typically doubt the intentions of the EU in supporting Central and Eastern Europe, the Baltic countries and the Western Balkans with these substantial programs and wave them away as disguised national interests of the core countries. The timing of the approval of these programs lends some credence to this skepticism. OBNOVA and CARDS were agreed in the aftermath of the two Balkan wars, a time when Western powers including the United States were concerned about possible spillover effect of traditional regional rivalries into neighboring countries. In the sense that West Europeans were defending their national interests by helping contain possible further conflict in the rest of the continent, this argument certainly stands. But there is a difference between the realist *real politik* of the national interest defined in terms of power, where coercion, war or other forms of overpowering the periphery (or weaker states) are a state's intentional choices (Morgenthau 1958), and the EC/EU's strategy of containing possible spill-over of conflict from the Balkans by sending technical assistance to the most vulnerable countries.

It is fair to also recognize that the EU did influence domestic policy and governance via these programs, as proponents of the EU as empire concept argue. In order for these countries to adopt and implement the *acquis*, they had to undergo far-reaching reforms which influenced their traditional political, economic and social interactions.

That said, Central and East European states showed that they *wanted* to change their domestic political and economic structures once they rejected communism. Post–Cold War developments inside Central Europe indicate that none of these countries were interested to experiment with communism or socialism any longer. Some, like Slovakia initially benefitted from leadership that did not endorse a Euro-orientation. Vladimír Mečiar cost Slovakia accession in the first wave of enlargement, together with the other Visegrad states. While Mečiar was a Euro-skeptic and a populist, he did not return the country to socialism. Others, like Belarus continue to benefit from leadership that errs on the authoritarian side of history. Belarus, however is not really interested in EU accession and has not applied for membership. Ukraine witnessed similar hesitance since its independence, in deciding whether it wanted to implement liberal reforms in line with a rapprochement to the EU or stick to a more state-centered political philosophy, in line with Russia's preferences. The crisis engulfing the country as of this writing is a direct result of a popular revolution reacting to former president Yanukovych's decision *not* to sign an association agreement with the EU, and accept a Russian agreement instead. The revolution led to the ousting of the president, new elections, and a continued state of conflict between the eastern part of Ukraine which is pro-Russian, and the Kyiv/Western part of Ukraine which favors integration with the EU. This is the ultimate example of Central European choice of the European project with all its downsides, as this Euro choice, expressed in a popular uprising in Ukraine, has not amounted to violent conflict in any other country in the region.

The EU's influence in how these states evolved since 1989 is a result of decisions made both among the periphery and the core, to move away from the past that divided them, into a future that brought them closer together. Both sides are responsible for this evolution, an aspect that is insufficiently contextualized by EU as empire scholarship.

The hierarchy assumption

This assumption is grounded in the following: What is the political relationship between the core and the periphery? In traditional empires, the relationship is one of political control of the core over the periphery (Doyle 1986, 51). The core 'both exploit[s] and rule[s]' the periphery, dictating what the periphery can and cannot do (Burbank and Cooper 2010, 2). Imperial leaders have as objective to 'maintain their political control over different groups in the society' (Eisenstadt 1963, 121). The hierarchy is unidirectional, from the core over the periphery.

EU as empire scholarship argues that relations between the core and the periphery during and after negotiations were unequal, with Brussels imposing its will and values on candidate countries. Political pressure from the core is embodied in policies and regulations that, as Zielonka identifies, amount to a form of political control over the post-Cold War candidates or new members. The fact that the core does not demand of its periphery – candidate states or new members – *reforms that it has not asked of the core itself* is not addressed. Instead of a unidirectional imposition of reforms, with the EU we see the slow bringing of new members to the levels of political culture and economic reform that long-time members of the EU have had to undertake themselves. As Kliewer and Stivachtis identify, EU's standards of economic and political performance are reflected in the policy of 'membership conditionality' and serve to determine which candidates are ready to undertake the responsibilities of membership, and which are not (Kliewer and Stivachtis 2007).

The pressure of the core of the EU on its Eastern periphery revolved around the implementation of the *acquis*, a body of some 2,500 laws stipulating rights and responsibilities that are binding on all members of the EU. It is revised and amended annually by all members to insure adaptation of institutional and bureaucratic structures in light of an enlarging and deepening Union. Central Europe could not possibly be ready for accession into a complex institution as the EC/EU when it first applied, as it was emerging from a political and economic culture that had little in common with the internal rules of the EC/EU. The imbalance between the two sides of Europe has been documented, with Central Europe falling well behind Western Europe in all aspects of political, economic and social life at the time of its emergence from communism. Central European accession was thus heavily dependent on the countries' ability to meet the requirements of the *acquis* in order to become a reliable and contributing member of the EU, rather than a burden and a drag on the entire community of states.

The amount of time it took Central Europe to fulfill the *acquis* was extensive, but a longer, historical view shows that lengthy accession talks are not uncommon. Historically, candidates have taken long years to join the EC/EU, partly because of vetoes or delays by current members against the candidacy of one country or another, and partly because of adjustments the candidates had to make in their domestic regulations in order to qualify for membership. For instance, the UK took five years to join in 1973 – from the moment the French veto was lifted in 1969 – but it really took twelve years to join, from the time it first applied in 1961. Comparatively, Bulgaria and Romania also took twelve years to join. Their application (1995) was followed by five years of delay as they were considered too poor, and economically, socially and politically unprepared for membership. From the start of accession negotiations, in 2000, they took seven years to negotiate their accession in 2007. Portugal and Spain took nine years to negotiate their membership in the EC (application in 1977, accession in 1986), due to their economic backwardness relative to the rest of the EC at the time of their applications.

Estonia, Latvia, Lithuania and Slovakia also took nine years from the submission of application (1995) until accession date (2004); while Hungary and Poland took ten years (application in 1994, accession in 2004). Greece, a country that was considered at the time of its accession application economically backward and was re-democratizing after a lengthy military regime, took six years to join (application in 1975, accession in 1981); Austria, a more advanced country also took six years to join (application in 1989, accession in 1995). The Czech Republic and Slovenia, considered more advanced politically and economically relative to the rest of Central European candidates took eight years to join (Europa n.d.-b). A lengthy accession process to bring candidate countries in line with expectations of the core is thus not new, nor relegated to Central Europe.

Another important difference between the empires of the past and EU governance is reflected in the equal rights of Central Europeans to share responsibilities of leadership and governance, on par with states that have been members since 1952. Slovenia held the rotating presidency January through June 2008, the Czech Republic held it from January through June 2009. Hungary held the rotating presidency from January through June 2011, followed by Poland for the remaining six months. Lithuania held the rotating presidency July through December 2013. Latvia is slated to hold the presidency in the first half of 2015, Slovakia in the second half of 2016. Estonia and Bulgaria will hold it consecutively in 2018, and Romania in the second half of 2019. The 'export of governmentality' feature of the EU-as-empire that Böröcz identifies is defined as a normalization, standardization and control mechanism of modern statehood over Central Europe (Böröcz 2001, 18). This definition begs the question as to why the EU is including newer members in the decision-making processes and power-sharing at all, an aspect scantly addressed by the scholarship. As of this writing, the Polish Prime Minister has been elected to be the next chair of the European Council, which makes one wonder how successful the EU core is in imposing its leadership preferences on the newer members.

The image of Central Europe as helpless states, subordinated to the EU also suffers from post-accession realities such as these countries support of military action in Iraq, against Brussels' main stream thinking on the issue, which earned them an angry rebuke from then French president Chirac. Hungarian and Czech current opposition to tougher EU sanctions against Russia in response to Russia's meddling in Ukraine's crisis has thrown a wrench in the EU's ability to agree on a strategy towards Russia, another reality that puts into question the hierarchical nature of relations between the core in Brussels and the periphery of the newer members.

It is the case that during and after negotiations, EU members applied pressure on candidates to undertake reforms. Some scholars describe this pressure as 'truly imperialist' in building a '"cooperative and voluntary" empire . . . via the policy of conditionality' (Zielonka 2006, 55; Cooper 2001, 26). EU officials did travel to candidate countries to, first offer assistance where templates for legislation were missing, and second to insure that changes were made in accordance with the *acquis*. Incentives rather than punishment were offered to candidates moving towards reforms. Candidates adopted recommendations for policies and laws in what is seen by some as 'an exercise [in] a remarkable degree of control over Eastern Europe' (Zielonka 2006, 57). Yet, what the EU recommended was in line with common practice among members, so that when admitted, new members could be on an equal footing and contribute to the life of the organization. It remains unclear why proponents of the EU as empire concept see voluntary compliance with the EU's *acquis* as imperial in nature as long as candidates choose to comply. While differences of political culture, social and economic reforms, and ability to implement the *acquis* will remain between older members and newer ones, the hierarchical nature of the relationship between the EU and its newest members needs to be qualified, historically contextualized, and recognition offered for the power-sharing arrangements that govern it.

Summary

This chapter has attempted to address how recent empire scholarship views the EU as a rising, (negative), and new type of empire in relation to its newest, Central European members. It discussed the relevance of the empire analytical framework with respect to three basic assumptions of what constitutes a traditional empire: coercion, sustainability and hierarchy. The chapter finds that empire scholarship needs to more explicitly address and acknowledge all three assumptions, specifically as they pertain to the new Central European EU members. The historical context of EU accession needs to include an analysis of the drivers of enlargement that recognizes Central Europe as a main player. Power-sharing relations and sustainability issues also need to be factored in these analyses, if they are to make a convincing case that the EU is becoming a (modern type of) empire.

References

Ash, T. G. 1993. *In Europe's Name: Germany and the Divided Continent*. London: Jonathan Cape.

Avery, G. and F. Cameron. 1998. *The Enlargement of the European Union*. Sheffield: Sheffield Academic Press.

Bayer, J. 2005. EU Accession and Hungarian Politics. In A. Skuhra, (ed.), *The Eastern Enlargement of the European Union: Efforts and Obstacles on the Way to Membership*, 53–74. Innsbruck: Studien Verlag.

Beck, U. and E. Grande. 2007. *Cosmopolitan Europe*. Cambridge: Polity.

Becker, D. G., J. Frieden, S. P. Schats and R. L. Sklar. 1987. *Postimperialism: International Capitalism and Development in the Late Twentieth Century*. Boulder, CO: Lynne Rienner.

Behr, H. 2007. The European Union in the Legacies of Imperial Rule? EU Accession Politics Viewed from A Historical Comparative Perspective. *European Journal of International Relations* 13(2): 240–91.

Böröcz, J. 2001. Empire and Coloniality in the 'Eastern Enlargement' of the European Union. In J. Böröcz and M. Kovács (eds.), *Empire's New Clothes: Unveiling EU Enlargement*, 4–50. Central Europe Review.

Burbank, J. and F. Cooper. 2010. *Empires in World History. Power and Politics of Difference*. Princeton: Princeton University Press.
Burgess, A. 1997. *Divided Europe: The New Domination of the East*. London: Pluto Press.
Colas, A. 2007. *Empire*. Cambridge: Polity.
Commission of the European Communities. 1992. *Europe and the Challenge of Enlargement*, www.europarl.europa.eu/summits/lisbon/li3_en.pdf (accessed 15 November 2013).
Cooper, R. 2001. *The Next Empire*, www.prospectmagazine.co.uk/magazine/thenextempire/#.UtqbcbROmpo (accessed 10 January 2014).
Doyle, M.W. 1986. *Empires*. Ithaca: Cornell University Press.
Eisenstadt, S.N. 1963. *The Political Systems of Empires*. New York: The Free Press.
Europa. (n.d.-a). *Enlargement*, http://europa.eu/legislation_summaries/enlargement/index_en.htm (accessed 15 November 2013).
Europa. (n.d.-b). *Enlargement. From 6 to 28 Members*, http://ec.europa.eu/enlargement/policy/from-6-to-28-members/index_en.htm (accessed 1 December 2013).
Europe Agreement. 1993. *Between the European Communities and Their Member States and the Republic of Poland*, http://wits.worldbank.org/GPTAD/PDF/archive/EC-Poland.pdf (accessed 15 November 2013).
European Commission. 1990. *Communication: Association Agreements with the Countries of Central and Eastern Europe, A General Outline*. COM 398 final.
Ferguson, N. 2002. *Empire. The Rise and Demise of the British World Order and the Lessons for Global Power*. New York: Basic Books.
Fritsch, S and H-J. Uibopuu. 2005. The Baltic States and EU Accession. In A. Skuhra (ed.), *The Eastern Enlargement of the European Union: Efforts and Obstacles on the Way to Membership*, 209–33. Innsbruk: Studien Verlag.
Gheciu, A. 2005. *NATO in the 'New Europe': The Politics of International Socialization after the Cold War*. Stanford: Stanford University Press.
Gibbon, E. 2000. *The History of the Decline and Fall of the Roman Empire*. Abridged edition. London: Penguin Books.
Hardt, M. and A. Negri. 2000. *Empire*. Cambridge, MA: Harvard University Press.
Hardt, M. and A. Negri. 2004. *Multitude. War and Democracy in the Age of Empire*. New York: Penguin Press.
Harvey, D. 2003. *The New Imperialism*. Oxford: Oxford University Press.
Hobson, A. J. 1965. *Imperialism: A Study*. Ann Arbor: University of Michigan Press.
Kliewer, B. and Y. A. Stivachtis. 2007. Democratizing and Socializing Candidate States: The Case of the EU Conditionality. In Y. A. Stivachtis (ed.), *The State of European Integration*. United Kingdom: Ashgate.
Lenin, V. I. 1939. *Imperialism: The Highest Stage of Capitalism*. New York: International.
Lundestand, G. 1986. Empire by Invitation? The United States and Western Europe, 1945–1952. *Journal of Peace Research* 23(3): 263–77.
Marasceau, M. and E. Montaguti. 1995. The Relations Between the European Union and Central and Eastern Europe: A Legal Appraisal. *Common Market Law Review* 32(6): 1327–67.
Milland, G. 2007. *An EU Empire Will 'Rule Over Britain*,' www.express.co.uk/news/uk/13067/An-EU-Empire-will-rule-over-Britain (accessed 15 October 2013)
Mooers, C. 2006. ed. *The New Imperialists. Ideologies of Empire*. Oxford: Oneworld.
Morgenthau, H.J. 1958. *Politics Among Nations: The Struggle for Power and Peace*. 2nd ed. New York: Alfred A. Knopf.
Negri, A. 2003. *Reflections on 'Empire.'* With contributions from Michael Hardt and Danilo Zolo. Trans. by Ed Emery. Cambridge: Polity.

Negri, A. 2006. *Empire and Beyond*. Trans. by Ed Emery. Cambridge: Polity.
Nye. J. S. 2001. *The Paradox of American Power: Why the World's Only Superpower Cannot Go It Alone*. Oxford: Oxford University Press.
Official Journal L 347. 1993. *Free Trade Agreement Between the European Communities and Their Member States and the Republic of Hungary*, http://wits.worldbank.org/GPTAD/PDF/archive/EC-Hungary.pdf (accessed 1 November 2013).
Price C. P. and A. Landau. 1999. The Enlargement of the European Union: Dealing with Complexity. In V. C. Price, A. Landau, and R. G. Whitman (eds.), *The Enlargement of the European Union: Issues and Strategies*, 10–24. London: Routledge.
Sajdik, M. and M. Schwarzinger. 2008. *European Union Enlargement. Background, Developments, Facts*. Central and Eastern European Policy Studies 2. New Brunswick: Transaction.
Schumpeter, J. 1955. *Imperialism and Social Classes*. Cleveland: World.
Tatham, A. F. 2009. *Enlargement of the European Union*. Kluwer La International.
Waterfield, B. 2007. *Barroso Hails the European 'Empire,'* www.telegraph.co.uk/news/worldnews/1557143/Barroso-hails-the-European-empire.html (accessed 1 July 2013).
Zielonka, J. 2006. *Europe as Empire: The Nature of the Enlarged EU*. Oxford: Oxford University Press.
Zielonka, J. 2008. Europe as a Global Actor: Empire by Example? *International Affairs* 84(3): 471–84.

2 'Empire', 'governing from the distance', and the mitigation of violence

Towards a novel policy framework for the EU politics

Hartmut Behr

Introduction

The chapter engages a relation between two contested and complex concepts, those of 'empire' and 'governing from the distance'. Even though there are plenty of empirical examples that suggest a relation among these concepts, its theorization is inevitably a construct. The task of their theorization is aggravated by the very ambiguity and nebulosity of these concepts; however, the empirical significance of respective political phenomena make such theorization necessary in order to enhance our understanding of and finally our ability to act upon them. Such empirical political phenomena are many and relate to all forms of government that are organized over geographical and territorial dimensions that do not allow for a politics 'on the market place', i.e. that have to, in the words of Benedict Anderson, be (more often than not forcefully and violently) 'imagined', because the people comprised by the political body will never meet in person, never have immediate exchange, or create politics out of direct debate. Such political bodies and forms of government depend on some sort of instruments that enable 'governing from the distance' that are – so the chapter shall argue – inevitably violent and reminiscent of 'imperial' centre-periphery problematics. One can hypothesize that the need for, and subsequent problems of, such instruments is the graver, the vaster the territorial dimension of the political body, making – next to historical forms such as the British Empire, or more contemporarily such as the US or post-colonial rule – the European Union (EU) one prime present-day example of this theorization.

The problem

The concept of empire is difficult to grasp, not only terminologically but also in terms of a definition; this applies within a Western context (to which this chapter will be limited), let alone in a cross-cultural and global. This is no wonder, has the idea of empire a long history and thus withdraws from any meaningful identification and fixation due to changing empirical features and political contestations. Nevertheless, there seem to be significant formative principles[1] due to which we can uphold and use this notion and relate it to certain empirical features. But we need to unlearn that empire is a concept that could be defined. But what is it instead?

The English term 'empire' goes back to Latin '*imperium*', but also to '*patrocinium*'. In both, according to their use in Marcus Tullius Cicero (*De re publica*; *De legibus*), we find formative principles, observable across time and space, that provide coherence to and solder empirical phenomena. One of these principles is geopolitical, thus relates to the geographical and territorial dimension of a political body, and can be analyzed according to the theorem of 'governing from the distance'. However, the English word 'empire' is the product of an etymological history in which the widths and depths of the Latin '*imperium*' and '*patrocinium*' have been narrowed down and bereft of meaning. Thus – in the English language – we end up with no adjective to describe and analyze the politics of an empire other than 'imperial' which, however, does only cover a minimum of the semantics of Latin '*patrocinium*' and '*imperium*' which indeed comprise so manifold meanings as 'power', 'command', 'rule', 'authority', 'patronage', 'protection', and 'responsibility'; and they all can, but are by no way limited to be exercised in an '*imperial*' way through force and military might, i.e. how the English 'imperial' implies.[2] According to original widths and depths of '*imperium*' and '*patrocinium*', they can also be exercised, however, in a responsible or benevolent, thus more legitimate way. So, what do we learn from this?

Two things at least: *first*, a general epistemological insight, namely that – to speak with Friedrich Nietzsche – we cannot 'define what has history'. Empire' is (just) one example that illustrates this anti-historicist and genealogical view. *Second*, there are nevertheless formative principles of what we would call 'empire' or 'imperial', in a narrower or wider sense, in the latter case being aware of also benevolent and benign forms of 'imperial' rule. In conclusion, this means that 'empire' must empirically articulate itself other than, and different to, conceptualizable typologies and is identifiable 'only' through formative principles (which, however, must be a matter of empirical experience and observation).[3] Such formative principles can be many; one of them is 'governing from the distance', manifesting a geopolitical centre-periphery constellation that is characterized by asymmetries and inequalities.

While there is plenty of literature across different disciplines that focuses on empire in relation to the geopolitical pattern of centre-periphery, including power asymmetries and inequalities (much of this literature discussed in Behr, 2007; Foster, 2014), the violent character of 'governing from the distance'-policies is a much lesser researched question. Therefore, this question will be discussed in the next section.

'Governing from the distance' and political violence

We want to approach the question of political violence in relation to 'governing from the distance' from an epistemological perspective. In this regard, the problem seems to be that all policies that are supposed to and organized in order to govern over vast geographical and territorial dimensions evince some difficulties in building fora for public deliberation and civil society institutions.[4] Subsequently, such policies are necessarily ignorant of contextual, culture-specific factors that influence political thought and political agency in those 'remote' regions and localities. They are inevitably neglecting situated knowledge and practice(s) and can therefore be called intrinsically violent. Examples of such histories of violence and resistance against it are many and reach in the history of Western empires from local resistance in Gallia against Roman reign; from all kinds of separatist movements in the wake of (imperial) nation-building insisting on local traditions, languages, habits, and ways of life; to colonial and postcolonial practices in the context of the so-called 'standards of civilization' (including historical, but also 21st century policies and discourses around EU enlargement and EU Neighborhood Policies); to worldwide EU peacebuilding and democratization universalities and forms of local resistance against them; to anti-Brussels sentiments that seem contemporarily strongest in France and the UK after the European election.[5] Thus, two questions arise: *first*, how to better understand theoretically the triangular relation between situated knowledge and practice, 'governing from the distance', and political violence; and *second*, there seems to be a quandary in relation to the 'right' balance between local, context-situated and context-specific, on the one hand, and general, universalistic approaches to and practices of politics, on the other hand, and their reconciliation in common institutions. Both questions will be discussed in the following subsections.

Situated knowledge and practices, 'governing from the distance', and political violence

We witness a huge debate about the relation between situated and perspectivist or universal and general knowledge. These debates span philosophy, history, politics, sociology, literature studies, and ethnography and are too comprehensive to review here. There seems to be, however, a clear stance on behalf of situated and perspectivist knowledge in all hermeneutic inspired research across, but also prior to the institutional establishment of at least some of the mentioned disciplines.[6] Not always began the researcher with hermeneutic episteme and methods, and, as intriguingly narrated by Susanne Hoeber-Rudolph, the conviction that context-specific methods are necessary for social and political research is often a matter of actual research experience in the field that requires the non-ideological openness of the researcher for eventually profound methodological shifts of his or her own work.[7] From such a, let us call it, *hermeneutic* viewpoint[8] on knowledge production and political practice as context-specific, local, and perpectivist, the ideational background that underpins all 'governing from the distance'-practices as well as these practices themselves appear as imposition of universal and universalized knowledge claims on and intervention in local contexts.

It is helpful here to understand and differentiate political violence. For such differentiation, I suggest the violence triangle of Johan Galtung consisting of the forms of direct, structural, and cultural violence (see Galtung, 1969, 1971). The imposition of universal(alized) knowledge and political practices occurs in all three forms. Empirically, these forms manifest to divergent degrees depending on the historical contexts of imposition and the actor. For example, direct violence seems obsolete in present-day EU impositions of its knowledge claims and practices, as in its 2004 Enlargement and contemporary Neighborhood Policies, for instance. However, structural and cultural violence appears very virulent.[9] The manifestation of violence looks different, of course, if we looked at the imposition of knowledge and practices in cases of present-day humanitarian intervention or historical forms of colonial and imperial politics where all three forms, including direct violence, become manifest.[10]

In all cases, however, 'governing from the distance'-practices and related knowledge claims seem to ignore situated epistemologies and ontologies, are thus nonperspectivist and in one or another form violent. Hence, the question arises of whether governing can operate *without* imposition at all, thus with varying to no degrees of ignorance of local contexts and subsequently, too, with varying to no degrees of violence. We here receive a more substantial answer from nonutilitarian ethical discussions in political philosophy than from studies on government and governmentality, because respective philosophical discussions inform us about a general pattern of political action that, too, underpins governing actors and institutions.

This pattern concerns the ethical dilemma and tragedy involved in every action. According to anti-utilitarian views, political action and employed means can never be justified by possible ends. This is not necessarily because of principled arguments against such functionalism, but rather because utilitarianism assumes that ends could be known and were predictable. Contrary to this, an anti-utilitarian position feels theoretically and empirically reassured that there are always inadvertent and accidental consequences of our actions that can neither be foretold nor controlled. Any justification of means by ends would thus be impossible.[11] Consequently, any action is inherently and inevitably caught-up in the production of inadvertent and nonpredictable consequences. It therefore can never be ethically pure and is intrinsically tragic if such consequences – what is always possible and likely – were harmful to others. Only he who thinks is innocent, as metaphorically Johann Wolfgang von Goethe says.[12]

Governing, however, is acting, and acting always interrupts the innocence of thought and reflection, is tragic, always ethically corrupted, by manifesting through its action an essentialist 'here and now' as if such 'here and now' existed (see Heidegger 1923–1944, also 2006 and 2007). And the manifestation and consolidation of such 'here and now' is inevitably ignorant of contexts: as much as it might try to take into account context-specific contingencies and conditions, the beginning of action is the ending of such respect of and accountability to context. The imposition of a distinct 'here and now' on behalf of certain consequences always triggers, too, inadvertent and uncontrollable consequences, excluding other possible 'heres and nows'. Action and governing is unescapably violent, and this even more the case if and when conducted and implemented 'from the distance' as the uncontrollability and context-insensitivity increases with distance. So, if this violent nature of governing cannot be eliminated, how can it at least be mitigated?

Balancing 'local' and 'universalistic' approaches and practices

To summarize the argument so far: any form of governing is inevitably violent since as a form of action it opens-up the likelihood of and manifests inadvertent consequences that are neither predictable, nor controllable. These consequences, as well as well-intended consequences, too, do eliminate, and in the very moment of action also ignore, alternative possibilities for action. The greater the geographical distance of governing and the remoter (and unfamiliar) the contexts, the greater and more harmful and violent are this elimination and ignorance.[13] This relation would argue against any kind of universal knowledge and practice and embrace the significance and relevance of localities. However, this embrace cannot and should not be unconditional, because each locality (and singularity) is just as contingent and conditional as every perspective on and each attempt to understand it. Empirically, European knowledge, practices, and related values are and shall not assumed or claimed to be universal, however, this does not result in an unconditional embrace of local knowledge, practices, and values. Conditional and contingent knowledge and practice – emerging from the temporality of being and the transformativities of individual and collective existence – indeed result in the unconditional embrace of difference(s),[14] however, it might well be, at least the possibility cannot be excluded, that local knowledge and practices are either directly harmful and violent themselves or harmful and violent to values that are perceived as a matter of heart from, for instance, European perspectives.[15]

Examples of humanitarian intervention (or nonintervention) is a point in case; also one might not dismiss fully and in total ideas from the 'standards of civilization', the Copenhagen criteria, or from ENPs; i.e. precisely, we are aware of the advantages of rule of law over the rule of kinship; are not prepared to accept racist violence, gender discrimination and gender violence, homophobia, etc. etc. as much local legitimacy as respective practices and worldviews might enjoy, as much as related phenomena might also have been existent in European history and are not fully eliminated present-day; and as much – as some postcolonial arguments would hold – as related phenomena might be reasoned by Western colonial practices.[16]

However, such (well founded) unwillingness to accept, does, on the other hand, not justify the (as discussed above) imposition of own (in this case, 'European') knowledge, practices, and values. This quandary appears unresolvable. It can be framed, in other words, as the problem between 'universalism and particularism' or between 'identity and difference'. While there are important arguments against universalism as (directly, structurally, and culturally) violent, and in favor of particularism, localities and their situated knowledge traditions and related practices, we need to be aware of one practical and one epistemological reason for (some kind of) universalism: *first* and practically, there might be, whether we like it or not, discrete, local practices that are universal, imposing essentialisms, and violent themselves why we need a normative framework to critique them; and *second* and epistemologically, we need some kind of universal ontology in order to (be able to) perceive of differences as equal, i.e., some vision of humanity that allows us to embrace difference(s) and, too, to critique their informing ontologies, epistemologies, and practices. However, respective universalities must and shall not be imposing and hierarchical.[17]

The philosophical answer to this question about a referent point for such kind of universalism and humanity lies, I suggest, in an active de-essentializing project that actively neutralizes universal, essentialist claims of all kind and origin through persistent critique, and that therefore can operate as a universal frame perceiving differences without essentializing them. However, this *philosophical* answer needs to translate into a practical policy framework. Therefore, the deconstructive character of such a de-essentializing, critical project needs some kind of reconstructive direction that informs agency; put differently: critique needs to be guided and is no end in itself; again differently: acting and governing are inevitably tragic, but this does not suspend the question of political agency and of *how* to act. In the remaining chapter I want to suggest a policy frame that is aware of the tragic of political agency, corresponds to such de-essentializing, critical project, but translates these into a practical proposition, applying to the EU as to any other political actor.

The action principle that translates the de-essentializing, critical project into a policy frame is the maxim of the reversibility and revocability of consequences. If consequences are neither controllable, nor predictable, if the tragic is therefore intrinsic to political action; and if universalism is imposing, violent, and essentializing; however, some kind of universalism needed: the only way towards and for action under those conditions consists in the principle that consequences are (at least) not irreversible. The nonirreversibility of consequences appears as policy yardstick that mitigates the always violent and essentializing articulations of action and governing – even if just momentarily and transiently for the very moment where action breaks through and manifests – and that directs critique towards a democratic, accountable, and humane end.[18]

The idea that policies must not bring about irreversible consequences has been initially formulated in the early discussions on environmental justice and generational accountability. First publications emerged in German academic debates under the term *Umweltgerechtigkeit* in the early 1980s in the context of the emergence of the Green Party, then as 'environmental justice' in US and subsequently in UK debates from the 2000s to present-day. A fundamental difference to the argument developed here is, however, that whereas most debates on environmental justice[19] assume accountability of environmental degradation to arise *after* it happened, so to say in relation to the settling and elimination of consequences, the argument here holds that policies that lead to irreversible consequences are to be avoided in the first place. The axiom developed here, in contrast, identifies policies as ignorant of conditions intrinsic to knowledge and practice always when and if policies are conducted which are of irreversible consequences.

Examples from EU politics to illustrate this point are many: We can refer to some examples that will be discussed below in this volume in greater detail and find that there are four policies analyzed that contradict the political norm of reversibility. Thus, we conclude that the EU could to much better in mitigating political violence inevitably caused by its 'governing from the distance'-practices. As we learn from Joszef Boeroecz's analysis of EU imperial geopolitics, the EU contracts agreements that are hierarchical and asymmetrical. This is especially the case with Eastern European nations, but also nations from outside the EU in its neighbourhood. Empirical articulations of this finding manifest in examples analyzed by Aylin Güney and his argument about the essentialization of geopolitical identities in and through EU politics; in politics critically studied by Yannis Stivachtis alongside the framework of politics of conditionality; as well as in Robert Phillipson's analysis of the unequal treatment of certain groups within the EU identified by language according to what he calls 'linguistic imperialism'. All these practices can be assessed according to the normative framework of 'reversibility' and 'irreversibility' while politics according to the former are inclined to mitigate political violence. The analyses presented here unfortunately portray a negative picture in that we observe EU politics that follow, create, or reason irreversible consequences, at least medium term; i.e. consequences that result from these practices are in need of further policies that are supposed to turn these consequences back, including the timeline according to the political processes in the EU decision-making apparatus and, of course, the actual success of these policies. As we learn from Russell Foster's chapter, there is an underlying intellectual pattern in EU politics that traces through centuries of European history and manifests in a social and political discourse on '*imperium*' in which the EU partakes. In this discourse we find the self-righteous proclamations about a (West) European civilizing mission, combined with discourses on the responsibility to civilize in the own image. This intellectual pattern seems to be underlie irreversible politics, but is itself characterized by a high degree of irreversibility, especially due to its century-lasting engraining in (Western) European self-understanding.

The drafting of policies that are informed by and include their own reversibility consequently appears as a dictum and policy frame for democratic and accountable politics, not only in terms of generational accountability, but also in terms of intrinsic conditions of human knowledge and agency. The ability to turn back the wheel of consequences, or to prevent policies with irreversible consequences in the first place appears as the only accountable political agency for an actor as the EU that is involved in turbulent world politics promoting policies 'governing from the distance' and building 'imperial' structures. Thus, the argument here is less engaged in demonstrating empirically that and to what degree the EU can be seen as a form of empire, but rather builds on evidence of the existence of respective centre-periphery relations and 'governing from the distance'-policies and discourses and is interested in the question of how to mitigate arising forms of violence and how to (re) integrate them in a framework of accountable politics that coincides with intrinsic conditions of human knowledge and agency.

The dictum of avoiding policy irreversibilities appears as such a framework. Of course, the subsequent question arises, how to specify, define, and/or measure irreversiblities? Also, at which scale and scope of consequences to speak of their irreversibility? These are questions for further elaboration. Time horizons seem to play a crucial role for addressing these questions; as well as institutional designs that allow to negotiate 'local' and 'universal' claims and that help to avoid irreversible politics.

Conclusions

Since political violence is inevitably an aspect of governing, and even more so of 'governing from the distance', the political responsibility is to mitigate the violence incremental to politics and its consequences. Regardless of what type of violence results from certain policies, political responsibility needs a normative framework for its conceptualization as well as, too, for the possibility to become a guideline for political agency. An effective normative framework – maybe the most effective due to resulting from an inherent condition of political action and human knowledge itself – is provided by the notion of the reversibility (or non-irreversibility) of politics. Reversibility means literally the possibility to reverse consequences of once action; and if such consequences are violent in its effect on contemporary societies and future generations, then violence can be mitigated through reversing such consequences. This framework is a powerful device for political analysis and action, and is suggested here for studying and assessing EU politics as well as for political action in the EU. Much analysis in the following chapters in this volume links, or can be linked, to this analytical framework of reversibility/irreversibility since they emphasize in their analyses essentializing EU policies that can be read alongside a reversibility/irreversibility spectrum. According to such a reading, the hypothesis can be suggested that the more policies are of an essentializing character the more irreversible they and their consequences are.

This chapter is among the first attempts to develop and suggest a novel policy framework of a reversibility/irreversibility spectrum. The author is fully aware that this needs more elaboration; the following key questions are to be addressed in further elaborations: (1) It seems to be important to accomplish clarification about the timeline when and from when on consequences can be called irreversible; (2) further, it appear necessary to elucidate the type and scale of violence inherent in and resulting from certain policies in relation to strategies of reversion; (3) the notion of reversibility of consequences must be applied and explained in relation to present populations and future generations; (4) the reversibility/irreversibility spectrum must be related to and interpreted against the background of the notion of responsibility; and (5) the normative character and the question of the foundation of its norms of a reversibility/irreversibility spectrum must be expounded. There are certainly more issues and questions and this list is by no way seen as comprehensive, but these five concerns appear as most urgent for further elaboration of what is a powerful framework for present EU politics and beyond.

Notes

1 See more on this notion in footnote 3.
2 For this discussion, see further: Champion, 2004; Erskine, 2010; Folz, 1969; Kiely, 2010; Richardson, 2008. In addition to these epistemological uncertainties, a literature review of research on 'empire' demonstrates significant differences and incompatibilities in their attempt to define and/or conceptualize empire – even looking at the *same* empirical phenomenon –, resulting in the conclusion that we cannot grasp a concept of empire. For an excellent discussion, see Foster, 2014.
3 I write here 'only' in inverted commas, signalizing that this 'non-conceptualizability' of empire and, more generally, of social and political reality and experience is *not* a deficiency of political or social theories and by no means of 'reality' (how could it?), but the very nature of our always historical and temporal experience of politics; and we do not have more than this experience: who would hold reality in hands? And who would know *what* it is? See in this regard Martin Heidegger who writes in 'Prolegomena zur Geschichte des Zeitbegriffs': "Die Frage nach dem Sein (. . .) ist eine sogenannte Bestimmungsfrage. Nicht gefragt ist, ob es so etwas wie Sein überhaupt gibt, sondern gefragt ist, was damit gemeint ist, was darunter verstanden ist, nämlich unter 'Sein'" (1923–1944, 193); also: "Als könnte aus der echten Ontik die Ontologie abgelesen werden. Was ist denn echte Ontik, wenn nicht echt aus vor-ontologischem Entwurf" (*Sein und Zeit*, 1929, Gesamtausgabe, Volume 2); furthermore: "Nirgends unter den Dingen finden wir das Sein" (2007, 7). For further discussion, see also Hartmut Behr, 2014. Against this background of temporal ontology, I speak here of *formative principles* of a thing-experienced, rather than of a concept of a thing or its conceptual determinability which is always fixation, determination, identification, and terminability of something that is, however, always in flux.
4 The large body of literature on globalization and civil society demonstrates related empirical and conceptual problems, see for example Baker and Chandler, 2005; Glasius, Lewis, Seckinelgin, 2004; Keane, 2003. For an early account of the same problematic and argument against geographically distant political authorities, see the *Anti-Federalist Papers* in the US constitutional debate in the 1770s and 1780s.
5 See representative literatures, including Euro-Barometer: Anderson, 1983; Behr, 2007; Berger, 2004; Berger, Donovan, Passmore, 1999; Boeroecz, 2001; Citron, 1989; Chandler, 2010; Donnelly, 1998; Eisenstadt, 1963; Engelbrekt, 2002; Escobar, 1995; Gong, 1984; Hansen, 2002; Richmond, 2010; Richmond, 2011; Richmond et al., 2011a; Richmond et al., 2011b; Said, 1994; Sinopoli, 1994; see also http://ec.europa.eu/public_opinion/archives/eb/eb80/eb80_publ_en.pdf.
6 Important main literatures include: Foucault, 1970; Habermas, 1978; Nietzsche, 2008; Ringer, 1997; Rorty, 1984; Simmel, 1918; Simmel, 1980; Taylor, 1983, 1985. As we can conclude from this, by no means whatsoever is the emphasis of conditionalities and contingencies of knowledge (claims) a 'postmodern' (or poststructuralist) accomplishment, but has been stressed upon by plenty movements and authors before and independently, many of which are dishonestly ignored by many so-called 'post' thinkers, who often proof to be too superficial historians of political thought.
7 See Cook, 2005; Hoeber-Rudolph, 2005; also Morgenthau's reference to K. Mannheim's notion of *Standortgebundenheit*; see Mannheim, 1936, 1984; Morgenthau, 1962. Most interesting and admirable in this regard of individual openness to epistemological and methodological shifts is Almond, 1990.

8 To summarize: a viewpoint that is aware, *first*, of the mutually constitutive, affective, and interactive relation between researcher and 'object under study', and subsequently, and *second*, that both in their relations to each other need to be understood, thus ontologically and epistemologically engaged, in each moment and context of their actuality.

9 See for further discussion, Behr, 2007, 2012. This view and assessment might be different, however, if we looked at EU immigration politics and the institution of refugee camps in Africa through which we can observe consequences that can be classified as direct violence.

10 See hereto particularly the main focus and findings of postcolonial studies and their emphasis on historical and continuing forms of power asymmetry between Europe/the West and the colonized/postcolonial world of the past and respective subordination of alterity; instead of many, see Chakrabarty, 2000; Chakravorty, 1988.

11 Important here, the phenomenological insight of Alfred Schuetz into the character of social action as always hypothetical and a 'project-on-draft'; see Schuetz, 1972.

12 For this anti-utilitarian position, see amongst others Morgenthau, 1945.

13 This relation does of course not apply in reverse, is thus not supposing that violence is generally the greatest the remoter the victim is.

14 As argued in Behr, 2014.

15 Thus, the unconditional embrace of differences does not mean the unconditional acceptance of their informing worldviews.

16 An example in this point might be the observation in Rothermund (1993, 1995) that the cast system in India today developed into a hierarchical relation between the different casts through the British colonial bureaucratic rationality of vertical classification.

17 These and resulting arguments below in the next paragraph are further discussed and developed in Behr, 2010 and 2014.

18 This policy frame of the reversibility of consequences has been outlined in Behr, 2013, is further discussed in Behr, *Conditions of Critique: Towards Humane and Democratic Politics*, paper delivered at the second workshop of the international network 'Classical Realism Meets Critical Theory', Ottawa University, June 21–22, 2014, and shall be developed in a future book project.

19 See, for example, Schlosberg (2007), Dobson (1999), and Rhodes (2003).

References

Almond, Gabriel A. 1990. Clouds, Clocks, and the Study of Politics. In: *A Discipline Divided: Schools and Sects in Political Science*, edited by Gabriel A. Almond, 32–65. Boston, MA: Sage.

Anderson, Benedict. 1983. *Imagined Communities. Reflections on the Origin and Spread of Nationalism*. London: Verso.

Anti-Federalist Papers, The. 1986. Edited and with an Introduction by Ralph Ketcham. New York: New American Library.

Behr, Hartmut. 2007. The European Union in the Legacies of Imperial Rule? EU Accession Politics viewed from a Historical Comparative Perspective. *European Journal of International Relations* 13: 239–262.

Behr, Hartmut. 2010. *A History of International Political Theory: Ontologies of the International*. Basingstoke: Palgrave Macmillan.

Behr, Hartmut. 2012. EU-rope: History, Violence, Peripheries', *Review of European Studies* 4(3): 7–17.

Behr, Hartmut. 2013. Security Politics and Public Discourse: A Morgenthauian Approach. In: *Interpreting Global Security*, edited by Mark Bevir, Oliver Daddow, and Ian Hall, 160–176. London: Routledge.

Behr, Hartmut. 2014. *Politics of Difference – Epistemologies of Peace*. Global Horizons Book Series. London: Routledge.

Berger, S. 2004. Representations of the Past: The Writing of National Histories in Europe. *Debate: A Review of Contemporary German Studies* 12(1): 73–96.

Berger, S., Donovan, M., and Passmore, K. (eds.) 1999. *Writing National Histories Western Europe since 1800*. London: Routledge.

Boeroecz, Jozsef. 2001. Empire and Coloniality in the "Eastern Enlargement" of the European Union. In Jozsef Boeroecz and Melinad Kovacs (eds.) *Empire's New Clothes: Unveiling EU Enlargement*, 4–50, www.ce-review.org.

Chakrabarty, Dipesh. 2000. *Provincializing Europe: Postcolonial Thought and Historical Difference*. Princeton. Princeton University Press.

Chakravorty, Gayatri. 1988. Can the Sub-altern Speak? In: *Marxism and the Interpretation of Culture*, ed. by C. Nelson and L. Grossberg, 271–313. Urbana: University of Illinois Press.

Champion, Craig. (ed.). 2004. *Roman Imperialism: readings and sources*. Cambridge, MA: Cambridge University Press.

Chandler, David. 2010. *International Statebuilding: The Rise of Post-Liberal Governance*. London: Routledge.

Chandler, David and Baker, Gideon (eds.). 2005. *Global Civil Society: Contested Futures*. London: Routledge.

Citron, Suzanne. 1989. *Le mythe national. L'historie de France en question*, Paris: Les Éditions Ouvrières.

Constitutional Convention Debates, The. 1986. Edited and with an introduction by Ralph Ketcham. New York: New American Library.

Cook, Ian *et al.* 2005. Positionality/Situated Knowledge. In David Atkinson et al. (eds.), *Cultural Geography: A Critical Dictionary of Key Concepts*. London: I. B. Tauris.

Dobson, Andrew. 1999. *Fairness and Futurity: Essays in Environmental Sustainability and Social Justice*. Oxford: Oxford University Press.

Donnelly, V. 1998. Human Rights: A New Standard of Civilization? *International Affairs* 74(1): 1–23.

Eisenstadt, Shmuel N. 1963. *The Political System of Empires*. Glencoe, IL: Free Press.

Engelbrekt, Kjell. 2002. Multiple Asymmetries: The European Union's Neo-Byzantine Approach to Eastern Enlargement. *International Politics* 39(1): 37–51.

Erskine, Andrew. 2010. *Roman Imperialism*. Edinburgh: Edinburgh University Press.

Escobar, Arturo. 1995. Beyond the Third World: Imperial Globality, Global Coloniality and Anti-Globalisation Social Movements. *Third World Quarterly* 25(1): 207–230.

Folz, R. 1969. *The Concept of Empire in Western Europe: from the Fifth to the Fourteenth Century*. Frome: Edward Arnold.

Foster, Russell. 2014. *Tabulae Imperii Europaei: Mapping European Empire*, forthcoming. London: Routledge.

Foucault, Michel. 1970. *The Order of Things: An Archaeology of the Human Sciences*. London: Tavistock Publications.

Galtung, Johann. 1969. Violence, Peace, and Peace Research. *Journal of Peace Research* 6(3): 167–191.

Galtung, Johann. 1971. A Structural Theory of Imperialism. *Journal of Peace Research* 8(2): 81–117.

Glasius, Marlies, David Lewis, and Hakan Seckinelgin, (eds.). 2004. *Exploring Civil Society: Political and Cultural Contexts*. London: Routledge.

Gong, Gerrit W. 1984. *The Standard of 'Civilization' in International Society*. Oxford: Clarendon Press.

Habermas, Jürgen. 1978. *Knowledge and Human Interests*, translated by Jeremy J. Shapiro. London: Heinemann Educational.

Hansen, Peo. 2002. European Integration, European Identity and the Colonial Connection. *European Journal of Social Theory* 5(4): 483–98.

Heidegger, Martin. 1923–1944. Prolegomena zur Geschichte des Zeitbegriffs. *Gesamtausgabe*, II. Abteilung: Vorlesungen 1923–1944, Bd. 20, Frankfurt/M: Vittorio Klostermann.

Heidegger, Martin. 1962 [1929]. *Being and Time*. Translated by John Macquire and Edward Robinson, New York: HarperCollins. [German edition 'Sein und Zeit', *Gesamtausgabe*, I. Abteilung: Frühe Schriften, Band 2, Frankfurt/M: Vittorio Klostermann.]

Heidegger, Martin. 2006. Identität und Differenz. *Gesamtausgabe*, I. Abteilung: Veröffentlichte Schriften, Band 11, Frankfurt/M: Vittorio Klostermann.

Heidegger, Martin. 2007. Zur Sache des Denkens. *Gesamtausgabe*, I. Abteilung: Frühe Schriften, Bd. 14, Frankfurt/M: Vittorio Klostermann.

Hoeber Rudolph, Susanne. 2005. The Imperialism of Categories: Situating Knowledge in a Globalized World. *Perspectives on Politics* 3(1): 5–14.

Keane, John. 2003. *Global Civil Society?* Cambridge: Cambridge University Press.

Kiely, Ray. 2010. *Rethinking Imperialism*. Basingstoke: Palgrave Macmillan.

Mannheim, K. 1936. *Ideology and Utopia*. London: Routledge.

Mannheim, K. 1984. Die Methoden der Wissenssoziologi. In *Ideologiekritik und Wissenssoziologie*, edited by Kurt Lenk, 203–12. Frankfurt am Main: Campus.

Morgenthau, Hans. J. 1945. The evil of politics and the ethics of evil. *Ethics* LVI (1): 1–18.

Morgenthau, Hans. J. 1962. The Intellectual and Political Functions of a Theory of International Relations. In *Politics in the 20th Century, Vol. I, The Decline of Democratic Politics*, edited by Hans J. Morgenthau, 62–78. Chicago, IL: University of Chicago Press.

Nietzsche, Friedrich. 2008. *On the genealogy of morals*. Oxford: Oxford University Press.

Rhodes, Edwardo Lao. 2003. *Environmental Justice in America*. Bloomington: Indiana University Press.

Richardson, J. 2008. *The Language of Empire: Rome and the Idea of Empire from the Third Century BC to the Second Century AD*. Cambridge: Cambridge University Press.

Richmond, Oliver P. 2010. Resistance and the Post-Liberal Peace. *Millennium* 38(3): 665–92.

Richmond, Oliver P. 2011. *A Post-Liberal Peace*. London: Routledge.

Richmond, Oliver P. *et al.* 2011a. The Emerging EU Peacebuilding Framework: Confirming or Transcending Liberal Peacebuilding. *Cambridge Review of International Affairs* 24(3): 449–69.

Richmond, Oliver P. *et al.* 2011b. The EU's Peace-as-Governance Model: More than pacification. In H. Carey (ed.), *The Effect of European Governance Policies on Human Rights and Democracy*. Lanham: Lexington Books.

Ringer, Fritz. 1997. *Max Weber's Methodology: The Reunification of Cultural and Social Sciences*. Cambridge, MA: Harvard University Press.

Rothermund, Dietmar. 1993. *An Economic History of India: from Pre-colonial Times to 1991*. London: Routledge.

Rothermund, Dietmar. 1995. *Indien. Kultur, Geschichte, Politik, Wirtschaft, Umwelt: Ein Handbuch*. Muenchen, C. H. Beck.

Rorty, Richard. 1984. The Historiography of Philosophy. In: *Philosophy of History: Essays on the Historiography of Philosophy*, ed. by Quentin Skinner, J. B. Schneewind, Richard Rorty, 49–75. Cambridge: Cambridge University Press.

Said, Edward. 1994. *Culture and imperialism*. New York: Vintage Books.

Schlosberg, David. 2007. *Defining Environmental Justice: Theories, Movements, and Nature*, Oxford: Oxford University Press.

Schütz, Alfred. 1972. *The Phenomenology of the Social World*, translated by George Walsh and Frederick Lehnert, with an Introduction by George Walsh. London: Heinemann.

Simmel, Georg. 1918. Vom Wesen des historischen Verstehens. *Geschichtliche Abende im Zentralinstitut für Erziehung und Unterricht*, Heft 5, Berlin.

Simmel, Georg. 1980. *Essays on Interpretation in Social Science*. Translated and edited with an introduction by Guy Oakes. Manchester: Manchester University Press.

Sinopoli, Carla M. 1994. The Archaeology of Empires. *Annual Review of Anthropology* 23: 159–80.

Taylor, Charles. 1983. *Social Theory as Practice*. New York: Oxford University Press.

Taylor, Charles. 1985. *Philosophy and the Human Sciences*. Cambridge: Cambridge University Press.

3 The uses and misuses of the imperial paradigm in the study of European integration

Jan Zielonka

Introduction

Empire represents a type of political organization in which the metropolis exercises control over diverse peripheral actors through formal annexations and/or various forms of informal domination. This short definition may well be uncontroversial, but can one classify as empire a unique if not postmodern polity such as the European Union? (Nunes 2011; Telo 2009) The EU does not have a clearly defined center of authority. Member states, however small and poor, are formally equal. Exercise of power within the EU has been highly institutionalized. Besides, the EU is currently in a deep crisis and one could ask whether the term 'empire' can be applied to it. However, the term 'empire' refers to the organizational characteristics of certain actors and not to their overall prowess. All empires have their moments of glory and demise. Despite the crisis, the EU represents a vast territorial unit with sizeable power and resources. The EU often imposes severe domestic constraints of formally sovereign actors, including its own member states. Like all empires, the EU has also a civilizing narrative if not a civilizing mission: it claims to be an indispensable agent of modernity and peace in Europe and beyond. This chapter will try to establish whether the EU does indeed look, walk and talk as empires. If the EU is a kind of empire, what are the implications for understanding the evolving nature of European politics? And has the Euro crisis undermined the EU's imperial credentials?

The politics of paradigms

Paradigms and concepts should help us to comprehend the complex reality, but this is easier said than done. Paradigms always simplify the reality and do not represent a true representation. As Emanuel Adler (1987, 4) once observed, 'paradigms "are not true" or "false" in any naive sense. Rather they take us further (or less far) and are theoretically more or less fruitful.'

Moreover, the use of paradigms is seldom objective. It reflects not only competing academic agendas, but also ideological prejudices and political preferences. Three decades ago the term social 'class' has been dominant in the public discourse, but it is no longer so after the 'victory' of neo-liberalism over Marxism (and despite the ever larger gap between the rich and the poor in Europe and

America.) States classified as 'failed' have become 'legitimate' targets for foreign intervention. A growing number of illiberal regimes subject themselves to electoral scrutiny because they want to be seen as democratic and not autocratic. Using the term 'empire' to characterize the European Union is not necessarily an 'innocent' exercise either.

Some scholars, activists and officials use the term 'empire' to show that Europe is on par with other global giants: America, Russia and China. In this version the EU is being presented as a benign and universal force for good. Through the skillful use of law and trade the EU pacifies the international environment, spreads prosperity, and enhances democracy in its vast neighborhood and beyond (Hettne and Söderbaum 2005; Beck and Grande 2007).

Other scholars and activists (but very few officials) use the term 'empire' to show Europe's colonial atavism and its record of manipulating formally sovereign states either outside or inside the EU. In this version the EU is presented as a malign international actor utilizing its sizable economic and political leverage in a selfish and arrogant manner (Chandler 2006; Böröcz and Kovács 2001). Both versions are correct and false to some degree. History shows that empires can be either benign or malign; they can chiefly rely on incentives or coercion; they can be modest regional affairs or manifestations of grandeur with global ambitions and reach. The EU often represents the force for good, but sometimes it also does stupid if not evil things as the people of Bosnia have experienced. The EU can be generous and selfish at the same time; it can be bold or paralyzed; overconfident or wary; confused or strategic.

Adding adjectives to the 'term' empire is not of much help either. The EU has been labelled as 'normative empire,' but all empires are normative; i.e. they pursue policies reflecting their norms and values (Laïdi 2008a, 2008b). The EU was also labelled a non-imperial empire, but this seems to be a contradiction in terms (Telegraph 2007). All empires pursue imperial policies of some kind or else they are not empires.

Despite all above mentioned complications it is hard to do without paradigms. To call the EU *sui generis* suggests that it can hardly be explained or compared to other economic or political units (MacCormick 1999). Labelling the EU as an 'unidentified political object' (UPO) suggests anything-goes policies of a rather mysterious origin and nature.[1] Besides, the UPO represents a paradigm of some sort, however poor. Alternatives are not any better. The EU is certainly not a state and nor is it a typical international organization. What is it then?

In other words, the EU needs to be conceptualized in one way or another. The imperial paradigm is certainly not perfect, but it can be quite revealing. This is because a research agenda focused on empires invites us to consider factors that are often seen in a different light by international relations' scholars or even ignored altogether (Zielonka 2012, 502). The imperial paradigm puts power at the center of analysis and devotes a special attention to order, hierarchy and structure in international politics. While scholars of International Relations construct abstract models of multi-polarity, students of empires analyze systemic discrepancies between the imperial center and its peripheries. The imperial paradigm also focuses on the scope and structure of governance, the nature of borders, and narratives framing policies, so-called civilizing missions. These topics are usually neglected by students of International Relations focusing on interstate conflict, diplomatic negotiations, political leadership, and national interests. The imperial paradigm does not differentiate between domestic and foreign affairs the way it is being done by the statist paradigm. Empires hardly ever possess fixed and hard borders and they often find it impractical to differentiate between external and internal policy. Borders between the imperial center and peripheries tend to be fuzzy, with peripheries able to drag the center into their parochial conflicts and extract side payments. This explains why students of empires are more at ease explaining the cascading economic interdependence, transnational jurisdictions and multiple cultural loyalties than students of interstate politics and international organizations.

What is empire?

There are many definitions of empire as there are many definitions of democracy, nation, class, or state (Colas 2007; Doyle 1986, 136–38; Eisenstadt 1963; Hardt and Negri 2000; Parker 2010, 113–14). All major concepts in the social sciences are imprecise and inconsistently employed. Each individual definition of empire emphasizes its different features. Some definitions put emphasis on control and domination while other on asymmetric political order and center-periphery relations. However, control and domination can be exercised through various combinations of military, economic and cultural means. It can also be formal or informal to various degrees; it can be flexible or rigid. Asymmetry between the center and periphery can also differ. Some peripheral actors are given access to the metropolis decision-making and resources, while others are kept at a distance or even subject to open discrimination and exploitation. The nature of both metropolis and peripheral actors can also differ. The center can be centralized or decentralized to various degrees; it can be united or ridden by internal conflicts; it can be strong in military and economic terms, but it can also be relatively weak.

Territorial expansion is also emphasized by numerous definitions of empires, even though this expansion does not need to be one-directional. In other words, empires can expand, shrink and then re-expand again in different historical periods. However, they differ from ordinary states which have their borders more or less fixed. Some definitions emphasize external territories of empires: France and Britain had overseas empires. Other definitions emphasize internal territorial aspects of empires; the Habsburg Monarchy or Russia were empires chiefly because of their internal structure.

Cognitive factors also feature differently in individual definitions of empires. Some definitions assume that the metropolis has a master plan of imperial conquest. Other definitions envisage empires rising quietly through uneven modernization and social differentiation with no specific plan or intention. Some actors are proud to be empire; they may even claim a special mandate from the heaven to run their empire. Other actors are empires in default or disguise. They may well have numerous imperial features, but they do not call themselves empires; they may even think that calling them by this name represents an insult.

Difficulty to define empires precisely stems from their very long history. One does not need to agree with John Darwin's (2008, 491) claim that the 'whole history of the world is an imperial history,' but there is no doubt that empires existed for a much longer period than nation-states. Different historical periods generated different sorts of empires. The Ottoman Empire shared only some common features with the British Empire. It would therefore be naïve to expect that contemporary empires will perfectly resemble any of their predecessors.

For me, the term 'empire' represents a vast territorial unit with global military, economic and diplomatic influence (in Badie, Berg-Schlosser and Morlino 2001). Moreover, an empire must have a record of acting in a way that imposes significant domestic constraints on a variety of formally sovereign or autonomous actors (Cohen 2004). These actors are seen as a kind of periphery to be governed by the imperial center. The rule over peripheries is justified by the empire's civilizing mission or vocation. In other words, empires must have an imperial vision of themselves or a *mission civilisatrice* of some sort towards their external environment (Pomeranz 2005, 34–5; Münkler 2007, 98–102).

EU as empire

There is little doubt that the EU has some of the key imperial features. EU territory is vast and it enlarged several times in its relatively short history. Most of Europe is now under the EU's governance. EU borders span from the outskirts of Asia, to North Africa and the Middles East. The EU is also a very powerful international actor. With nearly 500 million inhabitants, a quarter of the world's GNP, and around 40 per cent of the world merchandise exports and with the comprehensive array of economic, legal, diplomatic and military instruments at its disposal, the EU is able to exercise significant influence in various parts of the world. The Euro is now the world's second most important international reserve and trade currency, giving major influence to the EU globally. European norms and regulations are progressively being adopted across the world, even prompting accusations of 'regulatory imperialism'[2] (Wall Street Journal 2008, A16). Consider, for instance, EU financial market regulation, regulation on data privacy, food and health protection, environment or criminal justice (Bach and Newman 2007). Europe is also the largest provider of developmental aid. Although the EU does not have its own army, it contributed to international peace and security missions in such different and often remote places as East Timor, Congo, Sudan, Mali, Somalia, Afghanistan, Iraq, Lebanon, Bosnia, and Georgia.[3]

The EU is not just a powerful international actor with impressive trade leverage, in particular. It is, above all, a very bullish, intrusive, and expanding actor. Like all empires, it tries to assert political and economic control over various peripheral actors through formal annexations or various forms of economic and political domination. This kind of imperial politics is most pronounced in Europe's ever larger neighborhood. Consider, for instance, the process of EU enlargement eastward based on strict, comprehensive, and demanding conditionality (Behr 2007; Stivachtis and Webber 2011). In its essence enlargement was about asserting the EU's political and economic control over the unstable and impoverished eastern part of the continent through a skilful use of political and economic conditionality. True, the post-communist countries were not 'conquered' but invited to join the EU, and they did so quite eagerly. Moreover, at the end of the accession process they were offered access to the EU's decision-making instruments and resources. Nevertheless, the discrepancy of power between the EU and the candidate states was enormous and one wonders how much actual freedom the candidate countries could ever have had in the accession negotiation process. In fact, the Union has from the start made it clear that the candidate countries must adopt the entire body of European laws before entering the Union. And this *acquis communautaire* contains some 20,000 detailed laws and regulations. The EU not only told the applicants what they should do – in terms of legislation or administrative reform – but it also sent representatives to specific ministries to guide and monitor the required changes (Zielonka 2007, 44–6).

A similar type of assertiveness and intrusiveness can also be traced in EU policies vis-á-vis its Southern and Eastern neighbors.[4] The latest generation of EU trade agreements on offer to EU neighbors, the Deep and Comprehensive Free Trade Agreements (DCFTA), explicitly demand from them to harmonize their trade-related legislation with EU standards and the *acquis communautaire.* Likewise, the numerous EU programs of cooperation on environment, enterprise policy, competition, transport, border management, and education are based on the partner country's regulatory convergence with the EU (Sarto 2014). The EU trains administrative elites in these neighboring countries to comply properly with the EU demands; it even pays the salaries of dozens of government officials in these countries to coordinate training activities and facilitate smooth adoption of the EU regulatory standards there.

In the Balkans the EU intervention is even more direct and pronounced. Kosovo and Bosnia-Herzegovina are *de facto* semi-protectorates governed by European officials under the formal auspices of the United Nations. European institutions and EU members are by far the largest donors to these countries. They have their peacekeepers and police forces on the ground there. Most of the laws and institutions in these countries are being set up and run under the EU supervision. EU officials frequently intervene in detailed economic and fiscal provisions. For instance, in the case of Bosnia-Herzegovina the EU envisaged a detailed package of 18 major reforms to be implemented in this country. One of the objectives was to create and maintain efficient and effective customs controls and to support reform of the taxation system, in particular the introduction of Value Added Tax (VAT). The Union subsequently spelled out an elaborate procedure of monitoring, evaluating and conditioning these reforms and created a 'Bulldozer Committee' to push through simplification of tax codes and boost public revenues with a country value added tax (CEC 2004; Knaus and Marin 2003).

Although the EU's imperial agenda is most pronounced and effective in Europe and its neighborhood, this does not mean that the EU does not try to assert its authority in other parts of the world, however distant. Trade leverage also allows the Union to effectively shape the global agenda in this field. And the field is quite broad and includes not only trade in goods but also in services which represents the largest part of EU's GDP. The field also includes investment, competition, banking, accounting, government procurement, trade facilities, and other related matters. In fact, the EU is already one of the most influential regulators in the world. The EU, together with the U.S., produces around 80 per cent of international norms and standards that regulate global markets, including the dollar and the Euro (Sapir 2007, 12). For instance, China has already applied EU regulations to its motor industry, food safety, and the GSM standard is used for mobile communications, cordless phones and technologies that are delivering broadband to tens of millions of customers globally (Document No 2438 2006, 3). Various regulatory regimes advocated by the EU dictate to domestic actors across the world what they can or cannot produce if they want to export to the EU. Some regulations on environment or food safety may appear to be mere technicalities, but their adoption often has major economic, if not political, implications for the targeted countries. EU regulatory regimes also subject these actors to extraterritorial scrutiny and arbitration. Consider, for instance, the European Court decision to effectively prohibit the merger of two U.S. companies (General Motors and Honeywell Bull.) The Microsoft case is another good example here. And as already mentioned the EU also uses trade to meet its foreign policy objectives.

EU policies may well be guided by self-interest, but the EU claims and probably believes that they are also good for those on the receiving end. The EU sees itself as an agent of peace, democracy, sustainable growth, and good governance. Its policies are said to represent a unique project congruent with the deeper forces of modernization and cross-border integration. They are supposed to contribute to order, development, and cooperation by spreading institutional structures and rules of legitimate behavior (Ashton 2012). In essence, the EU has its own civilizing mission which is one of the key characteristics of empires (Zielonka 2013; Lucarelli and Manners 2006).

The EU and other empires

The EU may well possess some basic features of empires, but it is certainly a rather peculiar empire. The EU does not have a single state in its core, but is composed of 28 states which share the authority through rotating presidency in some fields and communitarian institutions in other fields. In fact, the EU has not a clearly defined center of authority and it certainly does not have an emperor. Key EU institutions are located in cities of Brussels, Luxembourg, Strasbourg and Frankfurt. Headquarters of various EU regulatory agencies show an even more complex map of authority ranging from Copenhagen (environment) and London (pharmaceutics) to Parma (food safety) and Heraklion (information security).[5] The Presidency of the European Council travels from one European capitol to another every six months (and it is handled by individual member states rather than cities). Powers of the office of the President of the European Council or of the President of the European Commission are anything but imperial, despite occasionally immodest political rhetoric displayed by the office holders. The EU has a so-called Common Foreign and Security Policy, but it is not in charge of the police and the military within its borders. When the EU wants to send soldiers under its flag it has to negotiate with member states their individual military contribution and the mode of envisaged military engagement. The result is usually the lowest common denominator with only some member states contributing soldiers to EU operations with other offering only token support if any.

In this sense the EU is not an empire like nineteenth-century Russia or Britain. The EU resembles more the Holy Roman Empire, especially in its medieval period (Wilson 2011; Beller 2006). The Holy Roman Empire was a complex multi-ethnic and multi-religious mosaic of European principalities, duchies, counties, Free Imperial Cities, and other units. It gradually developed through the middle ages and existed until its dissolution in 1806. The Holy Roman Empire had no official capital and the imperial center moved from one European city to another. Different imperial institutions were also placed in different cities. For instance, Vienna was the imperial 'Residenz' city for a long time, but the 'Eternal Diet' was in Regensburg. (Before 1594 the Diet had convened in different cities).

The office of the Holy Roman Emperor was traditionally elective, and the power of the emperor was limited. While individual kings, princes, and lords within the empire were vassals and subjects who owed the emperor their allegiance, they also enjoyed numerous privileges that gave them a large degree of autonomy if not sovereignty within their territories (Osiander 1994, 2001).[6] The emperor has not had his own standing imperial army. If needed, he had to use his own military forces (in his capacity as king of one or more territories within the empire) and negotiate with other members of empire the use of their soldiers for the requested purpose. In essence, the Holy Roman Empire like the contemporary EU was always a highly 'plurilateral' and decentralized unit unable or unwilling to forge a fully fledged political unification.

The EU is also different from contemporary empires such as the United States of America (Bacevich 2002; Ferguson 2004; Grazia 2005; James 2006; Maier 2006). The U.S. is a classical federal state with a strong center, especially in the field of defense and foreign policy. The U.S. President is the sole commander-in-chief, and he runs foreign policy with limited input from Congress. The EU is a kind of post-modern (or neo-medieval) polity with a 'plurilateral' or 'polycentric' structure of governance. Each time there is a crisis its 27 member-states have to negotiate the notion of common interests and decide who will take the lead in implementing the adopted policy. The U.S. is a formidable military power; it has more than 700 military installations located in over 130 countries worldwide. The EU is a formidable civilian power; its 'imperial' instruments are chiefly economic and bureaucratic.

U.S. borders are fixed, while EU borders undergo regular adjustments, both in territorial and functional terms. There is no major disjunction between administrative boundaries, military frontiers, cultural traits, and market transaction fringes in the United States. In the EU we have different and only partly overlapping legal, economic, security and cultural spaces. Successive enlargements have allowed the EU to acquire new territory, but they have produced ever more variable geometry.

Both the United States and EU effectively constrain the sovereignty of their respective peripheries, but the nature of their peripheries differ and so the policies vis-à-vis them. The United States basically has no internal peripheries, although the case of Puerto Rico and other so-called 'non-incorporated territories' complicates the issue. (Puerto Rico is part of the United States by special arrangement and has commonwealth status). In the case of the EU, the definition of periphery is quite confusing. The EU, EMU and Schengen have different memberships, creating different peripheries and centers. Moreover, some states formally outside the EU such as Switzerland and Norway adopted numerous EU laws and bonded their economies with the EU. Candidates for EU membership and even candidates for EU help, however symbolic, are also asked to adopt EU laws. This process of exporting EU governance to the neighboring states brings them *de facto* closer to the EU or even leads to mergers through the EU enlargement. The U.S. often helps its peripheries, but it does not contemplate mergers through enlargement.

The nature of U.S. and EU relations with their respective peripheries is also different. The power imbalance and its hard borders make it difficult for peripheral actors to gain access to U.S. decision-making. These relations are by their nature hierarchical, and the hierarchy is basically perpetual. Even America's closest allies are not recognized as equals. They are asked to support American policies and share the burdens. The EU is more exposed to all sort of instability in its peripheries and neither willing nor able to practice a policy of containment let alone conquest. To use Ulrich Beck's and Edgar Grande's EU policies towards peripheries are based on 'overcoming national borders, voluntarism, consensus, transnational interdependence and the political value added accruing from cooperation' (2007, 53). The EU's territorial acquisitions are negotiated and endorsed by parliaments in the incorporated countries.

Both the EU and the U.S. see themselves as engines of modernity, security and welfare in their peripheries. They both want to spread noble values such as democracy, human rights and free trade. However, their respective 'civilizing missions differ in both their scope and nature. The U.S. normative agenda is truly global and universal while the EU agenda is chiefly regional with no ambition to become an 'indispensable nation' (as the Americans are fond to describe themselves (Ikenberry 2002, 296).[7] Europeans tend to claim technocratic or institutional superiority while Americans tend to claim military and ideological superiority.

Magali Gravier has grasped well the difference between contemporary America and Europe by observing that for the U.S. empire is chiefly a matter of foreign policy, while for the EU it is chiefly a matter of domestic policy. In other words, the U.S. has an empire, while the EU is an empire (2014).

Empire in crisis?

The financial crisis that has shaken the Western world in 2008 has affected both the U.S. and the EU. The Obama administration in the U.S. has adopted a more cautious global policy than the Bush administration and it also faced serious budgetary pressures affecting many federal agencies including the Pentagon. However, the fundaments of the American empire still seem firm and there is no prospect of the American state disintegrating. The fundaments of the European empire seem shakier in comparison and the EU is facing a serious prospect of disintegration.

For a long time the Euro seemed to be on the verge of collapse as the EU leaders proved unable to regain control over mounting private and public debts. Some measure of control has eventually been regained satisfying financial markets, but the policies adopted by the EU have antagonized citizens in both creditor and debtor states. Anti-European populism on the left and right of the political spectrum was the result with serious electoral implications. Therefore in due time we may see some countries leaving the Euro, Schengen or even the single market with damming prospects for the EU itself. Further enlargements were put on halt in the meantime leaving the EU with no effective means for addressing challenges emanating from the dramatic events in Ukraine and North Africa.[8] The EU lost much of its sex appeal throughout the crisis and its civilizing mission does not appear as credible and attractive as several years ago (Zielonka 2014; Krastev 2012; Soros 2012). Is the EU still an empire of some sort with its power dramatically declining?

The definition offered earlier argued that empires represent an unbounded type of political authority. It did not focus on the relative ability to exercise this authority. In other words, empire is about a system of rule and not about prowess. Empires can be fairly ineffective and incompetent; they may be in crisis or even declining (Motyl 2001; Kennedy 1987). Moreover, power is a relative concept. The EU may well be weakened by the crisis, but for small and troubled neighbors it still represents a formidable power in both material and ideational terms.[9] In early 2014 this was fairly apparent in Ukraine where the activist at the Maidan square were happy to side with the EU against Russia even though the former was not particularly skillful and forthcoming (*The New York Review* 2014; Speck 2014).

That said every empire is a specific agent that governs the relationship with its periphery. Empire is not a synonym of hegemony. Hegemony is chiefly about the use and misuse of power with vaguely defined agency (Wallerstein 2004; Joseph 2002; Gilpin 1981; Cox 1983). Empire is about specific actors. These actors or agents may be coercive or benign, centralized or decentralized, rising or falling. Control and domination exercised by empires can be formal or informal to various degrees; it can be economic, political, or military to various degrees; it can be effective or ineffective to various degrees. In short, the European empire can be fairly unsuccessful and in the midst of a profound crisis. Yet, there can hardly be a European empire without the EU or another independent agent/actor that would take its place.

The recent crisis has suggested that the EU may not survive as an independent agency for several reasons. First, the crisis has generated a profound conflict within Europe's metropolis. Greece, Spain, Portugal, and Italy are not the EU's 'southern peripheries' as they are often being presented in the media. They are members of the Euro-zone which according to the official rhetoric represents Europe's integrative core. Formally they are having the same access to the EU resources and decision-making as Germany, France, Austria, Finland or the

Netherlands. Today key members of this EU's core are head to head in an ongoing conflict about their budgetary deficits and surpluses as well as over the means for addressing them.

Second, since early days of the crisis the EU looked like it simply rubber stamped decisions made in Berlin and other capitals of creditor countries. The European Commission and other key EU institutions have not been allowed to play any crucial role in handling the crisis. The Fiscal Compact Treaty, the key instrument for handling the crisis, was launched by then French President Sarkozy and the German Chancellor Merkel, with little consultation with other EU members. In order to avoid a possible veto by some EU member states, the Fiscal Compact was not formally part of the EU treaty framework and it could thus enter into force with only 12Euro-zone members ratifying it. Not surprisingly, it was seen as a symbol of legal and political manipulation.

Third, although creditor countries used the EU to impose austerity measures on the debtor countries, they have declined to equip the EU in any significant financial or legal resources. Proposals to increase the EU overall budget have been vetoed and so have been the proposals to introduce Eurobonds or Euro-rates within the common currency zone. Serious treaty changes have also been ruled out.

Of course, this all may change in the future. After all, the EU has a good record of overcoming successive crises (Kühnhardt 2008). The problem is that the latest crisis seems to be deeper and more multifaceted than the previous ones. More crucially, it is hard to envisage a scenario that will boost Europe's imperial fortunes. A federal prospect is currently more distant than ever. Public opinion polls show low trust in the EU and politicians are unable to agree on anything resembling a political union.[10] Creation of a political union would require putting the EU in charge of economic supervision, taxation, redistribution and social welfare (Verhofstadt 2006).[11] No wonder member states are reluctant to endorse such a major transfer of their sovereignty to Brussels. Moreover, an EU in charge of such major economic policies would need to have stronger democratic legitimacy. As the famous saying dating back to the American war on independence goes: 'no taxation without representation.' The EU is unable and unwilling to offer such representation for various complex reasons.

Nor is there any serious prospect of transforming the EU into a Germany-led empire (Beck 2013; Collignon 2007; Bulmer and Paterson 2013). Germany is by far the most powerful country on the continent and during the crisis it was able to push through EU policies prepared in Berlin. However, these policies have generated political conflicts rather than harmony; probably they are also economically unsustainable. Moreover, because of its traumatic history Germany has a particular aversion to the imperial project. Germany seems also too self-centered and inward looking to be able to act as the engine of empire. To be successful in generating and sustaining an empire, Germany would need to be more tolerant and generous. Moreover, Germany would need to generate security and stability and its current policies achieve the opposite regardless of presumably good intentions. If neither the United States of Europe nor *Bundesrepublik* Europa are viable options, can the EU remain as it is?

Conclusions: A post-imperial Europe

The EU may return to its imperial glory provided that it is able to reform itself. Reforms need to diagnose correctly the 'illness' and apply an appropriate cure. The currency crisis may well be overcome, but undertaken policies to save the Euro generated a profound crisis of socio-economic cohesion and of political trust. So far, the EU has no cure for regaining the public trust and for providing greater convergence between its numerous member-states. The reforms currently discussed in European circles may make the situation even worse. For instance, giving more powers to the European Parliament containing a sizable group of Euro-sceptic EMPs is likely to undermine further the Parliament's legitimacy.

In the absence of some internal or external shocks it is fair to assume that the EU will continue to exist, but with ever less powers and resources. It will probably be transformed into a public relations tool with no effective means for addressing economic, social, and political challenges. Member-states will search for solutions to these challenges outside the EU frame. This is something that they have practiced in the field of European foreign policy for many years, for instance. Member states always treated the CFSP (Common Foreign and Security Policy) framework as one among many institutional tools of their foreign policy. They often preferred to act within the United Nations framework or via the OSCE, Council of Europe or NATO. Foreign and security policies were often being carried out by formal or informal coalitions of the willing, contact groups, or bilateral initiatives. The same attitude is likely to be adapted to many other functional fields if the current EU institutions were to be judged ineffective and illegitimate. Moreover, other actors than states are likely to step into the field of European politics proper. For instance, some large European cities have become the engines of the European economy and the key centers for trade and investment. However, they do not have a seat at the EU decision-making table dominated by many small states with rather parochial agendas. The same can be said about some important transnational NGOs, public or private. It is hard to see these influential actors supporting the EU structure that prevents them to punch their real weight.

This does not necessarily herald the end of European integration, but it suggests the end of the EU being the key embodiment of integration. Needless to say, an EU deprived of major powers and resources would not be in a position to practice the imperial politics of the past two or three decades. The next two or three decades will tell if any of the above mentioned scenarios are indeed correct.

Notes

1 The term 'unidentified political object' was coined by Jacques Delors. See www.notre-europe.asso.fr/article.php3?id_article=168&lang=en.

2 The article cites examples of EU efforts to cow large American firms such as Microsoft, Qualcomm and MasterCard with antitrust laws. Other frequently cited examples of the European 'regulatory imperialism' include the Reach legislation on chemical products and the ban on the importation of chlorine-rinsed poultry.

3 For a list of the ongoing missions and operations see www.eeas.europa.eu/csdp/missions-and-operations/.
4 So-called European Neighbourhood Policy (ENP) launched a decade ago relates to such diverse countries as Algeria, Egypt, Israel, Jordan, Lebanon, Libya, Morocco, the Palestinian Authority, Syria, Tunisia, Ukraine, Moldova, and Belarus. See Commission of the European Communities (2003). See also, Council Conclusions.
5 There are more than 30 such regulatory agencies located in different cities of Europe. For details see http://europa.eu/about-eu/agencies/index_en.htm.
6 The term 'sovereignty' entered the diplomatic discourse only after the Treaty of Westphalia of 1648.
7 The term 'indispensable nation' has been attributed to Madeleine Albright.
8 Although Croatia joined the EU and Latvia joined the EMU in 2013. For the official list EU prospective members see http://europa.eu/about-eu/countries/index_en.htm.
9 For a sophisticated analysis of power see Lukes (2005) and Galtung (1971).
10 Between 2007 and 2012, trust in the EU has fallen from +10 to –22 points in France, from +20 to –29 points in Germany, from +30 to –22 points in Italy, from +42 to –52 points in Spain, from +50 to +6 points in Poland, and from –13 to –49 points in the UK. See Torreblanca and Leonard (2103).
11 For an analysis of different version of a political union, see, e.g. Dullien and Torreblanca (2012).

References

Adler, Emanuel. 1987. *The Power of Ideology*. Berkeley, CA: University of California Press.

Ashton, Catherine. 2012. Speech by European Union High Representative for Foreign Affairs and Security Policy Catherine Ashton in the European Parliament on the annual report on CFSP, 11 September 2012, Strasbourg, www.eu-un.europa.eu/articles/en/article_12568_en.htm.

Bacevich, Andrew J. 2002. *American Empire: The Realities and Consequences of U.S. Diplomacy*. Cambridge, MA: Harvard University Press.

Bach, David, and Abraham Newman. 2007. The European regulatory state and Global Public Policy: Micro-Institutions, Micro Influence. *Journal of European Public Policy* 14(6): 827–46.

Badie, Bertrand, Dirk Berg-Schlosser, and Leonardo Morlino. 2001. *International Encyclopedia of Political Science*. Thousand Oaks, CA: Sage.

Beck, Ulrich. 2013. *German Europe*. London: Polity Press.

Beck, Ulrich, and Edgar Grande. 2007. *Cosmopolitan Europe*. Cambridge: Polity Press.

Behr, Hartmut. 2007. The European Union in the Legacies of imperial rule? EU Accession Politics Viewed From a Historical Comparative Perspective. *European Journal of International Relations* 13(2): 239–62.

Beller, Steven. 2006. Back to the Middle. *The Times Literary Supplement* 8 December.

Böröcz, József, and Melinda Kovács. 2001. Empire's New Clothes: Unveiling EU-Enlargement. In *Central Europe Review*. www.ce-review.org.

Bulmer, Simon, and William E. Paterson. 2013. Germany as the EU's Reluctant Hegemon? Of Economic Strength and Political Constraints. *Journal Of European Public Policy* 20(10): 1387–405.

Chandler, David. 2006. *Empire in Denial: The Politics of State-Building*. London: Pluto.

Cohen, Jean. 2004. Whose Sovereignty? Empire Versus International Law. *Ethics and International Affairs* 18: 1–24.

Colas, Alejandro. 2007. *Empire*. Cambridge: Polity.

Collignon, Stefan. 2007. *Bundesrepublik Europa? Die demokratische Herausforderung und Europas Krise*. Berlin: Vorwärts Verlag.

Commission of the European Communities. 2003. *Wider Europe — Neighbourhood: A New Framework for Relations with our Eastern and Southern Neighbours* (Communication from the Commission to the Council and the European Parliament), http://eeas.europa.eu/enp/pdf/pdf/com03_104_en.pdf.

Commission of the European Communities, Brussels, SEC (2004) 375, Commission Staff Working Paper: Bosnia and Herzegovina, Stabilisation and Association Report 2004 {COM(2004)205}.

Cox, Robert W. 1983. Gramsci, Hegemony and International Relations: An Essay in Method. *Millennium: Journal of International Studies* 12: 162–75.

Darwin, John. 2008. *After Tamerlane: The Rise and Fall of Global Empires, 1400–2000*. London: Bloomsbury Press.

Document No 2438. 2006. Europe in the World. *Communication from the Commission to the European Council of June 2006*. Document No 2438: 3.

Doyle, Michael W. 1986. *Empires*. Ithaca, NY: Cornell University Press.

Dullien, Sebastian, and José Ignacio Torreblanca. 2012. *What Is Political Union?* London: European Council on Foreign Relations, http://ecfr.eu/page/-/ECFR70_POLITICAL_UNION_BRIEF_AW.pdf.

Eisenstadt, Shmuel N. 1963. *Political Systems of Empires*. New York: Free Press.

Ferguson, Niall. 2004. *Colossus: The Price of America's Empire*. New York: Allen Lane.

Galtung, Johan. 1971. A Structural Theory of Imperialism. *Journal of Peace Research* 8: 81–118.

Gilpin, Robert. 1981. *War and change in World Politics*. New York: Cambridge University Press.

Grazia, Victoria de. 2005. *Irresistible Empire: America's Advance Through Twentieth-Century Europe*. Cambridge, MA: Harvard University Press.

Hardt, Michael, and Antonio Negri. 2000. *Empire*. Cambridge, MA: Harvard University Press.

Hettne, Björn, and Fredrik Söderbaum. 2005. Civilian Power or Soft Imperialism? EU as a Global Actor and the Role of Interregionalism. *European Foreign Affairs Review* 10(4): 535–52.

Ikenberry, G. John. 2002. American Unipolarity: The Sources of Persistence and Decline. In *America Unrivalled: The Future of the Balance of Power*. Ithaca, NY: Cornell University Press.

James, Harold. 2006. *The Roman Predicament: How the Rules of International Order Create the Politics of Empire*. Princeton, NJ: Princeton University Press.

Joseph, Jonathan. 2002. *Hegemony: A Realist Analysis*. New York: Routledge.

Kennedy, Paul. 1987. *The Rise and Fall of the Great Powers: Economic Change and Military Conflict from 1500 to 2000*. New York: Random House.

Knaus, Gerhard, and Felix Martin. 2003. Travails of the European Raj. *Journal of Democracy* 14(3): 60–74.

Krastev, Ivan. 2012. A Fraying Union. *Journal of Democracy* 23(4): 23–30.

Kühnhardt, Ludger. 2008. *Crises in European Integration: Challenges and Responses, 1945–2005*. Oxford: Berghahn Books.

Laïdi, Zaki. 2008b. *Norms Over Force: The Enigma of European Power*. Basingstoke: Palgrave Macmillan.

Laïdi, Zaki. 2008a. The normative empire: The Unintended Consequences of European Power. *Garnet Policy Brief* 6.

Lucarelli, Sonia, and Ian Manners. 2006. *Values and Principles in European Union Foreign Policy*. London: Routledge.

Lukes, Steven. 2005. *Power: A Radical View*. 2nd ed. London: Macmillan.

MacCormick, Neil. 1999. *Questioning Sovereignty*. Oxford: Oxford University Press.
Maier, Charles S. 2006. *Among Empires: American Ascendancy and Its Predecessors*. Cambridge, MA: Harvard University Press.
Motyl, Alexander J. 2001. *Imperial Ends: The Decay, Collapse, and Revival of Empires*. New York: Columbia University Press.
Münkler, Herfried. 2007. *Empires: The Logic of World Domination From Ancient Rome to the United States*. Cambridge: Polity.
New York Review. 2014. Fascism, Russia and Ukraine. *The New York Review of Books* March 20.
Nunes, Isabel Ferreira. 2011. Civilian, Normative, and Ethical Power Europe: Role Claims and EU Discourses. *European Foreign Affairs Review* 16(1): 1–20.
Osiander, Andres. 2001. Sovereignty, International Relations and the Westphalian myth. *International Organization* 55(2): 251–87.
Osiander, Andres. 1994. *The States System of Europe, 1640–1990: Peace-Making and the Conditions of International Stability*. Oxford: Clarendon Press.
Parker, Noel. 2010. Empire as a Geopolitical Figure. *Geopolitics* 15(1): 113–4.
Pomeranz, Kenneth. 2005. Civilizing' Missions, Past and Present. *Dædalus* 134: 34–45.
Sapir, André. 2007. Europe and the Global Economy. In *Fragmented Power: Europe and the Global Economy*, 1–12. Brussels: Bruegel Books.
Sarto, Raffaella A. Del. 2014. *Normative Empire Europe: The EU, Its Borderlands and the Arab Spring*. Paper presented at Copenhagen Business School, 'Imperial Soft Power and Governance beyond Borders: The EU's Relations with North Africa and the Middle East', 23–24 January.
Soros, George. 2012. The Tragedy of the European Union and How to Resolve It. *New York Review of Books*, 27 September, 2012, www.nybooks.com/articles/archives/2012/sep/27/tragedy-european-union-and-how-resolve-it/.
Speck, Ulrich. 2014. What the West Must Do for Ukraine. *The New York Times*, 23 February.
Stivachtis, Yannis, and Mark Webber. 2011. Europe after Enlargement. *Journal of European Integration* 33(2): 101–249.
Telegraph. 11 July 2007. José Manuel Barroso, President of the European Commission. *The Telegraph*, www.telegraph.co.uk.
Telo, Mario. 2009. Introduction: The EU as a Model, a Global Actor and an Unprecedented Power. In *The European Union and Global Governance*, 1–40. London: Routledge.
The Oxford English Reference Dictionary. 1999. 2nd edition. Oxford: Oxford University Press.
Torreblanca, Jose Ignacio, and Mark Leonard. 2013. The Remarkable Rise of Continental Euroscepticism. *The Guardian*, 24 April, http://ecfr.eu/content/entry/commentary_the_remarkable_rise_of_continental_euroscepticism129.
Verhofstadt, Guy. 2006. *The United States of Europe*. London: Federal Trust.
Wall Street Journal. 2008. Europe v. U.S. business. *Wall Street Journal*, January 17: A16.
Wallerstein, Immanuel M. 2004. *World-Systems Analysis: An Introduction*. Durham, NC: Duke University Press.
Wilson, Peter H. 2011. *The Holy Roman Empire 1495–1806*. Second Edition. Basingstoke: Palgrave/MacMillan.
Zielonka, Jan. 2014. *Is the EU Doomed?* Cambridge: Polity Press.
Zielonka, Jan. 2013. Europe's New Civilizing Missions: The EU's Normative Power Discourse. *Journal of Political Ideologies* 18(1): 35–55.
Zielonka, Jan. 2012. Empires and the Modern International System. *Geopolitics* 17(3): 502–25.
Zielonka, Jan. 2007. Chapter 2. In *Europe as Empire. The Nature of the Enlarged European Union*, 44–46. Oxford: Oxford University Press.

4 European Union

Imperial geopolitics and enforcements chains

József Böröcz

Introduction

Over the last five centuries or so, West European societies have played a central, and exceptionally privileged, part in the history of global capitalism. Some of the geopolitical and economic foundations of that centrality and privilege have recently begun to show powerful signs of erosion. This chapter regards the supra-state public authority of the European Union as an instrument of a strategic coalition among west and central European capital, state apparatuses and populations, aiming to optimize their geopolitical position under the new conditions. The key instrument of this new global adjustment – termed, here, *enforcement chains* – bears a clear resemblance to the asymmetrical linkages that constituted the geopolitics of power for supra-state empires throughout much of history.

Geopolitical transformations

The world scene in geopolitics is undergoing two major transformations. First, starting in the last decade of the 20th century, the end of the Soviet-centered version of state socialism took out a defining feature of the remarkably complex, multidimensional geopolitical arrangement of the preceding era. The world of the Cold War was simultaneously

- bipolar – to the extent it involved a military conflict between the USSR and its Warsaw Pact and COMECON allies on the one hand and the wealthiest capitalist states on the other, integrated into NATO, the European Union and a host of other supra-state organizations – ,
- antagonistic – as for the irreconcilable "system conflict" revealed in the situation of state socialism embedded in an otherwise capitalist world – ,
- highly competitive – as revealed in the two sides' rivalries for military, economic and political supremacy and opportunities to subdue each other and establish control over the rest of the world, variously referred to as the "Third World," the "global South," or the periphery of the world-system – and
- hierarchical – increasing the steepness and the rigidity of the system that arranges the world's societies into a single global income pyramid, inherited

> from the world of colonial empires only to reach magnitudes unprecedented in the history of humankind during the Cold War era.

The collapse of the Soviet bloc rearranged all four aspects of the post–Cold War world. It removed one end of the bipolar logic, leaving the other "pole" in a position that was, at least in some dimensions, that much more powerful. The end of the Cold War brought about an unprecedented military supremacy for the "West," and especially for the United States. It also reduced the magnitude of the "system conflict" by moving a contiguous bloc of erstwhile state socialist societies – just about 10% of the total world economy[1] at the time – back into the fold of capitalist mode of production. It diminished, at least for a generation, the ability of most of the erstwhile state socialist societies to compete successfully in the ever more closely integrated global capitalist system and reduced both their living standards and their global economic weight[2] to historically unprecedented lows. In some cases this was exacerbated by the breakup and otherwise fragmentation of erstwhile federal or quasi-federal state socialist states in east- and south-central Europe and northern Eurasia. As a result, the overall steepness of global state-to-state income inequality increased further, only counterbalanced by the concomitant rise of some of the largest, and, over the last century or so, poorest, societies on the global income ladder. And that takes us to the next ongoing change in global geopolitics.

A second global geopolitical transformation of the recent decades has to do with the decline of the structures of primacy and hegemony in the world capitalist system. The great, as yet unresolved riddle concerning this transformation is whether the by now undeniable loss of position of the United States (Chase-Dunn et al. 2005), the world's most powerful capitalist state for over a century,[3] a decline particularly palpable since the beginning of the 21st century (Wallerstein 2006) signals "just" the end of a "systemic cycle of accumulation" (Arrighi and Silver 2001), leading to yet another a *hegemonic transition* (ibid.), not unlike previous historical shifts such as those summarized by Giovanni Arrighi as

> [the] Genoese-Iberian cycle, stretching from the fifteenth through the early seventeenth centuries; a Dutch cycle, stretching from the late sixteenth through the late eighteenth centuries; a British cycle, stretching from the mid eighteenth through to the early twentieth centuries; and a US cycle, stretching from the late nineteenth to the current phase [. . .].[4]

The historic question for the global geopolitics of our times is whether the world is experiencing (1) a shift in which the state occupies the hegemonic position in the otherwise, by and large unchanging, hierarchical structure of governance of the capitalist world economy, (2) a transformation of global capitalism to a system with a different systemic architecture that is different from that which had been in effect over the last five centuries or (3) an end to capitalism, *tout court*.

In order for the least sweeping, "hegemonic transformation" interpretation (see 1, above) to hold true, we would need to see, at a minimum, the surfacing of yet another single, powerful capitalist state actor capable of wielding such tremendous concentration of some key resources that it is able to wrest global hegemony from the United States and prevent all other actors from taking it from it for a substantial amount of time.

A transformation in the systemic architecture of world capitalism (see scenario 2, above) would involve the emergence of a different *kind* of global capitalism. Whether that would take place by globalizing some, already existing, currently domestic or regional but not yet global, features a different, perhaps non-west-European variety of capitalisms, by the construction of some kind of power-sharing, or condominium, arrangement wherein a coalition of actors would form a strategic entity to dominate the world jointly, or some other, hitherto imperceptible, new form of capitalism, is impossible to tell at this juncture. Whichever of those alternatives would be realized, the ensuing global transformation would constitute a very noteworthy departure, indeed, from the logic of all four hegemonic cycles the history of world capitalism has seen hitherto. Given the degree to which the pairing of military supremacy and nonmilitary aspects of political and economic hegemony characterizes the current system, such a transformation would involve, perforce, far-reaching rearrangements between the relationship of "national" capitals and states. It would also redefine what we understand today as the tension between limited, quasi-national sovereignties on the one hand and the global interstate system on the other.

The third alternative (3, above) implies that we would see the formation of a global arrangement in which the logic that holds the world together today – based on profit-based accumulation through global commodity production – would be replaced by a system based on a different underlying logic. By now we have over 200 years' worth of social science, as well as literary, ethical and political writing, not to mention progressive art, journalism and social movements, anticipating the emergence of such a new, postcapitalist system, and reasonable arguments have been made to the effect that such a transformation will require a sudden and radical form discontinuous social change. And yet, we have not seen sociopolitical forces that have managed to achieve the "systemic" objective of replacing global capitalism with an alternative global logic.

Meanwhile, even if the least sweeping "hegemonic-transition" scenario (alternative 1, above) should unfold, it is clear that *no west European or North American state is currently in a position* to become a contender for the position of the new hegemon. In other words, even if a "simple" hegemonic transition were to take place, it would undoubtedly involve a major shift, a paradigm-changing departure from the by-now five-centuries-long history of capitalism. Throughout that history, west European and North American states and for-profit corporations have passed the hegemonic position to each other and keep all non-west-European–non-North-American societies out of contention for that position. Closely tied to the location of the global hegemon, the first 500 years of global capitalism had a distinctly "Western" character, keeping the rest of the world under tight "Western" geopolitical, economic as well as military and cultural control, an exclusion and subjugation that has affected over 90% of the world's population. The current transformation should thus be recognized as unique, at the very least to the extent that the hitherto hegemonic actors that have repeatedly insisted on as the "superior," "Western" social, political, military, moral and cultural "foundations" of their hegemony are unlikely to be at the helm of geopolitical control over the world.

Clearly, the prospect of such tectonic transformations foreshadows the danger of sharp global geopolitical conflicts, military or otherwise. Such conflict has been postponed by the collapse of the Soviet bloc: As shown elsewhere (Böröcz 2009b), the gains in relative global economic weight that the emerging non-west-European giants have managed to achieve have, until recently, been offset by the catastrophic losses experienced by the erstwhile Soviet bloc of former-state-socialist societies. The collapse of the Soviet bloc acted as a historic "buffer," postponing a looming global conflict over "the West's" losses in relative economic weight, and the attendant decline in "Western" geopolitical power on a global scale (ibid.).

However, that period of relative geopolitical quiet, gained at the expense of reducing the economic performance of eastern Europe and northern Eurasia, is now over; most societies of the erstwhile Soviet bloc seem to be at the limit of their ability to reduce their economic weight and have, hence, exhausted their global "buffering potential" (ibid.). No other part of the world except "the west" seems to show the concentration of material resources whose global share could be reduced in order to accommodate the rising Asian giants' need for some "room at the top." To put this history in perspective, the post-state-socialist losses of at least some of the post-state-socialist states, both in terms of per capita GDP and global economic weight, have been considerably greater than the respective losses of the USSR during World War II.[5] Based on this, even if we subscribe to the least ambitious, "hegemonic transition" reading of the current world transformation, the world has, clearly, entered into a situation of open struggle for control over global economic resources, as reflected in a new competition for global economic weight.

Resolution in this struggle is likely to take place in the interaction space among the world's most powerful public authorities. Global economic weight provides a useful insight into the dispersal of such power among the world's societies.

The distribution of the world's societies according to global economic weight is strikingly uneven.[6] Table 4.1 shows the top of the list of the heaviest actors in

Table 4.1 Geopolitical actors with the greatest global economic weight, top of the list, 2008.

Rank	*Global economic weight (%)*	*Unit*	*Cumulative weight (top-down %)*
1	18.6	USA	18.6
2	18	EU	36.7
3	17.5	China	54.1
4	6.7	India	60.8
5	5.7	Japan	66.5
6	2.5	Russia	69.0

Source: Computed from Maddison 2010.

terms of global economic weight. As the rightmost column indicates, the distribution of economic power in the world is so uneven that the top three actors – in order of magnitude: the USA, the European Union and China – together contribute more than half of the entire economic output of humankind. Of the six entries included in Table 4.1, five – the USA, China, India, Japan and Russia – are states in the conventional sense of the word; the European Union is a supra-state public authority with no monopoly over the means of coercion over its territory (Böröcz and Sarkar 2005).

Of the top six actors, Japan is an outlier in the sense that, in spite of its considerable economic weight (contributing approximately 5.7% of the world's total economic output), partly in conformity with its constitution imposed on it after World War II aiming explicitly to prevent the re-emergence of Japanese imperial militarism, partly due to some features of its specific geostrategic location, it has a very powerful local and regional presence but does not project itself as a serious contender for *global* influence. Meanwhile, Russia is, clearly, an eager and vigorous global geopolitical actor, in spite of its relatively smaller economic weight (with 2.5% Russia has less than half of Japan's heft).

Varied and combined legacies of empires

Each of the world's five top geopolitical actors is heir to a unique constellation of imperial historical heritage. Broadly speaking, humankind has seen two distinct geopolitical types of imperial structures: *contiguous* and *overseas* empires. Land-based, *contiguous empires* are hierarchical networks of political authority whose spatial structures resemble blots of ink spreading on a paper map (Böröcz and Sarkar 2012). Imperial possessions share land borders with each other, leaving little to no space un-covered by imperial rule among them. Internal structures of contiguous empires tend to be concentric, such that overland geometric distance from the imperial seat is also a reasonably good indication of an area's relative position in the political, economic and cultural hierarchies of the empire (ibid.) All empires built before the 16th century were of the contiguous type.

Overseas empires are a European invention: They were products of the colonial system. They follow, in contrast, a distinctive, spatially dispersed, network logic. Overseas empires are made up of a set of dyadic linkages (ibid.) between colonial possessions – usually some considerable distance away from Europe – and a dominant colonial power in Europe. At one end of the linkage we find the society that initiates, maintains and enforces this network arrangement; on the other, we see the subordinate society subjected to colonial domination (ibid.) Overseas empires are constituted by two parallel vectors of opposite directions: one of oppression and projected geopolitical power pointing from western Europe to the colony; the other of flows of value out of the colonial location into the colonial center.

The United States is a product of a white-settler colonial empire whose settler population claimed its independence from its former colonizing power in the late 18th century, i.e., a true latecomer in the world of modern imperial states. In this sense, the United States shows a unique combination of two kinds of imperial heritage – partly a land-based, contiguous empire, partly the center of a *meta-colonial system of global domination*. That US-centered global system of domination resembles some powerful features of a colonial empire due to the long-distance, vector-like shape of the linkages that constitute it, its propensity to indirect rule. This US-centered global structure of dominance was created in the period of the dissolution, and with the ruins, of western Europe-centered colonial empires during and after World War II. During the Cold War, the USA has built up an extremely large, technologically cutting-edge and lavishly funded military machinery which it has used during, and arguably even more since, the Cold War, as a key instrument in implementing a global imperial strategy. The United States is a unique, 21st-century strategic composite that combines elements of both contiguous and overseas types of empire.

China, the world's most populous state, is heir to one of the world's oldest contiguous empires, and its elites explicitly use that heritage as a resource and a guide for modern statecraft as well as identity discourse. China's basic geopolitical posture is that of extremely selective global engagement, with three key concerns: protection of the mainland, assertion of claims over territories that have been detached from the mainland during the revolutionary war, and a stubborn, long-term strategy of slow, incremental buildup of economic linkages, political influence and military weight. China has also been very vigorous in securing energy and raw materials resources for its future growth both in Asia and in Africa. To put China's low-key geopolitical behavior, as it underlies its economic ascent, in its proper context, it is important to remember that, as recently as the early part of the 19th century, China alone produced no less than one-third of the total economic output of humankind[7] – a weight to be contrasted with the catastrophically low figure at the point of the revolution, measuring approximately 4.6% in 1950 (Maddison 2010).

When India, the second most populous state in the world, gained its independence from the British Empire after World War II, it had a global economic weight of 4.16%,[8] i.e., slightly below China's – a figure to be contrasted with the approximately 25% estimate for 1820. In contrast to the other four main geopolitical actors, India, in spite of its extremely important strategic location, the size of its population and the strength of its armed forces, is not a member of the United Nations Security Council yet, and a considerable part of its geopolitical efforts are focused on attaining that objective. India's global geopolitical posture is also deeply shaped by its relatively recent, successful history of import-substitution industrialization as well as the remarkable flexibility, professionalism and acumen with which its educated elites and populous business-oriented middle-classes have incorporated in their life strategies, and use to their great advantage, the individual mobility opportunities offered by the advanced, highly globalized capitalism of the late-20th-early-21st century, especially within the space of the Anglophone context created by the now-defunct British Raj. On the other hand, India – a very diverse multi-denominational, multi-ethnic state saddled with grave social, economic and political inequalities – is also struggling with recurrent legitimacy crises, secession struggles, very taxing, large-scale border disputes and sovereignty conflicts with neighboring states, and a set of radical revolutionary peasant uprisings, all of which jointly pose a major challenge to the internal sovereignty and the overall capacity of the central state.

Russia is a direct heir to the USSR – that was, in turn, a direct heir to the Czars' Russia, one of the world's classical examples of contiguous, land-based empires. Geopolitics has a deep historical relevance for Russia: Even such defining concepts of classical geopolitics as the 'pivot' and the 'heartland' – two key notions of the new, quintessentially imperial science of geopolitics as proposed by its British founder, Halford J. Mackinder in 1904 – referred to central portions of the Russian Empire. Even after the breakup of the USSR into its 15 constitutive republics, the now post-state-socialist Russian Federation continues to be the world's largest state in terms of land area (it is almost twice as large as the next biggest state, Canada), and a multi-ethnic, resource-rich empire with a deep historical interest, and legacy, in global geopolitics. For a host of reasons having to do with Russia's physical centrality in northern Eurasia – forming a single land-based imperial link between Europe, China and the United States – its extremely strong military, its clear global supremacy in space exploration, and its breathtaking endowments in raw materials and energy sources far beyond hydrocarbon deposits, it would be difficult to overestimate the significance of geopolitics for Russian political thinking. Further increasing the geopolitical preoccupation of Russian politics is the fact that, simply because of the dissolution of the USSR, the reduction of its territory, and the dramatically increased complexity of international relations on its borders, the period since the end of the USSR has been an extremely intense and complex time for Russia, and much of the changes that took place has been openly considered a net loss from the perspective of Russian geopolitical strategy.

Finally, the European Union, similar to the United States, is heir to some key historical legacies of *both* the contiguous and the overseas type of empire. Clearly, the EU was conceived and created as a supra-state public authority whose key members were deeply enmeshed in colonial empire: Five of the EU's six founding members (Belgium, France, Germany, Italy and Netherlands) were colonial powers when they established the EU. Britain's accession was delayed (and in many ways its legacy of EU-"skeptical" politics is explained) by its reluctance to share the spoils of its empire through the EU's mechanism of the "sharing and pooling of sovereignty" (e.g., Wallace 1999). By 1994, all European erstwhile-colonial powers became member states of the European Union. Put differently, from the perspective of the real legacies of colonial history, the EU is but a meta-colonial association of former colonial powers. This conceptualization goes a long way in explaining the obvious unwillingness to participate in celebrating the European Union's "European" identity discourse on part of that, large segment of the world's societies outside of Europe whose history is marked by a considerably less jubilant memory of involuntary involvement in 'Europe' due to European-centered colonialism.

As a result of these colonial-imperial legacies, the EU enjoys privileged, "by default" access to the economic, political and social institutions of many now-independent states that had been colonized by European powers. The European

Union's system of treaties, rules and regulations shared with the independent states of the Global South systematically carry in them the legacies of colonial rule. This is so much so that the concept of 'dependency' – a foundational notion in the post-war sociology of development and underdevelopment – was initially proposed to refer to these surviving, or reproduced, post- and neo-colonial ties to the erstwhile colonizing powers in western Europe.[9] But this is just one aspect of the EU's imperial legacies (e.g., Baran 1957, 201–205; Frank 1979, 11; Blaut 1993, 55; Chase-Dunn and Hall 1997, 189–191).

The end of the colonial system took place in three main geopolitical steps. The early-to-mid-19th century wave of anticolonial nationalist movements brought independence to the white-settler societies of Latin America. The abolition of slavery, begun with the Haitian revolution of 1791–1804, occupied much of colonial policy during the 19th century and was not over until well into the 20th century. Finally, the third wave involved a process that took approximately one generation to unfold in the aftermath of World War II. The last wave of colonial liberation struggles resulted in a fundamental reorganization of global governance. Among those most strongly affected were the former colonizer states of Western Europe. From a tightly hierarchical network structure with west European powers at its center, the post-independence period saw a shift to European regionalism. In response to the triple challenge of the impossibility of war among west European societies, the precipitous loss of colonial power (and the resulting, partial reduction in effective control over global resources by west European actors) and the appearance of state socialism as a regional threat on their eastern borders, west European societies reinvented the idea of a pan-Europe (proposed earlier by several generations of European public intellectuals and statesmen only to be ignored until the post-World-War-II period) (Böröcz 2009a).

Two of those challenges – the question of war among European powers and the Cold War – were imperial concerns of the contiguous kind: They involved rivalries and rearrangements of territorial sovereignty along shared land borders in a supra-state context. The rearrangements so created – NATO and the EU on the one side and the Warsaw Pact and COMECON on the other – were recognizably centralized, with strongly concentric spatial features.

A recurrent theme in the *longue-durée* geopolitical history of west European statehood is their chronic size-impairment.[10] Re-phrased in the language of imperial politics, Western Europe's long-term historical disadvantage can be identified in its legacy of small statehood – i.e., the region's endemic inability to construct large and reasonably stable as well as coherent land-based empires.

The greatest global economic weight to have ever been achieved by a west European state is around 10% (registered by Britain at the height of its colonial rule at the end of the 19th century).[11] In contrast, the global economic weight of both China and India had never dropped below 15% until well into the second half of the 19th century.[12] And, a few years after Britain reached the historic apex of its global economic weight, its former colony, the United States, surpassed it in global weight.[13] In global terms, in other words, west European states have a history of continuous, and quite frustrated, struggles for global economic weight. Construction of the European Union can be seen as a solution of sorts to that problem.

The resulting land-based, concentrically hierarchical, contiguous supra-state public authority, i.e., the European Union, cannot be considered a state because it lacks, and explicitly excludes, the possibility of an executive apparatus of its own. Hence the EU is a new, and unique, institution, a supra-state public authority that is not, itself, a state. Meanwhile, it shows distinct features not only of the legacies of overseas colonial empires, but also that of land-based empires – without an emperor of course (Böröcz and Sarkar 2005; Zielonka 2006; Böröcz 2009a, a2014).

Enforcement chains

As Mahua Sarkar and I argued a decade ago (Böröcz and Sarkar 2005), any public authority that is not a state because it has no executive apparatus of its own faces a structural problem: How will its output in laws, regulations and other legal materials be enforced? The European Union has been remarkably creative in this regard: Execution of its legal output is done through a network-based system of executive arrangements, not unlike the subcontracted, distributed production schemes familiar from the economic sociology of flexible accumulation (ibid.). Given that the EU has no direct means of coercion of its own, its reliance on a distributed, subcontracted system (in which the member states as well as a large number of other contracting parties play a key role) implies that the EU is eternally locked into the imperative of creating and maintaining a network of contractual agreements with a large number of partners, making up for the EU's absent executive apparatus. A key to the European Union's remarkable success in being able to have its legal output be adhered to and, more broadly, to have its interests be taken into account, respected and followed in a global context is its flourishing, expanding, dynamic and in many ways highly adaptable system of legal-contractual ties with a huge number of actors both in- and outside its borders.

The key aspect of these contractual relationships is that they create agreements that they serve as *enforcement chains*: always hierarchical and typically asymmetrical, arrangements of authority in which the subordinate party undertakes to execute the legal output of the superordinate party.[14] As far as the EU is concerned, the most direct, and in many ways the simplest, contractual arrangement is membership. Membership is, in a very simple and straightforward manner, an explicit enforcement chain. The oft-quoted, elegant formula of the "sharing and pooling of sovereignty" (e.g., Wallace 1999) implies that, in exchange for specific rights and privileges in the decision making process, the newly contracting accession state undertakes to execute the legal materials of the Brussels center. As the ongoing fiscal crisis of a number of EU-member states indicates, this asymmetrical enforcement chain aspect of the EU-to-member-state relationship is crucial for the functioning of the EU, and the prospect of a protracted inability to overcome some structural rigidities threatens the survival of the EU as a whole.

Above, and in some of my earlier work, I used the analogy of subcontracted, distributed production to describe the European Union's strategy of reliance on both external and internal actors to provide for the execution of the EU's legal output, and to safeguard the EU's interests in a broader sense. In tying the EU's contemporary practices to the imperial legacies, it is important to recognize that the asymmetrical internal and external executive arrangements I have called enforcement chains are a key feature of the workings of contiguous empires throughout history. Fiefdom, imperial agreement, patent, kowtow are all asymmetrical enforcement mechanisms, so that the study of pre-capitalist political contractuality is, to a very large extent, about such enforcement chains and the symbolic practices surrounding them. In this, striking sense the European Union is a true heir to the legacies of *contiguous* empires (e.g., Zielonka 2006, 2007, 2008; Böröcz 2009a).

The European Union's intense reliance on contractual enforcement chains goes a long way in explaining the otherwise quite astonishing historic speed of the European Union's recent enlargements. Simply put, *all other things equal* (more about this later), it is in the interest of the European Union to keep increasing its membership, for two interrelated reasons. First, because a greater membership base provides it with a larger pool of enforcement agents (member states), with greater potential variation among them in terms of their specific abilities, strengths and weaknesses, and a greater historical heritage of reach and access both domestically and globally. Second, *ceteris paribus*, a greater European Union means a reasonably coherent global actor *with greater global economic weight*. A more diverse, more complex and more heavyweight EU is in a position to exert its influence on the outside world, including an ability to continue influencing the overall rules of conduct in the world economy.

Struggle for global geopolitical-economic influence has been a crucial consideration throughout the entire period of the EU's existence. At first, it was so primarily because of the need of west European societies for a recovery from the war damage. Then, the loss of colonies and colonial resources created a crisis of global influence for west European colonial states – something that could be counterbalanced by way of the "sharing and pooling" of west European states sovereignties and resources. During the Cold War, global influence, and, specifically, global economic weight, served as a powerful antidote to the perceived geopolitical threats from the Soviet bloc on the immediate borders of west European states. And, finally, the end of the Cold War coincided with the remarkable re-emergence of China and India (along with some other, less gigantic but – still considerable and economically fast expanding – societies, e.g., Vietnam and Indonesia, as well as Brazil) as increasingly powerful global economic actors. All this has forced the EU's hands toward enlargements in what can be considered, in historical terms, relatively fast and bold moves, clearly in spite of the considerable "cultural" and "civilizational" fastidiousness on parts of west European populations and political parties, and much bureaucratic foot dragging on part of the Brussels apparatus of the European Union.

The EU has a vested interest in enlargements, as I have argued above – "all other things equal". However, in reality, "all other things" are not equal. Consequently, the European Union's logic of enlargements (i.e., the idea that it will grow itself out of its size-impairment problem) has run into a set of real limitations created by some basic facts of economic, political and social geography. The then German Foreign Minister Joschka Fischer's famous speech at Humboldt University (2000) about the "finality" of enlargement already signaled the problem. To put it bluntly, the European Union seems to be running out of states to swallow.

In a recent study (Böröcz 2014), I considered a number of hypothetical scenarios for future enlargements of the European Union in the context of EU's global weight competition with China and India. Those scenarios included /0/ the option of doing nothing, /1/ the rapid completion of all pending enlargements in the Balkans and Turkey, /2/ conclusion of the Transatlantic Trade and Investment Partnership and its speedy transformation into a more ambitious integration, not unlike today's EU, as well as /3/ a hypothetical union with Russia. The empirical findings of this exercise can be summed up with much simplicity: None of these scenarios offer a resolution to the challenge of the European Union's endemic lack of growth.

China, currently just about *on par* with the European Union and the USA in terms of its global economic weight, is projected to continue its growth into the foreseeable future. So are India and the other large and growing economies in Asia. The only difference among the various scenarios is the amount of time it would take for China and India to surpass the EU (or, the EU's union with various potential geopolitical partners), ranging from a few years to maybe a maximum of one generation. In principle, there is no reason to expect that China's and India's upswings will run into hard limits; to be remembered is that, throughout much of history with written records on economic activity, both India and China have contributed between one-fourth and one-third of the total world economic output, *each*.

Strictly speaking, even a bold, expanded and expedited process of large-scale enlargements – i.e., the process of promoting applicant states and either of the two major geopolitical actors that could be, with a gigantic grain of salt, imagined as potential partners for enlargement of the European Union, to full membership – simply does not hold the promise that the geopolitical calculations for the European Union's global role would require. And this is of course without even taking into account the very significant differences in the models of *capitalisms*, in the plural, that set apart the various parties that would have to come together seamlessly in order for this calculation to be realistic.

Finally, the European Union has yet another set of tools for the creation of contractual enforcement chains at its disposal, beyond membership: Association Agreements and Trade Agreements. In addition to creating enforcement chains not unlike membership, Association Agreements also typically carry provisions for preferential access by EU-based corporations to the internal markets and the other resources of non-EU-member societies. Association Agreements *may* carry the promise of full membership, but most of them simply do not – and even if they do, such promises are not binding. Because of the steep conditions involved in full membership (a host of political, economic, social and even "cultural" criteria are specified, and fulfillment of those criteria is evaluated unilaterally by the EU through a remarkably non-transparent process), except for the recent history of "eastern enlargements," most Association Agreements do not lead to membership.

Since the collapse of the Soviet bloc in 1989–1990, the European Union has added 16 new member states. The new member states have added just over 2 million square kilometers of land area and, as of 2013, approximately 124 million new citizens to the European Union. 46% of the land area and 25.3% of the population of the current European Union came with the post-1990 enlargements. Thanks to the accession of Finland, Estonia, Latvia, Lithuania and Poland, the European Union now shares significant land borders with Russia; the admission of Poland, Slovakia, Hungary and Romania also created new EU land borders with Ukraine. In addition, the European Union has bilateral agreements with 31 countries, the Cariforum states as well as Central America, as well as customs agreements with Andorra, San Marino and Turkey.[15] And all that is in addition to the EU's bilateral trade agreements signed in the context of the World Trade Organization. All association and other, non-membership-generating agreements are essentially deals that provide preferential access to the internal natural, social and economic resources of the non-EU-member societies for EU-based capital, in exchange for tariff- and discrimination-free opportunities for EU-bound exports. Membership is so not on the horizon for such partners that association and partnership agreements do not even offer eased access to visas, let alone visa-free travel, etc. to the partner societies.

Empirical coda

At the time of the writing of this essay in 2014, global reporting on geopolitical issues is focused, to a large extent, on Ukraine, i.e., on the European Union's eastern borderlands. Following a five-month political crisis precipitated by then Ukrainian president Yanukovych's postponement of the Association Agreement with the European Union, the extralegal ouster of the sitting government in Kyiv, the bloodless military occupation of the Crimean peninsula by Russia and the highly problematic Crimean referendum results in favor of secession from Ukraine, on March 18, 2014, the President of the Russian Federation, the self-appointed Prime Minister of Crimea and the Mayor of the city of Sebastopol signed a treaty on Crimea's accession to the Russian Federation.[16]

Three major geopolitical actors, with clearly recognizable, but distinct, legacies of imperial structures, have directly participated in the Ukraine crisis: The European Union, the Russian Federation, and the United States. Of the three, Russia – closest to the contiguous historical model of empire among the three – gained an immediate short-term geopolitical victory by being able to annex Crimea (whose significance is not its size or economic potential but the access it provides to "warm seas" to the Russian Navy, made easier by its predominantly Russian-speaking population) without bloodshed. The United States has imposed a set of sanctions on Russia, with unclear effect. The ongoing civil war has tied down an unprecedented proportion of the resources and capacities of the Ukrainian state, made the prospect of a political *modus vivendi* for eastern Ukraine's Russian majority a virtual impossibility within the confines of the state of Ukraine, and re-drew the basic patterns of the post-1989 Russia–NATO relationship to the brink of a new era of military confrontation.

For its part, the European Union gained a significant, and little acknowledged, victory in this process. Three days after the annexation of Crimea to the Russian Federation, the acting government of Ukraine initialed "the core elements" of an Association Agreement[17] between Ukraine and the European Union.[18] Several steps have been taken to confirm and extend that process since then. Contrary to a slew of statements by a variety of politicians in Kyiv, Washington D.C. and Brussels – making vague allusions to that effect – membership in the European Union is definitely not on the table for Ukraine.[19]

Put in terms of our analysis above, the European Union has just added another state, with a population of 46 million, or approximately 9% of the EU's own population, with an appropriate state capacity, located in a high-intensity geopolitical space between the European Union and Russia, to its collection of the thirty-plus states tied to the EU by way of asymmetrical enforcement chains, without even the slightest promise of full membership in the European Union. Along with such, much discussed features as Russian nationalism and post-Soviet nostalgia, the contractual attachment of Ukraine to the European Union as an economic and political dependency plays a significant part in motivating secessionist, pro-Russia politics, and fueling the ongoing proxy war, in eastern Ukraine.

Notes

An earlier version of this paper has been published, in Castillan Spanish, as "Unión Europea: Geopolítica Imperial y Cadenas de Imposición" in Ángel Ferrero et al. (eds.) *El último europeo: Imperialismo, xenofóbia y la derecha radical en la Unión Europea*. Madrid: La oveja roja.

1 The source of this computation, as well as all others quoted in this chapter, is the widely used online data set produced by British economic historian Angus Maddison (2010).
2 For a detailed demonstration of this process, see Böröcz (2012).
3 For an analysis of the dynamics of the UK–US shift in global hegemony, see Böröcz (2009a).
4 Arrighi and Silver (2001, 260–261). See also Böröcz (2009a).
5 For more detail, see Böröcz (2012).
6 A coefficient of dispersion (standard deviation / mean) of the distribution of the world's states according to global economic weight is very high – approximately 3.4 for 2008 – i.e. more than three times greater than the distribution in terms of per capita GDP for the same year (Maddison 2010).
7 In 1820, China's global economic weight was approximately 32% of the total (computed from Maddison 2010).
8 4.16% (Maddison 2010).
9 For more on the colonial foundations of the EU, see Böröcz and Sarkar (2005).
10 For a detailed development and empirical demonstration of this argument, see Böröcz (2009a).
11 Computed from Maddison (2010). For more detail, see Böröcz (2009a).
12 Ibid.
13 Ibid.

14 This concept is created by reference to notion in the political economy of globalized, transnational business, called *value chains*, defined as: "the full range of activities required to bring a product or service from conception through the different phases of production, delivery to final consumers, and final disposal after use" (see, e.g., Sturgeon 2013, quoting Kaplinski and Morris 2001). What is common between the two notions is that the conception and full execution of the product/legal material is not performed at the same institutional location but through spatial displacement that involves the crossing of effective boundaries of formal sovereignty.

15 http://ec.europa.eu/trade/policy/countries-and-regions/agreements/ (accessed March 25, 2014).

16 http://rt.com/news/putin-include-crimea-sevastopol-russia-578/ (accessed March 27, 2014).

17 http://eeas.europa.eu/ukraine/assoagreement/assoagreement-2013_en.htm (accessed March 27, 2014).

18 www.reuters.com/article/2014/03/21/us-ukraine-crisis-eu-agreement-idUSBREA2K0JY20140321 (accessed March 27, 2014).

19 The words *accession* and *membership* hardly ever appear in the text of the agreement, and the few times they do occur, they refer to other processes, not membership in the European Union. See http://eeas.europa.eu/ukraine/assoagreement/assoagreement-2013_en.htm (accessed March 27, 2014).

References

Arrighi, Giovanni and Beverly Silver. 2001. Capitalism and World (Dis)Order. *Review of International Studies* 27: 257–279.

Baran, Paul. 1957. *The Political Economy of Growth*. Amherst, NY: Prometheus.

Blaut, J.M. 1993. *The Colonizer's Model of the World. Geographical Diffusionism and Eurocentric History*. New York: Guilford.

Böröcz, József. 2009a. *The European Union and Global Social Change: A Critical Geopolitical Economic Analysis*. Oxford, UK: Routledge.

Böröcz, József. 2009b. The 'Rise of China' and the Changing World Income Distribution. In Hung, Ho-fung (ed.), *China and the Transformation of Global Capitalism*, 86–108. Baltimore: The Johns Hopkins University Press.

Böröcz, József. 2012. Notes on the Geopolitical Economy of Post-State-Socialism. In Nina Bandelj and Dorothy J. Solinger (eds.) *Socialism Vanquished, Socialism Challenged: Eastern Europe and China, 1989–2009*, 103–124. Oxford, UK: Oxford University Press.

Böröcz, József. 2014. Geopolitical Scenarios for European Integration: The Decades to Come. Chapter 2 in Ferenc Miszlivetz and Jody Jensen (eds.) *Reframing Europe's Future: Challenges and Failures of the European Construction*. Oxford: Routledge.

Böröcz, József and Mahua Sarkar. 2005. What Is the EU? *International Sociology* 20(2): 153–173.

Böröcz, József and Mahua Sarkar. 2012. "Empires." Entry in Helmut K. Anheier, Mark Juergensmeyer, and Victor Faessel (eds.), *Encyclopedia of Global Studies*. Thousand Oaks, CA: SAGE. 476–80.

Chase-Dunn, Christopher K. and Thomas D. Hall. 1997. *Rise and Demise: Comparing World-Systems*. Boulder, CO: Westview.

Christopher K. Chase-Dunn, Andrew K. Jorgenson, Thomas E. Reifer, and Shoon Lio. 2005. The Trajectories of the United States in the World-System: A Quantitative Reflection. *Sociological Perspectives* 48: 233–254.

Fischer, Joschka. 2000. *From Confederacy to Federation – Thoughts on the Finality of European Integration*. Speech by Foreign Minister Joschka Fischer at Humboldt University in Berlin, May 12, 2000. http://germanhistorydocs.ghi-dc.org/sub_document.cfm?document_id=3745 (accessed September 27, 2014).

Frank, André Gunder. 1979. *Dependent Accumulation and Underdevelopment*. New York: Monthly Review Press.

Kaplinsky, Raphael and Mike Morris. 2001. *Manual for Value Chain Research*. Manual prepared for the IDRC. http://asiandrivers.open.ac.uk/documents/Value_chain_Handbook_RKMM_Nov_2001.pdf (accessed March 22, 2014).

Mackinder, Halford John. 1904. The Geographical Pivot of History. *The Geographical Journal* 23(4): 431–437.

Maddison, Angus. 2010. *Statistics on World Population, GDP and Per Capita GDP, 1–2008*, www.ggdc.net/MADDISON/Historical_Statistics/horizontal-file_02–2010.xls (accessed March 12, 2013).

Sturgeon, Timothy P. 2013. *Global Value Chains and Economic Globalization: Towards a New Measurement Framework*, May 2013, http://epp.eurostat.ec.europa.eu/portal/page/portal/european_business/documents/Sturgeon_report_Eurostat.pdf (accessed March 22, 2014), p. 11.

Wallace, William. 1999. The Sharing of Sovereignty: The European Paradox. *Political Studies* XLVII: 503–521.

Wallerstein, Immanuel. 2006. The Curve of American Power. *New Left Review*, 40, July–August: 77–94.

Zielonka, Jan. 2006. *Europe as Empire: the nature of an enlarged European Union*. Oxford, UK: Oxford University Press.

Zielonka, Jan. 2007. *Is Europe Turning Into a Neo-Medieval Empire?* www.europaeum.org/files/publications/Review/Spring2007_Zielonka.pdf (accessed March 24, 2014).

Zielonka, Jan. 2008. Europe as a Global Actor: Empire by Example? *International Affairs* 84(3): 471–484.

5 European Union, conditionality and empire

Yannis A. Stivachtis

Introduction

The purpose of this paper is to demonstrate that the European Union (EU) constitutes a modern form of empire. In so doing, it is divided into two main sections. The first section provides the paper's theoretical framework and examines the constitutive elements of 'empire'. To this end, the paper argues that the notion of 'empire' should be understood in relation to what goals a political unit intends to pursue and achieve rather than the instruments it might employ to achieve them. The second section constitutes the empirical part of the paper and focuses on the European Union. This part is further divided into three sub-sections. The first of those subsections examines the political goals the EU seeks to achieve in relation to global order and identifies the order supporting elements the EU seeks to export, namely its values and norms. The next subsection focuses on the policy of conditionality, which constitutes the instrument used by the EU to export its norms and values, while the final sub-section examines the subjects of the EU's conditionality policies. In this regard, the paper's emphasis is on three sets of states: the candidate for EU membership countries, the states that are part of the European Neighbourhood Policy (ENP), and the states that receive development assistance from the European Union.

European Union as empire: Theoretical considerations

In order to show why the EU constitutes a modern form of empire this section will begin by engaging in a critical examination of the constitutive elements of the traditional definitions of empire.

The concept of 'empire'

According to the *Oxford Dictionary Online* (2015), the term 'empire' is derived from the Latin term *imperium*, which initially referred to a "magistrate's power to command," but which gradually came to refer to the "territory in which a magistrate can effectively enforce his commands." Thus, an 'empire' may include regions that are not legally within the territory of a state, but are under the direct, or indirect, control of that state. In other words, the notion of 'empire' refers to a geographically extensive group of political units and peoples governed by an authority that, according to Hartmut Behr (see Chapter 2), 'governs from distance'. Since the existence of a political unit and the existence of an authority are elements that are related to the definition of any state, the defining element of 'empire' is ability of the imperial polity to 'govern from distance'.

But before we analyze further the question of how a polity could 'govern from distance', it is necessary to address some issues pertaining to the characteristics of empires because it is to those characteristics scholars refer when rejecting the notion of the EU as empire.

First, does the type of polity determine whether a political unit constitutes an empire? The study of the genealogy of the term 'empire' demonstrates that the Europeans began applying the designation of 'empire' to non-European monarchies, such as the Qing Dynasty as well as the Mogul and Median empires, eventually leading to the looser denotations applicable to any political structure meeting the criteria of imperium. This means that different types of political entities could qualify as 'empire'. In other words, an empire can be a nation-state (e.g. the French Empire), a polity characterized by overlapping authorities (i.e. the Holy Roman Empire), a federal state (it has been argued that the U.S. constitutes an empire) or a federation of states or a union of states, such as the European Union. As a supranational polity, the EU has created the necessary supranational political structures to govern itself as well as its relations with the rest of the world. Although an unusual political construction, the element of authority (both in its centralized and diffused versions) is present in the European Union.

Second, does the type of authority determine whether a political unit constitutes an empire? The answer is negative. For example, in the Medieval West, the title 'empire' had a specific technical meaning that was exclusively applied to states that considered themselves the heirs and successors of the Roman Empire. Among these were the Byzantine Empire, which was the actual continuation of the Eastern Roman Empire, the Carolingian Empire, the largely Germanic Holy Roman Empire and the Russian Empire. Yet, these states did not always fit the geographic, political or military profiles of empires in the modern sense of the word. To legitimize their *imperium*, these states directly claimed the title of *Empire* from Rome. The *sacrum Romanum imperium* (Holy Roman Empire), which lasted from 800 to 1806, claimed to have exclusively Christian principalities and was only nominally a discrete imperial state.

Unlike most states today, the Holy Roman Empire was not a highly centralized state as it had neither core nor peripheral territories and was not governed by a central, politico-military elite. Instead, it was divided into numerous individual entities governed by kings, counts, dukes, princes and bishops. In other words, political and religious authorities overlapped and worked in parallel. The Holy Roman Empire was headed by the emperor, who had the title of the 'King of the Romans' and had a political structure that included the Imperial Estates, the Imperial Diet, the Imperial Courts and the Imperial Circles. It also had an army, which was not a standing force and was composed by forces belonging to the princes who governed the various estates. Therefore, it could be argued that the European Union resembles the Holy Roman Empire in terms of its overlapping authorities and the types of supranational institutions. As a result, the EU can be seen as constituting an empire from within irrespective of whether its authority is centralized or diffused.

Third, it has been suggested that empires are typically formed from diverse ethnic, national, cultural and religious components (Howe 2002, 15). According to *The Oxford English Reference Dictionary* (1999s, 461), an empire is a multi-ethnic or multinational state with political and/or military dominion of populations who are culturally and ethnically distinct from the imperial (ruling) ethnic group and its culture. However, there are historical examples, such as the Athenian Empire or the Empire of Brazil, which indicate that the existence of multi-ethnic/national populations is not a defining characteristic of an empire. But even if it were, the EU could easily conform to this characteristic. In fact, the EU has become a multi-ethnic/national polity in two ways: first, because several of its constitutive units/states were already multi-ethic/national entities and second, by coming together to form the *Union* the Member States further strengthen the Union's multi-ethnic/national character. This *Union* was formed not as a result of a military conquest but the end result meant that the European Union exercises political dominion over the populations of the Member States who vary in terms of ethnic origins, cultures and traditions. This is the reason for which scholars like Jan Zielonka (2006) have made the argument that the EU resembles an empire from within. The question now becomes whether the EU behaves as an empire in its relations with the rest of the world.

In reference to its external relations, it is widely argued that the EU does not constitute an empire because it does not force states either to become members of the Union or pursue close relations with it. In other words, the elements of 'imposition' and 'force' are absent. It is not the EU that forces states to enter into a relationship with the Union but rather other states that voluntarily wish to do so. However, as it will be shown later in this paper, a series of proclamations by EU officials, the texts of various EU treaties and the European Security Strategy (ESS) point otherwise. Second, the elements of 'imposition' and 'force' are not necessarily defining elements of imperial relations. For example, some members of the Athenian Empire were not forced to become members of it. Instead, they saw it either as an opportunity to achieve certain benefits or as the only viable alternative. Likewise, Japan and Siam were not forced to implement that standard of 'civilization' but they did so in order to achieve certain objectives. Japan, for instance, did so in order to increase its status and role in world affairs (Stivachtis 1998, 91; Hishida 1905, 39). Likewise, Siam implemented domestic policies associated with the application of the standard of 'civilization' in order to avoid isolation (Stivachtis 1998, 93; Gong 1984). The same logic applies to the European Union. Third states may wish to join the Union or establish close relations with it either in order to achieve certain benefits, to avoid isolation or because it is the only viable alternative they have.

'Governing from distance': The defining element of empire

As it was suggested earlier, the defining element of 'empire' is the ability of the imperial polity to 'govern from distance'. However, the fundamental question is: how this could be achieved? What means are available to the imperial polity to achieve its objectives?

Those who disagree with the idea of the EU as empire usually suggest that the most fundamental and defining characteristic of empires has been territorial conquest through the use of military power. Since the EU does not do that, they argue, the Union cannot be considered an imperial polity.

Indeed, many empires in history have been the result of military conquest, incorporating the vanquished states into its political union. However, this has not always been the case. Historical examples indicate that a state could establish imperial hegemony in other ways. For example, the Athenian Empire did not begin or was exclusively based on military conquest, while Brazil declared itself an empire after separating from the Portuguese Empire in 1822. A weak state may also voluntarily seek annexation into the empire. An example is the bequest of Pergamon to the Roman Empire by Attalus III. The unification of Germany as the empire accreted to the Prussian metropole was less a military conquest of the German states than their political divorce from the Austrian Empire. Having convinced the other states of its military prowess, and having excluded the Austrians, Prussia dictated the terms of imperial membership. All these historical cases demonstrate that military conquest is one of the ways in which empires could come into being, but it is not in itself a defining element of empire.

As the above paragraph indicates, an imperial political structure can be established and maintained in two ways: first, as a territorial empire of direct conquest and control with force and second, as a coercive, hegemonic empire of indirect control achieved through 'governing from distance'. For example, the Roman Empire, the British Empire and the French Empire all pursued imperial policies that relied on the use of military force and territorial conquest. On the other hand, it has been argued that the United States constitutes a hegemonic empire that uses its instruments of coercion to exercise and maintain control over the international system (Johnson, 2000, 2004; Sandars 2000; O'Brien and Clesse 2002; Bacevich 2002, 2005; Mann 2003; Barber 2003; Simes 2003; Todd 2003; Harvey 2003; Ferguson 2004; 2005; Craig 2004; Kaplan 2005; Mandelbaum 2005).

Therefore, the issue of 'governing from distance' should be separated from the issue of the means through which 'governing from distance' is exercised. Military conquest and coercive diplomacy are certainly important means through which imperial policies are pursued, but they are not the only ones. As Alejandro Colas (2007) has demonstrated, economic and cultural means can also be used to create and maintain empires. Michael Hardt and Antonio Negri (2001) also argue that imperialism as we knew it may have ceased to exist, but empire is alive and well. They show that empire today is fundamentally different from the imperialism of European dominance and capitalist expansion in previous eras. Rather, today's empire draws on elements of U.S. constitutionalism, with its tradition of hybrid identities and expanding frontiers. In their book, Hardt and Negri link political transformation to cultural and economic changes in postmodern society that lead to new forms of racism, new conceptions of identity and difference, new networks of communication and control and new paths of migration. In their edited volume, Paul Passavant and Jodi Dean (2004) have reinforced the arguments advanced by Hardt and Negri. Finally, Tom Nairn and Paul James (2006, xxiii) define empires as polities that "extend relations of power across territorial spaces over which they have no prior or given legal sovereignty, and where, in one or more of the domains of economics, politics, and culture, they gain some measure of extensive hegemony over those spaces for the purpose of extracting or accruing value".

Since 'governing' territorial spaces beyond the legal territorial limits of the polity (from distance) is the essence of 'empire', the focus shifts to the notion of imperialism that refers to a policy of extending a polity's power and influence through various means, such as colonization, use of military force, or other means. Lewis Samuel Feuer (1989, 4) identifies two major subtypes of imperialism: the first is 'regressive imperialism' identified with pure conquest, unequivocal exploitation, extermination or reductions of undesired peoples, and the settlement of desired peoples into such territories. The second type identified by Feuer is 'progressive imperialism' founded upon a cosmopolitan view of humanity, that promotes the spread of civilization to allegedly backward societies to elevate living standards and promote civil and political liberties in territories lying beyond the legal boundaries of the imperial polity, with the allowance of people living in those territories to assimilate into the imperial society. The mechanics and implications of 'progressive imperialism' have been highlighted in the work of Brett Bowden (2009).

'Progressive imperialism' is related to the historical expansion of the European society of states and its gradual transformation into the contemporary global international society (Bull and Watson 1984; Watson 1992). In this process, the fulfillment of the standard of 'civilization' played an essential role in determining which countries would join the expanding international society and which will be left outside (Gong 1984). It is in this context that Hartmut Behr (2007) and Yannis Stivachtis (2008) have suggested that the EU currently pursues policies similar to those associated with the historical expansion of Europe. In other words, since the European policies and practices of the previous centuries were imperial, so are the current ones. Policies remain the same although different names are used to describe them. So, the standard of 'civilization' of the nineteenth century is today's 'conditionality'.

European Union as empire

As it was stated in the introductory part of this volume, there is a general consensus that the EU represents a new kind of power in international politics (Diez 2005, 2013; Manners 2002; Whitman 1998; Manners and Whitman 1998) and that it plays an ever increasing role in world affairs (Elgstrom and Smith 2006; Orbie 2009). To achieve its foreign and security policy objectives, the EU employs a range of instruments the use of which is guided by the objectives set out in various treaties as well as the European Security Strategy (ESS) (EC 2003 and 2008). For example, according to the 1991 Maastricht Treaty, the EU's foreign policy objectives included, among other things, the promotion of democracy and the rule of law and human rights. Likewise, the draft Constitutional Treaty and the Lisbon Treaty proclaimed that EU efforts aiming at preserving peace, preventing conflicts and strengthening international security would be guided by the principles that inspired its own creation and evolution and which are rooted in traditions of "democracy, human rights, fundamental freedoms and the rule of law" (cited in Tocci 2007, 7).

One of the most significant security threats identified in ESS has been bad governance (ESS 2003, 4). Therefore, spreading good governance, supporting social and political reform, dealing with corruption and abuse of power, establishing the rule of law and protecting human rights are viewed by the EU as the best means not only for increasing its own security but also building a more peaceful and stable international order. For example, the ESS notes that

> The quality of international society depends on the quality of the governments that are its foundation. The best protection for our security is a world of well-governed democratic states. Spreading good governance, supporting social and political reform, dealing with corruption and abuse of power, establishing the rule of law and protecting human rights are the best means of strengthening the international order.
>
> (EC 2003, 10)

In other words, the best protection for the EU's security is a world of well-governed democratic states and EU policies aimed at creating a stable international order that are to be guided by a set of principles, values and norms that reflect those of the European Union. José Manuel Barroso, recent President of the European Commission and Herman Van Rompuy, recent President of the European Council reiterated this approach by making it clear that the European values of respect for human dignity, freedom, democracy, equality, the rule of law and respect for human rights are "the values that the European Union promotes to make the world a better place for all" (EC 2010a; 2012) (Mocanu, 2010; Schimmelfenning and Scholtz, 2007). In other words, the EU has sought to conceptualize global order in terms of the spread and adoption of its values and norms.

EU efforts to promote a peaceful and stable international order have been highlighted by the debate about what kind of power the Union should utilize to achieve its objectives. Francois Duchene (1973) argued that the EU could become a global actor that does not rely primarily on military but on civilian means. But what are these civilian means? Hans Maull has defined a 'civilian power' as a state "whose conception of its foreign policy role and behavior is bound to particular aims, values, principles, as well as forms of influence and instruments of power in the name of a civilization of international relations" (Maull 1990, 92–3). According to this definition, EU's civilian power lies on the use of its norms, values and principles in an effort to 'civilize' international relations. In this context, the EU acts as the 'civilizer' whose duty is to create a peaceful and stable international order by 'civilizing' the 'barbarian others', thereby establishing a hegemonic and imperial type of 'civilizer–civilizee' relationship. Such a relationship brings to mind European relations with the rest of the world during the historical expansion of Europe and especially during the nineteenth century when the 'standard of civilization' became the mechanism regulating the relations of European powers with the non-European states (Gong 1984). Moreover, Maull's definition of 'civilian power' echoes that of 'progressive imperialism' advanced by Feuer.

Others have argued that if the EU wishes to play any meaningful role in world affairs it should develop its military capabilities and be ready to use them in pursuance of its foreign and security policy objectives. In other words, military means could be used to promote an international order based on EU values and norms. This militarization of the EU that has been highlighted by the Union's involvement in a number of international military operations is not without criticism. For example, Jan Zielonka (1998, 229) has argued that it weakens the EU's 'distinct profile' of having a civilian international identity. Others have pointed out that this militarization promotes an image of the EU as a potential hegemonic and imperial power (Whitman 1998).

Ian Manners (2002) has argued that a better understanding of the EU's role in world politics might be gained by reflecting on its normative power; a kind of power, which according to Johann Galtung (1973, 33) is of great significance because "the power sender's ideas penetrate and shape the will of the power-recipient". Manners claims that unlike what happened with historical empires and contemporary global powers, the EU's normative difference comes from its historical context, hybrid polity and political-legal constitution (Manners 2002, 240); a combination that has accelerated a commitment to placing European norms and principles at the center of its relations with the rest of the world (Clapham 1999) thereby universalizing them. For example, Manners notes that the EU has made its external relations informed by, and conditional on, a catalogue of norms which come closer to those of the European Convention on Human Rights and Fundamental Freedoms (ECHR) and the Universal Declaration of Human rights (UDHR) than most other actors in world politics (Manners 2002, 241).

However, as Thomas Diez suggests, the power that lies in the representation of the EU as a normative power should not be ignored (Diez 2005, 614) and that 'normative power' constitutes a form of hegemony (Diez 2013). Diez suggests that normative power connotes the characteristic of a Weberian type of power relationship which takes on a 'Lukesian twist in the form of a kind of hegemonic power', namely the power to shape the values of others (Diez 2005, 614). He notes that not only is the success of this representation a precondition for other actors to agree to the norms set out by the EU, but it also constructs an identity of the EU against an image of 'Others' in the 'outside world' (Diez 2005, 615). Diez argues that this has important implications for the way EU policies treat those 'Others', and the degree to which its adherence to its own norms is scrutinized within the European Union (Diez 2005, 614). In this sense, the discourse of the

EU as a normative power constructs a particular self of the EU, while it attempts to change others through the spread of particular norms. This does not mean that normative power cannot go alongside other forms of power, such as military, civilian and economic forms of power (Diez 2005, 620). For example, Helene Sjursen (1998, 122) has pointed out that it is entirely conceivable that military force is used to back up the spread of normative and civilian values.

The ESS makes it clear that a peaceful and stable global order requires the creation of democratic states and the spread of European values and norms across the globe. However, the ideas of a 'normative' or 'civilian power Europe' are not so innocent in the sense that the transmission of European norms and values is one way of shaping international order and serves as an alternative to economic and military means (Telo 2006; Merlingen 2007; Diez 2013). This position is contested by those who argue that the EU does not constitute an empire because it has been unable to effectively use the sources of its power in pursuance of a global order of its choice. However, this argument is absurd because it relates the idea of 'empire' to outcomes rather than intentions! The fact that an actor fails to achieve its objectives does not mean that it never had the intention of pursuing its policy goals (Holland 2002; Hurt 2003).

The EU uses a variety of tools, including political and economic conditionality as well as trade and development policies, to ensure the establishment of well-governed democratic states. As it is stated in ESS, "As the world's largest provider of official assistance and its largest trading entity, the European Union and its Member States are well placed to pursue these goals" (EC 2003, 10). Thus, contributing to 'better' governance through assistance programs, conditionality and targeted trade measures remains an important feature in EU's policy. Therefore, the remaining of the paper will be dedicated to the identification of the order supporting elements that the EU seeks to export, namely its values and norms; the discussion of the policy of conditionality as the means used by the EU to export its norms and values and the way in which conditionality applies to three sets of states: the candidate for EU membership countries, the states that are part of the European Neighbourhood Policy (ENP), and the states that receive development assistance from the European Union.

Norms and values of the European Union

The broad normative basis of the EU has been developed over the past fifty-five or so years through a series of declarations, treaties, policies, criteria and conditions. According to Manners (2002, 242), the five 'core' norms within the vast body of Union laws and policies, which comprise the *acquis communautaire* and *acquis politique*, include democracy, the rule of law, and respect for human rights and fundamental freedoms, all of which are expressed in the preamble and founding principles of the TEU, the development co-operation policy of the Community (TEC art. 177), the common foreign and security provisions of the Union (TEC art. 11), and the membership criteria adopted at the Copenhagen European Council in 1993. Among the four additional norms that Manners suggests, one can find 'good governance', which is implicit in the Copenhagen criteria but is also found in Romano Prodi's inaugural speech to the European Parliament (Prodi 2000), as well as Commission papers on 'EU election assistance and observation' and the 'White Paper on European Governance' (cited in Manners 2002, 242).

The principles of democracy, rule of law, social justice and respect for human rights were first made explicit in the 1973 Copenhagen Declaration on European Identity, although the centrality of many of these norms was only constitutionalized in the Treaty of the European Union (TEU). As Manners (2002, 243) points out, the EU is founded on and has as its foreign and development policy objectives the consolidation of democracy, rule of law, and respect for human rights and fundamental freedoms (TEU art. 6, art. 11 and TEC art. 177). Furthermore it is committed to pursuing these norms in accordance with the ECHR (TEU art. 6) and 'the principles of the United Nations Charter' (TEU art. 11, preamble to TEC). Lisbon Treaty's constitutional norms, such as democracy, rule of law, social justice and respect for human rights, represent crucial constitutive factors determining the EU's international identity.

But how does the EU transmit its norms and values to the broader international system in which it is embedded thereby increasing not only its security but also transforming it according to its interests?

EU trade and development policies have become powerful tools for promoting democratic reforms in third states. According to the ESS, for states that have placed themselves outside the bounds of international society, it is desirable that they rejoin the international community and that the EU should be ready to provide assistance (Sepos 2013: Holland 2002; Smith 2001). However, for those "who are unwilling to do so should understand that there is a price to be paid, including in their relationship with the European Union" (ESS 2003, 10). Consequently, the next section will discuss the EU's conditionality policy that constitutes the defining principle of the EU's relations with the rest of the world.

EU conditionality

The pressures of international anarchy and the need of certain states to maintain close relations with a regional international organization in order to achieve their goals and objectives enable the EU to define certain expectations and impose certain standards of behavior on the former. Therefore, pressures aimed at altering attitudes and policies can be equally applicable to all states irrespective of whether or not they seek EU membership.

Among notions of international influences on democratization, 'conditionality' represents a deliberate effort to determine the process' outcome through external pressure. This is achieved by specifying conditions or even preconditions for support, involving either promise of material aid or political opportunities. A special version is 'democratic conditionality, which emphasizes respect for and the furtherance of democratic rules, procedures and values. While other international organizations make such conditionality demands, it is the EU, which, most of all, has elaborated an extensive policy of 'democratic conditionality'. The latter has considerable leverage because the prize for compliance on the part of applicant states is full EU membership and on the part of countries that wish to establish close relations with the EU is often financial and development assistance.

Conditionality has been an essential feature of the EEC enlargement since the 1960s. The formulation of 'political conditions' has undergone considerable evolution over time expanded to include substantive democratic requirements. The real beginnings of 'political conditionality' thinking came in the early 1960s, when the issue of new membership was first under discussion although it did not actually take place until 1973. It was the European Parliament (EP) that took the initiative through its Political Committee to issue a report on the necessary political and institutional conditions for membership and association status of the EEC. The report stated clearly that "only states which guarantee on their territories truly democratic practices and respect for fundamental rights and freedoms can become members of the Community." The report also warned that "states whose governments do not have democratic legitimization and whose people do not participate in government decisions, either directly or through fully elected representatives, cannot aspire to be admitted into the circle of nations which form the European Communities" (Pridham 2005, 30).

Subsequent developments related to the relations between the EEC and the authoritarian states in Southern Europe (Greece, Spain and Portugal) proved essential in assisting the definition of 'political conditionality'. But it was the end of the Soviet Union, the collapse of communism in Eastern Europe, and the subsequent request of Eastern and Central European countries for EU membership that made 'political conditionality' a central feature of the EU enlargement (Kliewer and Stivachtis 2007, 146). The increasing role of the EU in world affairs also made 'political conditionality' a central feature of the EU's external policy.

Specifically, the formulation of 'political conditionality' became a more central and proactive part of the overall enlargement process, influenced partly by concern over special problems relating to post-communist politics (Pridham 2002b, 205–6). Since the end of the Cold War in 1989, the EU (then EEC) has made assistance and institutional ties – first informally and later formally – conditional on the fulfillment of democratic and human rights standards. Generally, these conditions become more stringent as external countries seek to upgrade their institutional ties with and assistance by the European Union. In January 1989, the European Parliament demanded that "reference to human rights should figure" in the Trade and Cooperation Agreements the EEC was beginning to negotiate with the Central and Eastern European countries (CEECs) and should be mentioned specifically in the negotiating mandates given to the Commission. In April 1989, the European Council made resumption of the negotiations with Romania conditional upon the country's compliance with its human rights commitments in the CSCE framework. In November of the same year, the Paris European Summit established that "initiatives aimed at the countries of Eastern Europe as a whole are applicable only to those which re-establish freedom and democracy" (cited in Schimmelfennig, Engert and Knobel 2006, 30). During his visit to Belgrade in May and June 1991, Jacques Santer, President of the Council, stated that

Yugoslavia's passage from the Cooperation agreement to association "hinges on political conditions such as . . . progress in establishing democracy and respect for human rights and the rights of minorities" (cited in Schimmelfennig, Engert and Knobel 2006, 30).

After the dissolution of the Soviet Union, the European Commission confirmed that "negotiating . . . new types of agreements has to be subject to political conditions." In May 1992, the European Council underscored that "respect for democratic principles and human rights . . . as well as the principles of a market economy, constitute essential elements of cooperation and association agreements between the Community and its CSCE partners" (all cited in Schimmelfennig, Engert, and Knobel 2006, 30). Henceforth, the EU added a clause to the agreements that stipulated a suspension of the agreements if partner countries failed to comply with these principles. In November of the same year, the European Council approved guidelines for PHARE, the EEC's main program of assistance to the CEECs, which made aid conditional upon the "state of advance of the reforms in each of the beneficiary countries." On this basis, Croatia and Serbia-Montenegro have long been denied PHARE aid. In July 1993, the new regulations of the aid program for the former Soviet republics (TACIS) strengthened conditionality too: "the level and intensity of the assistance will take into account the extent and progress of reform efforts in the beneficiary country" (cited in Schimmelfennig, Engert and Knobel 2006, 30).

Finally, at its Copenhagen Summit in June 1993, the European Council established the "stability of institutions guaranteeing democracy, the rule of law, human rights and respect for and protection of minorities" as the *sine qua non* for accession to the European Union. The Copenhagen political conditions have been elaborated on in the European Commission's (EC) Opinion of 1997 and from 1998 in the regular annual reports on candidate countries. The political conditions have been tied in with EU's programs of financial assistance, the accession partnerships, and the whole pre-accession strategy (Papadimitriou and Phinnemore 2004; Knill and Lenschow 2005). It is worth mentioning that additions have been made to the original criteria, notably in the inclusion of the fight against corruption, prompted by growing evidence of widespread corruption in most post-communist states.

Since the end of the Cold War, the protection of human rights and the attainment of good governance have been gradually becoming fundamental conditions in determining EU relations with its neighbors as well as the recipients of its development assistance. Therefore, elements of order present in the EU are exported beyond the EU boundaries, at least in three different ways. First through the EU's Enlargement Policy candidate states are obliged to adopt norms, rules and practices compatible with those of the European Union. Second, through the implementation of the European Neighbourhood Policy (ENP) states located in the EU's periphery and which are eager to establish advantageous relations with the EU are encouraged to adopt norms and practices compatible with those of the European Union. Finally, states that wish to be partners of the EU's Development

Policy and recipients of EU's aid are encouraged to adopt policies, norms and practices compatible with those of the European Union.

EU conditionality and candidate states

The pressures of international anarchy following the end of the Cold War, the collapse of the Soviet Union, and the dissolution of Yugoslavia pushed a number of states, such as those of Eastern and Southern Europe as well as those of the Former Soviet Union to seek membership of the EU in order to avoid isolation, improve their security and extract certain economic benefits. These needs have enabled the EU to define certain expectations and impose certain standards of behavior on those states thereby transmitting elements of the EU order beyond the EU borders. But how does this process work and what mechanisms does the EU use to achieve its objectives?

Applicant states seeking admission into the EU hope to gain social, political, and economic benefits that are associated with being a member state. However, before the EU acknowledges an applicant state as a member, the applicant state's behavior must be modified to fit within liberal norms. Conditionality of acceptance uses a reward system to entice applicant states to adopt EU norms. The European Commission relies upon five 'levers' of conditionality: (1) access to negotiations and further stages in the accession process; (2) provision of legislative and institutional templates; (3) aid and technical assistance; (4) policy advice and twinning projects; (5) monitoring, demarches and public criticism (Grabbe 2006, 261).

If the EU conditions are not met, the EU has three reinforcement strategies available for use: reinforcement by reward, reinforcement by punishment, and reinforcement by support (Schimmelfennig and Sedelmeir 2005a, 108; 2005b). Reinforcement strategies use social power to award desired behaviour while discouraging undesirable behaviour. Reinforcement strategies differ from persuasion in two fundamental ways: first, reinforcement polices are exercised in an asymmetrical power structure where incentives and disincentives are used to entice applicants to adopt desired norms; and second, reinforcement polices look to modify state behavior over time (Schimmelfennig, Engert, and Knobel 2003, 498).

The substance of the reinforcement strategies involves two components: material incentives and social reinforcement (Schimmelfennig 2005a, 109). Material incentives involve tangible rewards. These rewards include but are not limited to the following: financial assistance, market access, technology experience and participation in decision. The second substantive component is social reinforcement. Schimmelfennig (2005a, 109) suggests that 'sociopsychological' rewards, such as international recognition and public praise influence applicant states to adopt desired norms.

The EU's potential for impacting democratization in candidate states varies between three broad stages: first, pre-negotiations (when the Copenhagen criteria have to be satisfied before negotiations commence); second, actual negotiations (when political conditions as updated are monitored regularly); and third, once membership begins when the EU's direct leverage over new entrants begins to weaken, but at the same time the indirect effects of European integration in helping to consolidate democracy increase through the very intensification of networking that goes with membership (Pridham 2002a, 957). Although the deeper effects of integration are most likely through the embedding of new democracies within the EU itself, the most decisive stages when direct effects are most effective remain the pre-negotiation and accession negotiation ones. During the first phase, negotiations may be blocked by a country's failure to satisfy the political conditions, while during the second phase, negotiations may be interrupted or terminated if a negotiating country reverses its fulfillment of the political conditions, or chooses seriously to violate anyone of them.

The procedure for dealing with the failure of candidate states to meet the prescribed 'political conditions' begins with the issuing of advance warnings in the annual regular report, and the European Commission would then set up an official visit to the country concern at the highest level. There would follow a period allowing for suitable action by the government. Failure to take any measures would be recorded in the next annual report. Eventually, if no measures are taken, then the matter would go to the European Council which would be responsible for halting negotiations for membership (Pridham 2002a, 958). Thus political monitoring of applicant countries is almost continuous. This procedure reflects the EU view of democratization as a 'rolling process' and not as a state that is reached at a certain point of time.

Accession countries respond formally by making necessary institutional changes and passing relevant legislation. However, as the cases of Bulgaria and Romania (Stivachtis 2007) as well as those of Eastern and Central European states (Grabbe 2006; Schimmelfennig and Seldenmeir 2005b; Schimelfenning, Engert and Knobel 2003) have illustrated, their full satisfaction, including their implementation in practice, is not always easy to achieve due to financial, political and social constraints facing the candidate countries. But since joining the EU has been identified as a policy priority, national governments are obliged to adhere to the EU conditions even if this means loss of popularity.

EU conditionality and the European Neighbourhood Policy (ENP)

The pressures of international anarchy facing former Soviet Republics following the end of the Cold War and the collapse of the Soviet Union in conjunction with their need to address serious economic and developmental problems pushed these states to seek close relations with the EU in order to achieve their goals and objectives with the hope that one day they may be able to join it (Engelbrekt 2002). Facing political and social instability due to their economic problems the states of the southern and eastern shores of the Mediterranean also sought to establish closer relations with the European Union. The EU was quick to realize that its security was intimately connected to the stability of the countries geographically embedded in its neighborhood. The establishment of the ENP reflected the need of all parties concerned.

However, the presence of asymmetrical interdependence between the EU, on the one hand, and its neighboring states on the other, enabled the EU to request, if not impose, the implementation of certain standards of behavior from or on those states seeking thereby to transmit elements of the EU order beyond the EU borders. But how does this process work and what mechanisms does the EU use to achieve its objectives?

While candidate states have to follow the EU *acquis*, there has been discussion regarding the specific role that the EU should take in the promotion of democratization in countries that are neither acceding countries nor candidates. As the European Commission states, the ENP is meant to allow its member to work "together with partner countries, to define a set of priorities, whose fulfilment will bring them closer to the European Union" (Commision Communication 2004). Even though candidacy may not be a short-term goal for some of these states, the EU nevertheless emphasizes the importance for building communication and shared values related to issues like security, democracy, human rights, political freedom, and trade liberalization. According to the EU, stability for not just the member states, but also the surrounding regions can be ensured much more effectively with attention paid to these areas, which are clearly interrelated and hard to untangle from one another.

According to the European Commission (2003), there are many areas and situations that require attention in the aspect of assessing democratization and the protection of human right. Among them is a noticeable deficit in governance, which restricts the cultivation of shared democratic values. The marginalization of women and insufficiency of judicial systems in many countries also leads to a lack of political representation and development. Furthermore, democratization relies upon increased attention towards education programs, which often suffers funding inequality and inadequacy among external states. As a result, in 2001 the Commission laid out a set of policies that characterize the overall approach to democratization in external countries, and recommends: the promotion of consistent policies among states; a pro-active approach, focusing on political dialogue and assistance; and the adoption of a strategic approach, focusing on the implementation of specific projects (Commission Communication 2001).

Following the Communication from the European Commission to the Council and the European Parliament (EC 2003), the ENP was developed in 2004 with the objective of strengthening the prosperity, stability and security of the EU and its neighboring states. As such, it is based on the values of democracy, rule of law and respect of human rights (EC 2004). The ENP framework is proposed to the sixteen of EU's closest neighbors.[1] The ENP is manly a bilateral policy between the EU and each partner country. However, it is complemented by regional and multilateral co-operation initiatives, such as the Eastern Partnership (launched in Prague in May 2009), the Union for the Mediterranean (the Euro-Mediterranean Partnership, formerly known as the Barcelona Process, relaunched in Paris in July 2008), and the Black Sea Synergy (launched in Kiev in February 2008) (Mocanu 2010).

In the ENP framework, the EU uses financial and diplomatic means to ensure that there is a move towards democratization in third states. In other words, the EU uses a strategy of positive reinforcement where the reward for desired behaviour is financial assistance. States, in order to reap the benefits of the ENP must show commitment to the respect of human rights, political freedoms, and democratization. Moreover, the Union's neighbors, in order to take full advantage of the various benefits of the ENP, must pledge an adherence not only to human rights, but also to the values of democracy that the Union promotes.

In 2010–2011, the EU reviewed the ENP and put a strong focus on the promotion of deep and sustainable democracy, accompanied by inclusive economic development (EC 2011). Deep and sustainable democracy includes in particular free and fair elections, freedom of expression, of assembly and of association, judicial independence, fight against corruption and democratic control over the armed forces. The EU also stressed the role of civil society bringing about deep and sustainable democracy. The EU unveiled 'more for more' principle, under which the EU will develop stronger partnerships with those neighboring states that make more progress towards democratic reform.

Within the ENP the EU offers its neighbors a privileged relationship, building upon a mutual commitment to common values (democracy and human rights, rule of law, good governance, market economy principles and sustainable development). The ENP builds upon the legal agreements in place between the EU and the partner in question: Partnership and Cooperation Agreements (PCA) or Association Agreements (AA). Implementation of the ENP is jointly promoted and monitored through the Committees and sub-Committees established in the frame of these agreements. The European External Action Service and the European Commission publish each year the ENP Progress Reports. The assessments contained in the Progress Reports form the basis for EU policy towards each ENP partner under the 'more for more' principle. Thus the level of ambition of the relationship depends on the extent to which these values are shared.

Central to the ENP are the bilateral 'Action Plans' between the EU and each ENP partner. These set out an agenda of political and economic reforms with short and medium-term priorities of three to five years. ENP Action Plans reflect each partner's needs and capacities, as well as their and the EU's interests. Under the ENP Action Plans the EU works together with its partners to develop democratic, socially equitable and inclusive societies. Because the civil society plays an important role in contributing to democracy and good governance building in partner countries, the EU supports organizations via the Civil Society Facility. Moreover, the EU offers its neighbors economic integration, improved circulation of people across borders, financial assistance and technical cooperation toward approximation with EU standards. The European Commission provides financial support in grant form to partners; the European Investment Bank and the European Bank for Reconstruction and Development complement this support through loans.

The 'more for more' principle applies to all incentives proposed by the EU: policy developments as well as to financial assistance. Countries determinedly embarking on political reforms are offered, in addition to the incentives available to other partners, elements of market access: economic integration and development (DCFTAs), mobility of people (mobility partnerships), and a greater share of the EU financial support. In this context, the Commission has decided to set up specific programs both for the Eastern (EAPIC) and Southern (SPRING) neighbors that will allocate extra financial support only to those neighbors taking clear and concrete steps on political reforms.

The question then arises as to how to enforce these stipulations and how democratic principles should be insisted upon. Besides negotiation and diplomacy, financial incentives seem to be the most widely considered way of increasing democratization. While the EU includes the language of democratization in agreements made with third states, unlike candidate states following the Copenhagen criteria, there are no clear, concrete political ramifications for third states that do not further pursue democratization (Schimmelfenning, 2005b). Economic incentives and positive conditionality, like the financial aid given to particular programs or organizations in third parties is a popular way for the EU to influence democratization measures. Despite the criticism it has received (Sasse 2008), the ENP has served as a valuable tool for increasing democratization and security in the states surrounding the borders of the EU thereby promoting an EU-like global order.

EU conditionality and development assistance recipient countries

Facing pressures stemming from international anarchy as well as political and social instability due to their economic problems, the states of the developing and less developed world have sought to establish closer relations with the European Union. As in the case of the ENP states, the presence of asymmetrical interdependence between the EU, on the one hand, and the developing and less developed states on the other, has enabled the EU to demand the implementation of certain standards of behavior from those states if development assistance is to be provided (Sepos 2013; Tzifakis 2007). Consequently, the introduction and implementation of requested changes would assist the EU to transmit elements of its domestic order beyond the EU borders. But how does this process work and what mechanisms does the EU use to achieve its objectives?

The origins of the EU's development policy can be found back in 1957 when the European Economic Community (EEC) was created and its relations with the sub-Africa, the Caribbean and the Pacific states (ACP) were established. Following the decolonization process a new approach was needed to regulate the relations between the European states and the new independent states. The Yaoundé Conventions grounded the relations on a legal basis and provided the fertile ground for the enhancement of the partnership between the EEC and these states. Later the Lomé Conventions sought to provide a broader and enhanced relation between the partners. Lomé IV (1990–2000) became the first development agreement to incorporate a human rights clause as a "fundamental part of cooperation." An updated clause confirmed human rights as an "essential element of cooperation", signifying that any violation could lead to partial or total suspension of development aid by the EU after prior consultation of other ACP nations and the abusing party (Holland 2002).

When the Cotonou Agreement was established in 2000, it introduced a new approach to EU–ACP relations while preserving the fundamental instruments of the partnership from the Lomé Conventions including conditionality clauses on human rights (EC 2010a; 2010b). With the Cotonou Agreement, the EU changed its role from a sole aid provider to an international actor that would monitor on a regular basis the application of the political conditionality principles by its ACP partners (Marsh and Mackenstein 2005; Bretherton and Volger 2006; Tzifakis 2007). This clearly demonstrates the effort of the EU to exercise a greater influence on ACP countries to improve their poor conditions on human rights and promote 'good governance.' Thus EU development assistance became a motive for these developing countries to reform their policies and practices associated with democracy, the rule of law, social justice and respect for human rights.

The European Commission contends that stability and security are some of the most important factors for long-term engagement with third states. Thus, by focusing on 'good governance' in some of the most politically unstable regions, the EU seeks to address "the root causes of conflict and insecurity" (European Commission 2010b, 2). Established by the European Parliament in 1994, the European Initiative for Democracy and Human Rights (EIDHR) focuses precisely on the issue of democratization and the promotion on human rights in third countries (Commission Communication 2003). This primarily takes place through funding activities of non-governmental and international organizations. In 2003, the annual sum for the worldwide projects amounted to €100 million. Thus, the EIDHR was established as a mechanism for cooperation and as a "financing instrument for the promotion of democracy and human rights worldwide" (European Commission 2010b, 5).

The EU notes that the fact that the organization is the world's largest aid donor demonstrates a commitment to poverty alleviation and economic development across the globe (Commission Communication 2012, 1). The need to deliver aid, according to the 2012 Annual Report by EUROPEAID, cannot be removed from democratization efforts, or the further pursuit of human rights regimes(Commission Communication 2003). For example, the report places particular emphasis on the EU's relationship with Central Asian states, where it is "seen as a close political ally and trusted partner on whom they can rely on (sic) in the challenging transition process on which they have embarked" (Commission Communication 2012, 5). Similarly, the EU–Latin America/Caribbean (LAC) Madrid summit in May 2010 outlined greater political relations with Central and South American countries. Even in Southeast Asia, the EU works towards strengthening bilateral partnerships with countries to increase the promotion of democratization in the region, in the hopes of securing other regions in order to secure EU's interests (Commission Communication 2012, 6).

Although it has received considerable criticism (Sepos 2013; Holland 2002), EU development policy has served as a valuable tool for increasing democratization in the developing and less developed world thereby promoting an EU-like global order.

Conclusion

The purpose of this paper was to demonstrate why the EU constitutes a modern form of empire by investigating how the EU's policy of conditionality contributes towards the strengthening of an international order that reflects EU's interests and values. The paper suggests that the need of non-EU states to maintain close relations with the EU in order to avoid isolation, promote their security and extract economic and other benefits in conjunction with the presence of asymmetrical interdependence in favor of the EU have enabled the latter to define certain expectations and impose certain standards of behaviour on the former. Therefore, EU pressures aimed at altering attitudes and policies can be equally applicable to all states irrespective of whether or not they seek EU membership.

The paper demonstrates that the EU's norms, rules, and practices are transmitted globally in, at least, three ways. First, through the EU's Enlargement Policy candidate states are obliged to adopt norms, rules and practices compatible with those of the European Union if they wish to gain admission. Second, through the implementation of the European Neighbourhood Policy (ENP) states in the EU's periphery, which wish to establish advantageous and good neighboring relations with the EU, are encouraged to adopt norms and practices compatible with those Union. Third, states that wish to be partners of the EU's Development Policy and recipients of EU's aid are also requested to adopt policies, norms and practices compatible with those of the European Union. In doing so, the EU contributes towards the creation of a global order compatible with the EU's vision and interests. Put in different words, through the use of its conditionality policy, the EU attempts to create a normative international/global order by 'governing from distance.'

Note

1 The European Neighbourhood Policy (ENP) includes the following countries: Algeria, Armenia, Azerbaijan, Belarus, Egypt, Georgia, Israel, Jordan, Lebanon, Libya, Moldova, Morocco, Palestine, Syria, Tunisia and Ukraine.

References

Bacevich, Andrew. (ed.). 2002, *The Imperial Tense: Prospects and Problems of American Empire*. New York: Ivan Dee.

Bacevich, Andrew. 2005. *The New American Militarism*. Oxford: Oxford University Press.

Barber, Benjamin. 2003. *War, Terrorism and Democracy*. New York: Norton.

Behr, Hartmut. 2007. The European Union in the Legacies of Imperial Rule? EU Accession Politics Viewed from A Historical Comparative Perspective. *European Journal of International Relations* 13(2): 239–262.

Bowden, Brett. 2009. *The Empire of Civilization: The Evolution of an Imperial Idea*. Chicago: University of Chicago Press.

Bretherton C. and J. Volger. 2006. *The European Union as a Global Actor*. 2nd edition, London: Routledge.

Bull, Hedley and Adam Watson. (eds.). 1984. *The Expansion of International Society*. Oxford: Clarendon Press.

Clapham, A. 1999. Where is the EU's Human Rights Common Foreign Policy, and How Is It Manifested in Multilateral Fora? In P. Alston (ed.). *The EU and Human Right*. Oxford: Oxford University Press.

Commission Communication. 2001 (May 8). *The European Union's Role in Promoting Human Rights and Democratisation in Third Countries*. COM(2001) 252 final.

Commission Communication. 2003 (March 11). *Wider Europe – Neighbourhood: Anew Framework for Relations with Our Eastern and Southern Neighbours*. COM(2003) 104 final.

Commission Communication. 2004 (May 12). *European Neighbourhood Policy*. COM (2004) 373 final.

Council of the European Union. 2012 (June 25). *EU Strategic Framework and Action Plan on Human Rights and Democracy*. 11855/12.

Commission Communication. 2012 (August 6). *Annual Report 2012 on the European Union's Development and External Assistance Policies and their Implementation in 2011*. COM(2012) 444 final.

Craig, Campbell. 2004. American Realism versus American Imperialism. *World Politics* 57: 141–71.

Diez, Thomas. 2005. Constructing the Self and Changing Others: Reconsidering "Normative Power Europe." *Millennium: Journal of International Studies* 33(3): 613–36.

Diez, Thomas. 2013. Normative Power as Hegemony. *Cooperation and Conflict* 48(2): 194–210.

Duchene, Francois. 1973. The European Community and the Uncertainties of Interdependence. In M. Kohnstamm and W. Hager (eds.). *A Nation Writ Large? Foreign Policy Problems before the European Community*. Basingstoke: Macmillan.

Elgstrom, Ole and Michael Smith. 2006. *The European Union's Roles in International Politics*. London: Routledge.

Engelbrekt, Kjell. 2002. Multiple Asymmetries: The European Union's Neo- Byzantine Approach to Eastern Enlargement. *International Politics* 39(1): 37–51.

European Commission. 2003. *European Security Strategy: A Secure Europe in a Better World*. www.consilium.europa.eu/uedocs/cmsUpload/78367.pdf

European Commission. 2008. *Report on the Implementation of the European Security Strategy: Providing Security in a Changing World*. www.consilium.europa.eu/ueDocs/cms_Data/docs/pressdata/EN/reports/104630.pdf

European Commission. 2010a (April 1). *European Instrument for Democracy and Human Rights (EIDHR)*. Strategy Paper 2007–2010.

European Commission. 2010b (April 21). *European Instrument for Democracy and Human Rights (EIDHR)*. Strategy Paper 2011–2013.

European Commission. 2011. *A New Response to a Changing Neighbourhood: A Review of European Neighbourhood Policy*.

European Commission. 2012. *Joint Statement of José Manuel Barroso, President of the European Commission, and Herman Van Rompuy, President of the European Council on the Award of the 2012 Nobel Peace Prize to the EU*. http://europa.eu/rapid/press-release_MEMO-12-779_en.htm#PR_metaPressRelease_bottom

Ferguson, Niall. 2004. *Empire: The Rise and Demise of the British World Order and the Lessons for Global Power*. New York: Basic Books.

Ferguson, Niall. 2005. *Colossus: The Rise and Fall of the American Empire*. New York: Penguin Books.
Feuer, Lewis Samuel. 1989. *Imperialism and the Anti-Imperialist Mind*. New York: Transaction.
Galtung, Johann. 1973. *The European Community: A Superpower in the Making*. London: Allen & Unwin.
Gong, Gerritt. 1984. *The Standard of Civilization in International Society*. Oxford: Clarendon Press
Grabbe, Heather. 2006. *The EU's Transformative Power: Europeanization through Conditionality in Central and Eastern Europe*. Basingstoke: Palgrave.
Harvey, David. 2003. *The New Imperialism*. Oxford: Oxford University Press.
Hishida, Seiji G. 1905. *The International Position of Japan as a Great Power*. New York: Columbia University Press.
Holland, M. 2002. *The European Union and the Third World*. Basingstoke: Palgrave.
Howe, Stephen. 2002. *Empire*. New York: Oxford University Press.
Hurt, Stephen. 2003. Cooperation and Coercion? The Cotonou Agreement between the European Union and ACP States and the End of the Lome Convention. *Third World Quarterly* 24: 161–76.
James, Paul and Tom Nairn. 2006. *Globalization and Violence, Vol. 1: Globalizing Empires, Old and New*. London: Sage.
Johnson, Chalmers. 2000. *Blowback: The Costs and Consequences of American Empire*. London: Little, Brown.
Johnson, Chalmers. 2004. *The Sorrows of Empire*. New York: Holt.
Kaplan, Robert. 2005. *Imperial Grunts: The American Military on the Ground*. New York: Random House.
Kliewer, Brandon and Yannis A. Stivachtis, 2007. Democratizing and Socializing Candidate States: The Case of EU Conditionality. In Yannis A. Stivachtis (ed.). *The State of European Integration*, 143–60. Aldershot: Ashgate.
Knill, C. and A. Lenschow. 2005. Compliance, Competition and Communication: Different Approaches to European Governance and their Impact on National Institutions. *Journal of Common Market Studies* 43(3): 583–606.
Mandelbaum, Michael. 2005. *The Case of Goliath: How America Acts as the World's Government in the 21st Century*. New York: Public Affairs.
Mann, Michael. 2003. *Incoherent Empire*. New York: Verso.
Manners, Ian. 2002. Normative Power Europe: A Contradiction in Terms? *Journal of Common Market Studies* 40(2): 235–58.
Manners, Ian and Richard Whitman. 1998. Towards Identifying the International Identity of the European Union. *Journal of European Integration* 21(2): 231–49.
Marsh, S. and H. Mackenstein. 2005. *International Relations of the European Union*. London: Pearson Longman.
Maull, Hans. 1990. Germany and Japan: The New Civilian Powers. *Foreign Affairs* 69(5): 91–106.
Merlingen, Michael. 2007. Everything Is Dangerous: A Critique of 'Normative Power Europe. *Security Dialogue* 38(4): 435–453.
Mocanu, Oana. 2010. Brief Overview on the Conditionality in the European Neighbourhood Policy. *Romanian Journal of European Affairs* 10(4): 42–49.
O'Brien, Patrick and Almand Clesse. (eds.). 2002. *Two Hegemonies: Britain 1846–1914 and the United States 1941–2001*. Aldershot: Ashgate.
Orbie, Jan. (ed.). 2009. *Europe's Global Role: External Policies of the European Union*. Aldershot: Ashgate.

Oxford Dictionary Online. 2015. Empire. www.oed.com/view/Entry/61337

Papadimitriou, D. and D. Phinnemore. 2004. Europeanisation, Conditionality and Domestic Change. *Journal of Common Market Studies* 42(3): 619–39.

Passavant, Paul and Jodi Dean (eds.). 2004. *Empire's New Clothes*. London: Routledge.

Pridham, Geoffrey. 2002a. EU Enlargement and Consolidation Democracy in Post-Communist States – Formality and Reality. *Journal of Common Market Studies* 40(3): 953–73.

Pridham, Geoffrey. 2002b. The European Union's Democratic Conditionality and Domestic Politics in Slovakia. *Europe-Asia Studies* 54(2): 203–27.

Pridham, Geoffrey. 2005. *Designing Democracy: EU Enlargement and Regime Change in Post-Communist Europe*. New York: Palgrave.

Prodi, Romano. 2000. *2000–2005: Shaping the New Europe*. Speech to the European Parliament, Strasburg, 15 February.

Sandars, Christopher. 2000. *America's Overseas Garrisons: The Leasehold Empire*. Oxford: Oxford University Press.

Sasse, Gwendolyn. 2008. The European Neighbourhood Policy: Conditionality Revisited for the EU's Eastern Neighbours. *Europe-Asia Studies* 60(2): 295–316.

Schimmelfennig, Frank. 2005a. The EU: Promoting Liberal Democracy Through Membership Conditionality. In Trine Flockhart (ed.). *Socializing Democratic Norms*. Basingstoke: Palgrave.

Schimmelfennig, Frank. 2005b. *European Neighborhood Policy: Political Conditionality and Its Impact on Democracy in Non-Candidate Neighbouring Countries*. Austin, Texas.

Schimmelfennig, Frank, S. Engert and H. Knobel. 2003. Costs, Commitment and Compliance: the Impact of EU Democratic Conditionality on Latvia, Slovakia and Turkey. *Journal of Common Market Studies* 41(3): 495–518.

Schimmelfennig, Frank, S. Engert and H. Knobel. 2006. *International Socialization in Europe: European Organizations, Political Conditionality and Democratic Change*. Basingstoke: Palgrave.

Schimmelfennig, Frank and Hanno Scoltz. 2007. *EU Democracy Promotion in the European Neighbourhood*. Paper presented at the EUSA Biennial Conference, Montreal, Canada.

Schimmelfennig, Frank and U. Sedelmeir. 2005a. *The Politics of European Union Enlargement*. London: Routledge.

Schimmelfennig, Frank and U. Sedelmeir. (eds.). 2005b. *The Europeanization of Central and Eastern Europe*. Ithaca: Cornell University Press.

Sepos, Angelos. 2013. Imperial Power Europe? The EU's Relations with the ACP Countries. *Journal of Political Power* 6(2): 261–287.

Sjursen, Helene. 1998. Missed Opportunity or Eternal Fantasy?: The Idea of a European Security and Defense Policy. In J. Peterson and H. Sjursen (eds.). *A Common Foreign Policy for Europe? Competing Visions of the CFSP*. London: Routledge.

Smith, K. 2001. The European Union, Human Rights and Relations with Third Countries: Foreign Policy with an Ethical Dimension. In. K. Smith and M. Light (eds.). *Ethics and Foreign Policy*. Cambridge: Cambridge University Press.

Stivachtis, Yannis. 1998. *The Enlargement of International Society*. London: Macmillan.

Stivachtis, Yannis. 2007. The EU as an International Actor: 'Civilian', 'Normative' or 'Military' Power? In Yannis A. Stivachtis (ed.), *The State of European Integration*. Aldershot: Ashgate, 2007, 41–58.

Stivachtis, Yannis. 2008. The Standard of Civilization in Contemporary International Society: The Case of the European Union. *Contemporary Politics* 14(1): 71–90.

Telo, Marion. 2006. *Europe, a Civilian Power*. New York: Palgrave Macmillan.
The Oxford English Reference Dictionary. (1999). Edited by Judy Pearsall and Bill Trumble. 2nd edition. Oxford: Oxford University Press.
Tocci, Nathalie. 2007. *The EU and Conflict Resolution: Promoting Peace in the Backyard*. London: Routledge.
Todd, Emmanuel. 2003. *After the Empire: The Breakdown of American Order*. New York: Columbia University Press.
Tzifakis, Nikolaos. 2007. EU's region-building and boundary-drawing policies: The European approach to the Southern Mediterranean and the Western Balkans. *Journal of Southern Europe and the Balkans* 9(1): 47–64.
Watson, Adam. 1992. *The Evolution of International Society*. London: Routledge.
Whitman, Richard. 1998. *From Civilian to Superpower? The International Identity of the European Union*. Basingstoke: Macmillan.
Zielonka, Jan. 2006. *Europe as Empire: The Nature of the Enlarged European Union*. Oxford: Oxford University Press.
Zielonka, Jan. 1998. *Explaining Euro-paralysis: Why Europe is Unable to Act in International Politics*. Basingstoke: Macmillan.

6 Imagining 'Europe as an empire'

Competing/converging geopolitical imaginations and EU enlargements

Aylin Güney

Introduction

The collapse of the Soviet Union and the transformations of power in Europe at the end of the Cold War led to emergence of a 'new Europe' (Paasi 2001, 8). Europe had to define itself *de novo* within the new world order (Postel-Vinay 2007, 566). European Union (EU) enlargements, in this respect, are closely interrelated to the geopolitical imagination of the EU since they have further aggravated the discussion not only about the identity of the EU but also about its borders. Since the EU enlargements are "intimately connected to the discourse of Europe and therefore inseparable from its political and economic reality, they not only have important implications upon discursive re-definitions and re-demarcations of Europe" (Kuus 2005, 567), they can be considered as policies justified on the basis of geopolitical identity and imagination of Europe. Therefore, not only did Europe's borders shift with the enlargements as defining elements of this new territory but also the meaning of Europe's 'Other' had to change during these processes. For instance, the geographic category of Central and Eastern Europe, which was generally absent in European discussions throughout the Cold War period, was introduced back to the European imagination through the rhetoric of states from Central and Eastern Europe that successfully applied to join the EU in the post–Cold War period (Rumelili 2008, 101).

It is exactly at this point that mainstream political discourse started to tackle the issues related to the definition of 'Europe' and 'Europeanness', asking what constitutes Europe. The question of how the EU would construct its identity and draw its borders based on this identity also played a crucial role in the formation of a new geopolitical imagination of the EU. In this respect, "the contradictions and social consequences of emerging EU territorialities are clearly reflected in exclusionary and discriminatory practices with regard to non-EU Europe and citizens of 'third' states." Therefore, it is important to note the "bordering processes which take place in the form of the creation of distinctions between groups of people according to varying degrees of 'EU-Europeanness'"(Scott and Houtum 2009, 271).

According to critical geopolitics, it is the geopolitical identity, which shapes geopolitical imagination that, in turn, influences, to a great extent, the enlargement policies of the EU. This chapter, therefore, aims at analyzing geopolitical imagination(s) of the EU and its impact on the enlargement policies. To do that, it will first introduce the theoretical framework and analytical tools provided by critical geopolitics, which provide a useful approach for investigating the power of naming in the "imagined geography of Europe" (Hagen 2003, 489–91). Borrowing from Heffernan's definition of the use of the term 'geography' (Heffernan 1998, 6) "as an intellectual arena of ideas and beliefs" and that "Europe can not be interpreted as a singular historical evolution, but as a series of contested geographical discourses which change over time and across space", the chapter will explore factors which have affected different geopolitical imaginations of Europe which are shaped by geopolitical discourses. Second, it will assess how critical geopolitics can help us understand the construction of geopolitical discourses which have been used to justify EU's enlargement policies towards Central and Eastern Europe and Turkey.

Theorizing critical geopolitics and geopolitical imagination(s)

Critical geopolitics, as a body of scholarship emerged in the early 1990s with the aim of bridging the gap between geopolitics and international relations and "radically reconceptualize 'geopolitics' as a complex set and problematic set of discourses, representations and practices" (Power and Campbell 2010, 243). Inspired by Michel Foucault and Jacques Derrida, critical geopolitics has been "concerned with developing a mode of interrogating and exposing the grounds for knowledge-prodcution and of seeking to analyze the articulation, objectivization and subversion of hegemony" (Power and Campbell 2010, 243). Although initially it was aimed at portraying enemies and the geographical language used to portray the "terrain of international conflict as requiring military intervention" (Dalby 2008, 424), after almost twenty years, critical geopolitics is still relevant to address "culture that produces imperial attempts at domination in distant places" (413). This chapter will, therefore, try to analyze the geopolitical imagination of Europe as an empire and how this relates to the EU's enlargement policies.

In order to explain the link between geopolitical imaginations and enlargement policies of the EU, it is first necessary to explore how geopolitical imaginations are formed. Geopolitical imaginations form a very important dimension in theories of critical geopolitics. Tuathail and Dalby (1998, 4) regard them as "useful analytical tools to explain how certain conceptual spatializations of identity, nationhood and danger manifest themselves across a landscape of states, and how certain political, social and physical geographies in turn enframe and incite certain understandings of Self and Other, security and danger, proximity and distance." In other words, it is through geopolitical imaginations that one can identify the 'Other'. Hagen (2003, 490), for instance, defines 'imagined geography' as "ways of *perceiving*[1] spaces and places, and the relationships between them, as complex sets of cultural and political practices and ideas defined spatially, rather than regarding them as static, discrete territorial units." In this view, the constructions of regions reveal broad representations of world views. Therefore, "regional constructs should be approached as 'discursive formations, constellations of power, knowledge and spatiality'" (Gregory 1995, 29, cited in Hagen 2003, 490). Since the imagined geographies also represent ways in which a national or regional identity is defined against an outside group (Hagen 2003, 491), the imagined geography of Europe is crucial to understanding what is and is not European.

Geopolitical discourses are crucial in the constructions of geopolitical imaginations. Toal (2000, 126) argues that geopolitical discourses are not "mere conversations", but rather "are power structures in themselves, rhetorical strategies and representational techniques sponsored by particular institutions and political forces that struggle in the public arena". Smith (2002, 651) explains why discursive analysis is important in critical geography as well as in understanding EU enlargements. In addition to boundary-drawing practices of defining inside and outside, geopolitical discourses also shape geopolitical concepts revealing an identity dimension. In other words, "geographical concepts have boundaries which are constructed through ideas and meanings loaded onto them and therefore their contents often clearly reveal an identity-related political dimension" (Moisio 2002, 94). In the same vein, Paasi (2001, 10) argues, "identity is not merely an individual or social category, but also, and crucially, spatial, since ideas of territory, 'self' and 'us' all require symbolic, socio-cultural and/or physical dividing lines with the Other." Therefore, geopolitical discourses reveal how the 'Other' is constructed through both boundary-drawing and identity-forming exercises. On the other hand, Bialasiewicz et al. (2007, 406–7) point to the 'performative' aspect of the discourses, arguing that "discourse is not something which subjects use in order to describe objects"; it is that which

> constitutes both subjects and objects. For example, states are made possible by a wide range of discursive practices that include immigration policies, military deployments and strategies, cultural debates about normal social behaviour, political speeches and economic investments. They are either made or represented in the name of a particular state but that state does not pre-exist those performances.

Likewise, "geopolitical imaginations or ideas do not exist 'out there' or simply in texts and documents; they are implicit in practices and social action" (Agnew 2003, 127). Therefore, geopolitical discourses reveal the characteristics of both "language and practice" (Müller 2008, 322). In this respect, foreign policy emerges an important field where geopolitical imaginations are revealed. Therefore, "major changes in geopolitical contexts generally cause the reformulations of geopolitical visions and rearticulations of geographical representations necessary to justify foreign policy changes" (Mamadouh and Dijkink 2006, 357). At this point, it is through the geopolitical discourses which legitimize policies and power projection. "Since foreign policy can be perceived as a kind of boundary-drawing, popular representations of Others are part of larger processes whereby geopolitical imaginations are used during foreign policy formulation processes" (Tuathail and Dalby 1998, 4; Dalby 1998, 307–8). The discursive approach, therefore, shows "how geographical representations and geographical arguments for interrelations and delimitations are linguistically constructed and deployed as discursive strategies in political interaction" (Rueber and Walkersdorfer 2002, 42). In short, discourse is created, recreated and transformed intentionally, and that is why it is important and powerful (Müller 2008, 326).

Deconstructing Europe's geopolitical imagination(s) and EU enlargements

This chapter will now identify the main determinants of the EU's geopolitical imagination(s) to assess how such imaginations translate into enlargement policies. Despite its peculiar character and complex structure, the EU is considered as an international actor or 'European power' or even 'European Empire', with an increasingly important role in its 'neighborhood' (Bialasiewicz et al. 2009, 79). Bialasiewicz et al. argue that it is necessary to understand Europe's geopolitical vision, since "creating new spaces of influence for Europe is also a bordering exercise. As the borders of Europe shift, the strategies of inclusion and exclusion also shift." Dahlman argues that "debates surrounding the delimitation of the EU's 'geopolitical space' have long been marked by the broader existential question of just what (EU)rope was to become" (Bialasiewicz et al. 2009, 80). In these debates, Europe is mostly defined by 'what it is'. As Rumford argues, "the question of Europe's borders is given fresh impetus by the fact that there are many Europes and hence a plurality of European borders and they are not agreed upon by consensus. Different institutions and peoples construe the location, meaning and importance of Europe's borders in different ways." (Rumford in Bialasiewicz et al. 2009, 84). However, they all agree that the EU's bordering exercise is extremely important since it also defines its identity, which is why the theoretical perspective of critical geopolitics is important and relevant.

The debate regarding whether the EU is a "post-Westphalian state", a "neo-Medieval Empire" (Zielonka 2006, 1), a "Fortress Empire" (Armstrong and Anderson 2007) or "Sieve Europe"[2] (Walters 2004, 676) contributes to discussions aiming to clarify geopolitical imaginations of Europe. Anderson considers five competing visions of Europe's territorial future: 'Europe of nations', 'a federal European superstate', 'Europe of regions', a 'new medieval Europe' and, more recently, 'Europe as an empire'. Anderson claims that, while distinct, they nevertheless share certain "overlapping conceptions of political space and territoriality: *national, medieval* and *imperial*" (Anderson 2007, 9). Paasi (2001, 9) maps competing, yet mutually constitutive, visions of Europe, namely 'Europe as an experience', 'Europe as an Institution', 'Europe as a Structure', 'Europe as a set of Regions'. Given that the EU's most important and unique feature is perhaps its widening, or enlargement process, it is important, at this point, to identify the geopolitical imagination that justifies and shapes the EU's enlargement decisions.

In order to understand how EU enlargement policies are made and justified, it is necessary first to understand how Europe is imagined or constructed through the discourses of the European political elites as well as the EU institutions. This issue has been at the center of political debates in Europe for centuries.

The geography called 'Europe' has changed geographically and spatially over time. Analysis of geopolitical discourses in the current debate on EU enlargement reveals that there is no single construction of Europe, hence no single geopolitical imagination; rather, there have been different constructions of Europe(s) – different discourses, stemming from or reflecting various forms of power relations or ideological perspectives.

For analytical purposes and for the sake of simplicity, two main models of Europe can be identified: Europe as a neo-Medieval Empire, characterized by the EU motto, "Europe united in diversity", Europe as neo-Westphalian state, represented by the EU and characterized by a "Historical-Geographical Idea". Jan Zielonka (2006, 14–15) has proposed this distinction of two different models of EU integration. The chapter, however, claims that these distinctions are not that clear and that the geopolitical imaginations of the neo-Medieval Empire represented by the EU are very much influenced by the historical-geographical idea of the EU as a post-Westphalian state. This, in turn, has major implications for enlargement since it shapes the inclusion/exclusion patterns in general and with regard to Central and Eastern Europe and Turkey in particular. These two models will be elaborated below.

Neo-Westphalian geopolitical imagination: Historical-geographical Europe

Europe as a historical-geographical construction is important for understanding patterns of inclusion and exclusion in the creation of political and cultural distinctions. Paasi (2005, 581) argues that, while "most cultural traditions embrace ideas about 'Us' and the 'Other' in constructing and representing identity, the power of such dualisms has been especially important in Europe's cultural tradition". Therefore, it is necessary to understand what led to imagining Europe as a historical-geographical idea. The first important factor is border-drawing, in that borders draw a line between the European Self and the Other, thereby contributing to imagining/constructing Europe as such an idea. Consequently, how the discourses of Europeans draw borders becomes an issue. One of the many ideas of Europe is the idea of borders, and the history of Europe can be said to have been dictated by its borders, both within the continent and in relation to Other(s). That is, Europe's borders are mostly drawn as a result of political, and ideological considerations which play a significant role in shaping European identity (Mikkeli 1998, 135). In that respect, Europe's eastern border, the location and importance of which has been subject to debate since antiquity, has especially significant in defining European identity (136).

Regarding the historical idea behind European identity, Postel-Vinay refers to "Wigen and Lewis's work on meta-geography, focusing on the construction of Europe as a 'world region', and how the notion of world region is geneologically related to those of the continent and civilization", that is geography and identity, characterizing a world region "as a clearly historically situated geopolitical construct" (Postel-Vinay 2007, 559). She further argues that European geographers also developed the notion of 'continent', as a geographical spatial category. Subsequently, "Europeans' own 'writing of the earth' and its associated continental and civilizational geopolitics became an unavoidable cognitive reality both for nations under direct Western domination and others, such as the Ottomans, Persians or Chinese" (Postel-Vinay 2007, 560).

Because Europe's borders were drawn to denote a geographical entity distinct from Africa and Asia, Mikkeli (1998, 34–5) argues that one key turning point in both Europe's history and philosophical thinking about Europe was the fall of Constantinople in 1453, which led to a new definition of the idea of European unity. This strengthened Europe's sense of the Ottomans as a looming threat, so the term 'Europe' began to acquire heightened emotional charge. Contemporaneously, increasing familiarity of Asia and Africa led to glorification of Europe as a superior civilization, with Islam positioned as non-European. The westward influx of Turks during the Renaissance were seen as threatening European civilization, "leading to a prominent politics of cultural anxiety, expressed as mysterious, alien threats against West European societal values" (Mikkeli 1998, 36).

The shaping of these perceptions closely relate to what Anderson (2007, 3) argues is myth-making. He thinks that, behind cultural anxieties and proposed solutions, lie national/regional perceptions shaping myths and histories that are the tools of specific cultures, working to define contextually the who 'we' are (Dalby 1998, 296; Dijkink 1996, 11). Thus, Europe's first encounters with Turks led to the formation of a myth and collective memory, against which a European identity was moulded. The literature on European identity generally agrees that Europe's historical heritage rests on three pillars: Roman law and order, Christian faith and ancient Greece's critical spirit. A fourth pillar, the Enlightenment, is also sometimes added, to stress the significance of critical reason, accompanied by human rights, democracy, etc. (Mikkeli 1998, 195). Çırakman (2007, 20) argues, similarly, for three major turning points in the formation of European self-images vis-a-vis the Turks throughout the modern era, ie. since the sixteenth century: Christian Europe, liberal Europe and civilized Europe. At all three turning points, Europeans defined themselves relative to the Other – that is, the non-Christian, the non-free and the uncivilized.

These historical-geographic conceptualizations of Europe help explain why enlargement to include Turkey has constituted a major problem for the EU, since Turkey has become the main reference point for European identity discussions. The intensified debate about definition(s) of Europe and Europeanness have become closely linked to geography, politics and culture, which has created concerns regarding Turkey's EU future. Discourses positioning 'Turkey' as the 'Other' primarily attempt to draw a boundary between the EU and Turkey by arguing that they have different historical memories. Applying Gertjan Dijkink's comment (1996, 5) that myths and historical memories contribute to shaping political cultures embedded in the discourses in question, regarding Europe's image of Turkey, the Ottoman Empire's centuries-old psycho-historical legacy seems to play an important role, creating controversies for many Europeans about Turkey's European credentials. Such discourses mainly draw on historical myths about Turks and the Ottoman Empire, cultural and civilizational differences between Turkey and Europe, and geographical imaginings of Europe, locating Turkish territory within Asia or the Middle East rather than Europe. Whether the Ottoman Empire belonged to Europe or the East has also caused confusion. For instance, Europeans referred to the Ottoman Empire as 'the sick man of Europe' (Çırakman 2002, 1; Livanios 2006, 299), whereas in other times it was considered as part of the East.

The term 'Europe', especially after the Muslim conquest of Constantinople, increasingly referred to the rise of the Ottomans and their threat to Christianity. For Europeans, this threat was substantial until as late as 1683, when the Ottomans reached Vienna, and Turks represented everything negated in the European identity: savage, barbarian, despotic, oppressive, violent and a threat to European civilization (Muftuler-Bac 1997, 27). This negative perception of the geography and identity of Turkey included religious references: "Christian society represented a free society, whereas Turkish society, due to the prominence of Islam as a religion, was despotic, the antithesis of the values on which Western civilization was based" (Pettifer 1997, xxi). In short, perceptions of Turks as the 'Other' are deeply embedded in Europe's collective memory and played a role in their mythmaking and geopolitical identity.

One main reason why Turkey posed a challenge for future EU enlargements was the EU's search for a new identity, triggered both by eastward enlargement challenges and the question of who the EU's new Other(s) would be. Any debate over the new European geographical entity's borders created a new political challenge of whether to locate Turkey inside or outside and, consequently, to justify including Turkey in future enlargements. This inevitably led to two kinds of questions. The first were more inward-oriented, towards the EU itself: What is Europe? Where does Europe start and end? Where are the borders of Europe? What is Europeanness? What is European identity? The second set were outward-oriented, towards Turkey: Does Turkey really belong to Europe? Is Turkey European or Asian? Is Islam compatible with European values?

In particular, the emergence of a 'new Europe' has led to a reappraisal of Turkey–EU relations, with increasing emphasis on a dichotomy of geopolitical discourses related to Turkey's spatiality. In the post–Cold War period, a normative turn in discourses on Turkey marked the Turkey–EU relations. The main EU accession criteria, defined by the 1993 Copenhagen European Council, and which are generally referred to as 'Copenhagen Criteria' formed the basis of the relations until 2004. Paradoxically, the decision to open accession negotiations with Turkey on 3 October 2005 was largely overshadowed by competing and conflicting geopolitical discourses on Turkey's Europeanness, and thus on whether it should gain EU membership. Discourses focusing on Turkey's spatiality vis-à-vis the EU mainly followed two divergent and paradoxical patterns, reflecting different constructions of Europe in European leaders' geopolitical imaginations. The first set of discourses focused on designating Turkey as the new Europe's new Other. This Otherization of Turkey, especially in European leaders' recent discourses, relates to how Europe is constructed as a 'historical-geographical idea', and how future enlargements should depend on candidate countries' inclusion within it. This conception appeared in the discourses of those European leaders wishing either to exclude Turkey from European integration, or to establish some relationship other than full membership, including 'privileged partnership'. Conservative political leaders, such as Angela Merkel, stated: "We cannot take in everyone in Europe as a full member. . . . Our common position is a privileged partnership for Turkey, but no full membership."[3]

Analysis of European leaders' geopolitical discourses reveals a focus on two problems. First, the identity dimension: Turkey is not European since it lacks a shared historical, cultural and normative past, making it seem culturally too different to fit into the EU. Other important constructions of Turkey as the 'Other' in European leaders' identity-related discourses focus on geographical and civilizational/cultural factors. Certain European leaders' recent discourses show that Turkey's spatiality vis-à-vis Europe has been dealt with through what can be called norm and identity-based explanations. That is, EU governments and publics evaluate the material costs and benefits of admitting a new member state largely on whether the candidate apparently belongs to Europe from a normative perspective. In assessing Turkey's spatiality vis-à-vis the EU, these discourses mostly emphasize the important role of EU values, as reiterated during 2004 discussions on the draft constitution for the European Union. Then head of the Convention on the Future of Europe, Valerie Giscard d'Estaing, stated that "Turkey must never be allowed into the European Union," since "it has a different culture, a different approach, a different way of life."[4] Similarly, Dutch politician and former EU Single Market Commissioner, Frits Bolkenstein, explicitly stated that "Europe is a product of Christendom, the Renaissance, the Enlightenment and Democracy. Turkey just doesn't fit in," later adding that Turkey should remain outside the EU to "cushion" Europe against Syria, Iran and Iraq.[5]

In determining European identity, these leaders' discourses also reflected skepticism regarding Islam's role in Turkey. Such uncertainties also appeared in discourses in Germany. Former German Chancellor Helmut Schmidt argued that Europeans are strongly characterized by a Christian-based culture, meaning Turkey belongs to a completely different cultural sphere as it largely adheres to Islamic traditions located in Asia and Africa rather than Europe, while former French president Nicolas Sarkozy also doubted Turkey's suitability, claiming: "We have a problem of integration with Muslims that raises the issue of Islam in Europe. To say it is not a problem is to hide from reality. If you let a hundred million Turkish Muslims come in, what will come out of it?"[6] Likewise, former French prime minister Dominique de Villepin stated at a conference in 2006 that "the identity crisis that the Europeans experience is closely related to the speed of enlargement."[7]

The second dimension to European leaders' discourses concerns geography and border-drawing. Its proponents claim that Turkey is not European since, territorially, it lies more in the Middle East or Asia than Europe. Sarkozy has frequently emphasized Turkey's non-European character in geographical terms as well, claiming that "Turkey belongs to Asia Minor, not to Europe" , and that "Turkey has no place in the EU. . . . The EU must give itself borders and not all countries have a vocation to become members of Europe, beginning with Turkey which has no place inside the EU." French leader Valerie Giscard D'Estaing unambiguously stated that "Turkey's entry into the EU would be 'the end of Europe'. Turkey is a country that is close to Europe, but it is not a European country. Its capital is not in Europe, 95% of its population is outside."[8] In short, especially since the accession of the Central and Eastern European countries, various EU leaders, attempted to redefine Europe's borders based on historical-geographical idea of Europe. This geopolitical imagination excludes Turkey from Europe's future.

Neo-Medieval Empire/Europe as a project

The second set of conceptualizations regard Europe as a project with the characteristics of a neo-Medieval Empire (Zielonka 2006, 1). Agnew draws a useful distinction between thinking of the European concept as an 'idea' and a 'project', while criticizing their frequent conflation in much contemporary geopolitical discussion about the EU's future. For him, the former refers to historical debates about Europe as a geographical entity with unambiguously recognizable and definable borders, in support of the concept of Europe constructed as a historical-geographical idea. The latter refers to Monnet, Schuman, De Gasperi and Adenauer's postwar integration project to break down Europe's inter-state boundaries. Its primary objectives were to prevent the national enmities that had produced two devastating world wars and further Europe's postwar economic reconstruction, ie. the European integration process, eventually realized as the EU (Agnew 2005, 578).

Concern with European identity becomes relevant in the context of European integration especially with respect to enlargement. Anthony Smith (in Mikelli 1998, 210–20) argues that it is not easy to construct a common myth for European integration to create a common identity, claiming that the complicated myth of European identity actually lacks any shared common historical tradition; rather, there is 'unity in diversity'. This view emphasizes that Europe is constructed, imagined and project-based, on the philosophy of 'unity in diversity' rather than on common reference points, such as Roman civilization, liberalism, etc. (Öner 2008, 262). Thus, in this 'project of unification', Europeans' perceptions of integration have revealed diversity between countries. Antonsich (2008, 707) argues empirically that Europe today is a postnational space which, analyzed through an attachment perspective, has emerged "as the product of a plurality of voices". Thus Europe cannot be characterized by a single pan-European identity, but by multiple national identities. This view rejects conceptions of Europe as a historical-geographical idea since there is no perception of a common history, common values or well-defined geography.

Carl Dahlman (2004, 555) argues that the idea of Europe as coterminous with Christendom, or later with liberalism, is weakened by contrary examples, both within and beyond the continent. Europe's current identity has been further shaped by experience with projects of modernity, especially by how liberal market democracy has informed EU ideals. Others argue that, because European identity lacks common reference points, Europe and Europeanness remain mere constructions, with implications for people's daily lives by affecting the construction of boundaries and inclusion/exclusion strategies (Öner 2008, 262). This view, therefore, implies that there is no well-defined European 'Self' against which an 'Other' can be depicted.

This raises the question of 'What is Europe?' In 2002, President of the European Commission, Romano Prodi, asked the Institut für die Wissenschaften vom Menschen (Institute for Human Sciences) in Vienna to establish a group of Europeans to reflect on and advise him about the values particularly relevant to continuing European unification. One reflection group on "The Spiritual and Cultural Dimension of Europe" instigated a public debate in Warsaw on "The Borders of Europe" on 29 May 2003. One of its main objectives was to reflect on the cultural affinities and differences between the EU and its neighbors. "The central problem that emerged regarding the EU's future borders was a dilemma presented as 'openness versus viability', 'diversity versus cohesion', 'the logic of unity versus the logic of peace.'"[9] That is, the principle of inclusiveness, promoting enlargement to any country wishing to be European, as stated in Article 237 of the Rome Treaty, was challenged by concerns over the viability and cohesiveness of the project with an increased number of member states.[10] Schott's study (2007) reveals starkly different geopolitical imaginations between the member states and the European Commission. It is actually the this notion of 'unity in diversity' which leads to the conceptualization of the EU as a neo-Medieval Empire with the "territorialization of frontiers presented as multiple, competing geostrategies" (Walters 2004, 675). Walters identifies four groups, namely "networked (non)border, the march, the colonial frontier and the *limes*" (677). He argues that "although EU enlargement is mostly rationalized in terms of a discourse of markets, prosperity and stability, the eastern frontier, for example, at least in one crucial respect, represents a zone where an organized power meets its outside in a relationship of transformation and assimilation. It is the setting of an asymmetrical relationship in which the expanding power assumes a right to define what is appropriate and just." (688). However, he denies that "a distinctly European culture or way of life is being fabricated at the frontier". In his view, "one can associate the generation of a certain concept of Europe with the colonial frontier. The reinvention and popularization of the idea of Central Europe and the efforts to establish Western credentials for it is such an attempt" (690). Thus in his view, the *limes* is more relevant as a concept to use instead of frontier in explaining the EU's enlargement policies towards Central Europe versus neighborhood policies towards the Mediterranean. The *limes*, is a term used to denote the frontier between the Empire and the outside, which is always in motion. The *limes* aims "to create a zone of stability and peace around the Empire" (690–1), although it is an assymmetrical relationship which remains a permanent source of tension. The difference between the frontier and *limes* is therefore significant in that "the frontier is the challenge which sets in motion forces of creativity and innovation. The *limes* is also central to the polity, but as a different mechanism, as a consolidative, drawing a line and preserving what we have" (691).

As opposed to various European leaders who justified the exclusion of Turkey by conceptualizing Europe as a historical-geographical idea, some other European leaders had a different geopolitical imagination which was inclusionary of Turkey. In this respect, it can be noted that it is basically the discourses of the leaders in the Commission, who had a geopolitical imagination of the EU based on the idea of project. Their arguments mostly emphasized the civilizing mission of the EU and expectations on the part of the EU institutions from Turkey to fulfil the Copenhagen Criteria mentioned above. It is interesting to note that in the post-2004 period, the discourses of the Commission Presidents mostly emphasized Turkey's role as a bridge between Islamic world and Europe. The Commission President Romano Prodi stated:

> Turkey is endowed with unique characteristics among European countries: the combination of a secular, democratic state with a prevalently Moslem population. I am convinced that Turkey can bring a unique contribution to peace and regional stability at the beginning of this new century. Turkey's repeated call to fellow Moslem countries to actively promote democracy and human rights constitutes a powerful message.[11]

A systematic analysis of the speeches of the Commission Presidents and members reveal that the Commission's geopolitical imagination is based on the conceptualization of Europe as a project. The European values represented in the Copenhagen criteria is seen as the main determinant of inclusion/exclusion of an accession state. In a speech, Mr. Olli Rehn, the former member of the Commission responsible for Enlargement stated that

> the map of Europe is defined in the mind, not just on the ground. Geography sets the frame, but fundamentally it is values that make the borders of Europe. Enlargement is a matter of extending the zone of European values, the most fundamental of which are liberty and solidarity, tolerance and human rights, democracy and rule of law. According to the EU's treaties-which are its legal basis- the Union's doors are open "to all European states which respect its values and are committed to promoting them together.[12]

The contrast in the geopolitical imaginations of the EU member state leaders and the EU Commission as the main drive of integration especially regarding the enlargement to include Turkey are remarkable in some statements of the Commissioners. For instance, Olli Rehn, has stated that "those who talk continously abour privileged partnership are creating a vicious circle of reversed commitment, weakened conditionality and stalled reforms."[13]

Competing geopolitical imaginations of the EU

Paradoxically, the 'Europe as a project"conceptualization has been challenged by increasingly Euro-centric policies shaping enlargement especially after the CEE enlargement. As a neo-Medieval Empire having to pay attention to diversity, the EU has started acting as a post-Westphalian state in terms of enlargement policies. The penetration of Euro-centric or neo-Westphalian geopolitical imagination that has marked these policies. The reasons of Euro-centricism have been analyzed by Postel-Vinay who argues that "the idea of Europe was originally a civilization-based regional idea, but it was embedded in a repertoire engendered by the European geopolitical tradition which put Europe not only at the center of the world, but in a high-height position as well" (Postel-Vinay 2007, 565). Postel-Vinay further argues that:

> Euro-centricism has been at the heart of an international relations system from the era of European expansion until 1945 when the civilization/continent based 'bird's eye view' position passed to the United States and that the turning point of 1945 was not that the idea of Europe was no longer equated with the world, but that the union of Europe was a de facto condemnation of nationalism, or at the very least a safeguard against the potentially destructive tendencies of nationalism, experienced in the devastation of the Second World War.
>
> (Postel-Vinay 2007, 563–4)

Another view claims that the EU's postwar development, in attempting to integrate economically, and eventually politically, to prevent war and restore European peace, stability and prosperity, revived the historical-geographical construction of Europe as an 'idea'. However, the process of European integration did not at first stimulate debates on identity or Europeanness, since the relative stability of the European geopolitical order from the mid-1950s to the late 1980s discouraged serious critical assessment of the use of these concepts (Murphy 2005, 586). Only with the 1973 Declaration of European Identity, the EU attempted to define itself by linking defence of 'Western' values with the delineation of borders against non-European 'others'" (Busch and Krzyzanowski 2007, 107).

The turning point when the historical-geographical idea or geopolitical imagination penetrated the EU project was the Soviet Union's disintegration. The debates concerning the nature and meaning of Europe as a "historical, ideological and geographical construct" intensified after 1989 (Mikkeli in Murphy 2005, 586) due to "larger-scale geopolitical shifts that focused attention on Europe's changing world role". The 2004 Big Bang enlargement that included member states from Central and Eastern Europe profoundly "affected conceptualizations of Europeaness, challenging conventional assumptions" (Murphy 2005, 586), because the eastward shift in Europe's border also transformed both the meaning of East and West (Busch and Kryzanowski 2007, 108) and the definition of 'Other'. Thus, European integration was challenged by new questions concerning borders, identity and the wisdom of future enlargements. In short, the 2004 "enlargement introduced a new meta-geography with a bounded shape: an image of Europe as a socio-spatial entity" (Paasi 2005, 582).

This penetration of the idea of historical-geographical Europe through the changing geography of Europeanness created significant new challenges accompanying the reconfiguration of Europe's political and identity spaces, for example the rise of a 'new Iron Curtain' along EU/NATO countries' eastern boundaries (Paasi 2005, 587). Because there is free movement of people and goods within the EU, EU leaders, have sought to ensure that Europe's external borders remain carefully patrolled,making neighboring countries like Ukraine and Turkey significant territorial Others. Thus, the EU's expansion to include Central and Eastern countries has "shifted the perceptual boundary of Europeanness eastward rather than fundamentally undermining the tendency to dichotomize Europe along political-cultural lines" (Paasi 2005, 588).

Anthony Smith, for instance, refers to how the EU's eastern enlargement is constructed discursively in the works of EBRD (Smith 2002, 661). "The new geopolitical imagination of East and Central Europe away from the Mackinderian geopolitical role as a 'shatter belt' to its place as a potential 'Gateway Region' is important and as a result of geopolitical and geoeconomic interests" (Smith 2002, 648). Paasi (2005, 582) argues that "the eastern border of the Union seems to be a key territorial element in the construction of a 'European identity'."

In distinguishing between the 'temporal other' and 'geographical other' Diez (2004, 320), argues that

> while the European Union opened up the possibility of the construction of a political identity through a less exclusionary practice of temporal difference, geographical and cultural otherings have since the 1990s become more important in the discourse on European identity.

Borrowing from Waewer's characterization of Europe's other as 'Europe's own past', he argues that temporal othering pervades European integration discourses much more thoroughly than it seems (Diez 2004, 325). Moreover, he argues that during the process of European integration Europe's past

> as Europe's other was related to the European self: the self was also its other . . . When the Cold War ended representation of the CEE remained within the discursive logic of the past as other . . . as a threat not only to its own peace, but also to the peace of the EU.
>
> (Diez 2004, 325)

In this context, the political transformation of the CEE countries and their incorporation into the EU was seen as a means to maintain peace and stability in Europe. In support of this view, Postel-Vinay (2007, 566–7) points out the transformation of Europe's world role, which "implied a modification of the status of the 'idea of Europe', which from being a 'world order' became de facto a 'world region'. She argues that "especially in the post-1989 period, the EU's governmental elite faced a new reality that Europe was no longer a self-evident entity shaping the global world order, but had to define itself *within* that order. Europe was no longer The Civilisation, but rather a sort of local cosmology." According to

Postel-Vinay (2007, 567), it is at this point that the evolution of Turkey's position vis-à-vis the European Union has revealed a change:

> While Turkey had been regarded as a 'natural' partner of Europe as long as it 'naturally' fit into the Cold War order's definition of Europe's borders, the end of the bipolar order caused Europe's governing elite to reappraise the 'natural' dimension of Turkey-EU relations.

The geographical and historical arguments of Europe's leaders as seen above were made public due to this reason. As a complementary explanation, Hansen (2002, 496) notes how colonialism and decolonization in the European Union's former empire states has left its mark on some of them. He argues that the colonial legacy of European identity and European integration and the imaginary map of Europe and European Union are important. "National identities built on imperial pride, racial superiority and the sense of partaking in a communal European civilizing mission could be linked to the acquisition and retention of a colonial empire and the status as a great power (Hansen 2002, 494). Therefore, "national populism, already on the rise before September 11, has been strengthened among others, by threat scenerios of illegal immigration, Islamophobic readings of a possible Turkish accession to the EU and loss of control over borders." Partly as result of this, the reclamation of national identity and sovereignty and the emphasis on cultural-civilizational difference in defining what is or is not European have become mainstream political discourse (Scott and Houtum 2009, 1). Bilgin also sees a possible "drift towards a civilizational geopolitics that colored EU policy-makers' post–Cold War security discourse", arguing that "Giscard d'Estaing's intervention in the EU debate on Turkey's membership and the debate in Germany has shown that an understanding of geography shaped by civilizational geopolitics continues to influence the discourse of some in the EU" (Bilgin 2004, 286).

Thus, just as Central Europe (*Mitteleuropa*) was created first as a distinct imagined geography with an emphasis on its Western credentials, it was followed by a more dominant discourse of a 'return to Europe' that was much more easily justified as a policy to be followed within the EU's enlargement schemes (Hagen 2003, 508). However, as opposed to the CEE enlargement, Diez (2004, 328) argues that

> the discursive site where most of the othering of Europe against Islam is performed is Turkey. Historically, the Ottoman Empire was a synonym for the Muslim Other, while at the same time a power in Europe. Geographically, the line dividing Europe and Asia has traditionally been drawn through Turkey.

Agnew (2005, 577) identifies this as a major dilemma of literally "bounding the European project" in geographical terms, a dilemma posed by Turkey's EU accession process. Agnew (2003, 93) claims that "the Otherness of the Turks was a fundamental barrier to their participation in a civilisational geopolitics that drew hard lines around its European homeland." He further argues that this situation can only be resolved by addressing yet another dilemma: to think of Europe as an 'idea' (referring to historic debates about Europe as a geographical entity with borders that can be clearly recognized and accepted) *or*[14] as a 'project' (Europe's integration process aiming to remove intra-EU boundaries between the states of Europe to achieve peace, prosperity and stability) (Agnew 2005, 577–8).

Convergence of geopolitical imaginations: Towards a 'singular empire'?

As mentioned above, since the end of the Second World War, the EU's evolution has led to the formation of a new geopolitical entity with a Eurocentric vision, with the ultimate goal of achieving political unity for the greater good of its peoples and preventing future wars in the continent (Heater 1992, 195). Anderson notes that "Europe's multiple centers of power and lack of an organized and singular core" due to absolutism and nationalism prevalent in its history. Indeed, the few but powerful centers left Europe even further from becoming a singular polity, being singular only in the sense of 'unique', 'beyond the average' or 'extraordinary'. Europe's competing centers and the absence of a single domineering core were seen as a strength, stimulating Europe to pioneer transitions from feudalism to merchant capitalism and then to industrial capitalism (Anderson 2007, 23). While competitive multiplicity had contributed to development, it had also had catastrophic consequences.

The realisation of this, and the wish to forestall another European war, led the founders of the EU to instigate moves toward singularity by establishing the European Economic Community in 1957. However, as the EU's enlargement process continued during the following decades, they have generally led to changing geopolitical imaginations and instead of "creating consolidation and unity, it caused fragmentation into multiple Europes. It becomes more important to understand how these Europes are defined and demarcated, and how they interact with each other and with the rest of the world" (Kuus 2005, 569). The EU's history of enlargement and integration, therefore, can be seen as continuing Europe's territorial amalgamation and homogenization with the aim of strengthening its global position (Anderson 2007, 24).

Scott and Houtum (2009, 271) argue that "in contrast to inclusion/exclusion logic, one would want to see the EU as a new type of international actor whose potential strengths lie less in the state-like exercise of power and rather more in its ability to affect gradual social transformation." The main challenge for the EU, in this respect, is whether the EU could continue the desired scheme of singularity given all the competing internal differentiations due to a collection of separate national states with separate ideologies, which seems to be like the model of a 'Europe of nations' (Anderson 2007, 25). In other words, whether the EU will follow a model of 'neo-Medieval Empire' or a 'neo-Westphalian state'. For Scott and Houtum (2009, 273), "if the EU's apparent crisis of identity is indeed one of territoriality then assuming a neo-Westphalian guise is fraught with dangers and therefore misplaced. Without the political will to transcend local and national particularisms, the EU is in danger of forfeiting its idealism and thus its ability to positively influence developments within and beyond its borders." They continue:

> Unfortunately, what we see are policies of internal consolidation and external bordering that can be characterized as 'neo-Westphalian'. Thus, instead of much-needed debate on the renewal of the EU, issues related to security, territorial borders and definitive geographical definitions of the EU have tended to dominate political debates.

As a result, Europe conceptualized as a geographically-bounded entity universalizes EU-centric visions despite signs of postmodern 'de-territorialization' within Europe.

The EU enlargements to include CEE and exclude Turkey, can therefore be interpreted as a result of this resurgence of neo-Westphalian geopolitical imagination, which regards Europe as a historical-geographical idea and its penetration to the conceptualizations of Europe as a project. The discourses of EU member state leaders as well as the Commission presidents or members have revealed this paradox clearly. Although conceptualizing Europe as empire resonated well with the EU enlargements and the European Neighborhood policy, with the penetration of neo-Westphalian geopolitical imaginations after the 2004 enlargement came on to the EU's agenda introducing a new discourse based on historical-geographical conceptualizations of Europe, with "pro-West/anti-east prejudices in popular ideologies across Europe and with the danger of imperial overreach is echoed in the arguments of those who would exclude Turkey from EU membership" (Anderson 2007, 20).

"Europe's position and 'weight' in the world would depend on how it develops or fails to develop a singular, coherent polity. Europe would be even more extraordinary if it were to develop in empire fashion around a single dominant core" (Anderson 2007, 24) representing a single and inclusionary geopolitical imagination. Reconfiguration of geographical imaginations and geo-economic power in the 'new Europe' as recently experienced in the 'postconflict Balkans' (Smith 2002, 663), will continue to influence future enlargements of the EU. In this respect, Western Balkans and Turkey will constitute yet another reflection of the competing/converging geopolitical imaginations of Europe within the EU enlargement scheme, while also revealing how much the EU, as a 'project based on inclusion', will succeed in overcoming the notion of Europe as an 'idea based on exclusion'.

Notes

1 Emphasis added by the author of the manuscript.
2 Sieve Europe is a Europe open and vulnerable to all manner of transnational threats.
3 "German, French leaders emphasize opposition to Turkey joining EU," found at website: www.hurriyet.com.tr/english/world/11621541.asp (accessed on 25/01/2014).
4 Ian Black, "Turkey must be kept out of the union, Giscard says," found at website: www.theguardian.com/world/2002/nov/09/turkey.eu (accessed on 25/01/2014).

5 www.eudimensions.border-research.eu/content/newsletter/download/pdf/Newsletter_2_Eudimensions.pdf, p.3 (accessed on 25/01/2014).
6 www.journal-online.co.uk/article/2631-can_europe_handle_100_million_muslims (accessed on 25/1/2014).
7 http://news.bbc.co.uk/2/hi/europe/4656484.stm (accessed on 25/1/2014).
8 http://news.bbc.co.uk/2/hi/europe/2420697.stm (accessed on 25/1/2014).
9 Reflection Group initiated by the President of the European Commission and coordinated by the Institute for Human Sciences, *The Spiritual and Cultural Dimension of Europe. Reflection Group initiated by the President of the European Commission and Coordinated by the Institute for Human Sciences*, Vienna, Brussels, October 2004, p. 2.
10 Ibid., p.3.
11 Romano Prodi, President of the European Commission Official Visit in Turkey Turkish Grand National Assembly Ankara, Rapid Database 15/1/2014 SPEECH/04/16.
12 Speech by Mr. Olli Rehn Member of the European Commission, responsible for Enlargement "Values define Europe, not borders" Speech to civil society Belgrade" Rapid Database 24/1/2005 SPEECH/05/32.
13 Mr. Olli Rehn Member of the European Commission, responsible for Enlargement, "Europe's Next Frontiers" lecture at Bilkent University, Ankara, Rapid Database 04/10/2006, SPEECH/06/561.
14 Emphasis added by the author or the manuscript.

References

Agnew, J. 2003. *Geopolitics: Re-visioning World Politics*. 2nd ed. London: Routledge.

Agnew, J. 2005. Bounding the European Project. *Geopolitics* 10(3): 575–80.

Anderson, J. 2007. Singular Empire: An Empire once Again? In *Geopolitics of European Union Enlargement*, ed. W. Armstrong and J. Anderson, 9–29. London: Routledge.

Antonsich, M. 2008. European Attachment and Meanings of Europe: A Qualitative Study in the EU-15. *Political Geography* 27: 6.

Armstrong, W. and J. Anderson. 2007. *Geopolitics of European Union Enlargement: The Fortress Empire*. London: Routledge.

Bialasiewicz, L., D. Campbell, S. Elden and S. Graham. 2007. Performing Security: The Imaginative Geographies of Current US Strategy. *Political Geography* 26(4): 405–22.

Bialasiewicz, L., C. Dahlman, A. Gian Matteo, F. Ciuta, A. Jones and C. Rumford. 2009. Interventions in the new political geographies of the European 'neighborhood'. *Political Geography* 28: 79–89.

Bilgin, P. 2004. A Return to 'Civilisational Geopolitics' in the Mediterranean? Changing Geopolitical Images of the European Union and Turkey in the post-Cold War Era. *Geopolitics* 9(2): 269–291.

Busch, B. and M. Kryzanowski. 2007. Inside/Outside the European Union: Enlargement, Migration Policy and the Search for Europe's Identity. In *Geopolitics of European Union Enlargement*, ed. W. Armstrong and J. Anderson, London: Routledge.

Çırakman, A. 2002. *From the 'Terror of the World' to the 'Sick Man of Europe': European Images of Ottoman Empire and Society from the Sixteenth Century to the Nineteenth*. New York: Peter Lang.

Çırakman, A. 2007. Reflections of European Self-Images in Ottoman Mirrors. In *Remaking Turkey: Globalization, Alternative Modernities, and Democracy*, ed. F. Keyman. Lanham: Lexington Books.

Dahlman, C. 2004. Turkey's Accession to the European Union: The Geopolitics of Enlargement. *Eurasian Geography and Economics* 45(8): 553–74.

Dalby, S. 1998. Geopolitics and Global Security: Culture, Identity and the 'Pogo' Syndrome. In *Rethinking Geopolitics*, ed. G. O'Tuathail and S. Dalby. 295–313. London: Routledge.

Dalby, S. 2008. Imperialism, Domination, Culture: The Continued Relevance of Critical Geopolitics. *Geopolitics* 13(3): 413–36.

Diez, T. 2004. Europe's Others and Return of Geopolitics. *Cambridge Review of International Affairs* 17(2): 319–35.

Dijkink, G. 1996. *National Identity and Geopolitical Visions: Maps of Pride and Pain.* London: Routledge.

Hagen, J. 2003. Redrawing the Imagined Map of Europe: the rise and Fall of the 'center'. *Political Geography* 22: 489–517.

Hansen, P. 2002. European Integration, European Identity and the Colonial Connection. *European Journal of Social Theory* 5(4): 483–98.

Heater, D. 1992. *The Idea of European Unity.* Leicester: Leicester University Press.

Heffernan, M. 1998. *The Meaning of Europe: Geopraphy and Geopolitics.* London: Arnold.

Kuus, M. 2005. Multiple Europes: Boundaries and Margins in European Union Enlargement. *Geopolitics* 10(3): 567–70.

Livanios, D. 2006. The 'Sick Man' Paradox: History, Rhetoric and the 'European Character' of Turkey. *Journal of Southern Europe and the Balkans* 8(3): 299–311.

Mamadouh,V. and G. Dijkink. 2006. Geopolitics, International Relations and Political Geography: The Politics of Geopolitical Discourse. *Geopolitics* 11(3): 349–66.

Mikkeli, H. 1998. *Europe as and Idea and an Identity.* Houndsmills: Macmillan Press.

Mamadouh,V., and G. Dijkink. 2006. Geopolitics, International Relations and Political Geography: The Politics of Geopolitical Discourse. *Geopolitics* 11(3): 349–66.

Mikkeli, H. 1998. *Europe as and Idea and an Identity.* Houndsmills Basingstoke: Macmillan Press.

Moisio, S. 2002. EU Eligibility, Central Europe, and the Invention of Applicant State Narrative. *Geopolitics* 7(3): 89–116.

Murphy, A.B. 2005. The Changing Geography of Europeanness. *Geopolitics* 10(3), 586–91.

Müftüler-Baç, M. 1997. *Turkey's Relations with a Changing Europe.* Manchester: Manchester University Press.

Müller, M. 2008. Reconsidering the Concept of Discourse for the Field of Critical Geopolitics: Towards Discourse as Language and Practice. *Political Geography* 27: 322–38.

Öner, S. 2008. European Identity in the Context of the EU: Construction of European Identity in Civic and Cultural Terms. *Europolis. Journal of Political Analysis and Theory* 4: 261–86. www.ceeol.com/aspx/issuedetails.aspx?issueid=1bece515–4fda-4c08-a1f4–4350dc03 defb&articleId=37bd610c-8405–42fb-8a23–0d3ed29e87b8 (accessed on 19/1/2014).

Paasi, A. 2001. Europe as a Social Process and Discourse: Considerations of Place, Boundaries and Identity. *European Urban and Regional Studies* 8(1): 7–28.

Paasi, A. 2005. Remarks on Europe's Transforming Meta-Geography. *Geopolitics* 10(3): 580–85.

Pettifer, J. 1997. *The Turkish Labyrinth: Atatürk and the New Islam.* England: Penguin Books.

Power, M. and D. Campbell. 2010. The State of Critical Geopolitics. *Political Geography* 29: 243–46.

Postel-Vinay, K. 2007. The Historicity of the International Region: Revisiting the 'Europe and the Rest' Divide. *Geopolitics* 12(4): 555–69.

Rueber, P. and G. Walkersdorfer. 2002. The Transformation of Europe and the German Contribution-Critical Geopolitics and Geopolitical Representations. *Geopolitics* 7(3): 39–60.

Rumelili, B. 2008. Negotiating Europe: EU-Turkey Relations from an Identity Perspective. *Insight Turkey* 10(1): 97–110.

Schott, M. 2007. Geopolitical Imaginations about the European Union in Recent Political Discussions. *Tidjschrift voor Economische en Sociale Geografie* 98(2): 284–295.

Scott, J. W. and H. V. Houtum. 2009. Reflections on EU Territoriality and the 'Bordering' of Europe. *Political Geography* 28: 271–73.

Smith, A. 2002. Imagining Geographies of 'New Europe': Geo-Economic Power and the New European Architecture of Integration. *Political Geography* 21: 647–70.

Toal, G. 2000. Geopolitical Discourses: A new geopolitics series. *Geopolitics* 5(1): 125–28.

Tuathail G. and S. Dalby. 1998. Introduction: Rethinking Geopolitics. Towards a Critical Geopolitics. In *Rethinking Geopolitics,* ed. G. Tuathail and S. Dalby, 1–15. London: Routledge.

Walters, W. 2004. The Frontiers of the European Union: A Geostrategic Perspective. *Geopolitics* 9(3): 674–98.

Zielonka, J. 2006. *Europe as Empire. The Nature of the Enlarged European Union.* Oxford: Oxford University Press.

7 Europe's post-imperial condition

Kalypso Nicolaidis and Nora Fisher Onar

Introduction

As he prepares to fly to Venus at the start of his adventures in 1950, Dan Dare, who was to become the greatest comic-book hero of postwar Britain, enters a Whitehall-of-the-future dominated by an immense towering statue of a certain John Strachey. Why the honor? Strachey had been a senior member of the 1945 Labor government. But his greatest claim to popular fame (or infamy) was *The Groundnuts Scheme*, a dream which spoke to the spirit of the times. It was born in Strachey's mind when, as a senior wartime RAF staff officer, he had seen the great allied armada sailing through the Straits of Gibraltar in November 1942, carrying the British and American armies and their vast quantities of tanks, vehicles, munitions, and supplies to the shores of North Africa for the *Operation Torch* Landings. Strachey later wrote of how the spectacle inspired him with the thought that the course of history might again be changed if a second such armada was to sail to the shores of Africa, but this time carrying mighty shipments of tractors, ploughshares, fertilizers and armies of engineers and agricultural experts. It would thereby – in the most literal sense – plant the seeds of a huge productive potential, which might sustain a continuing independent world role for Britain. The background assumption – shortly unmasked as a delusion – that European rule would remain in Africa for generations to come – was unrelentingly shared on the mainland of Europe. Yet, ironically, it was such fantasies, whether dressed up by the traditional imperialist Right under the slogan of 'the Third British Empire' or projected in progressive guise by Strachey as laying the geopolitical foundations for an International Socialist Commonwealth that contributed to keeping Britain aloof from the emerging European integration project. Meanwhile, those engaged in that project hoped to implement the same dream, with or without Britain: a dream for which the shorthand expression Eurafrica came into being – pooling sovereignty in Europe and pooling colonial administration in Africa as two sides of the same coin (Hansen and Jonsson, 2013, 2015).

Strachey's dream never came to be. Groundnuts proved to be a fiasco and Eurafrica was forgotten. With decolonization and the Cold War, Europeans redirected their energy within. And while the modern nation-state versions of the erstwhile imperial metropoles remained shaped by their colonial pasts, Europe in its incarnation as the EEC and later the EU, sought to capitalize on the myth of its virgin birth and in the process redefine itself as a post-imperial peace project: post-imperial *within*, as no longer shall big European states bully smaller states into submission; post-imperial *without*, as no longer shall Europe impose its will and whims onto the rest of the world. The 'post' here would be about transcending the past and committing once and for all to the spirit and letter of multilateralism.

Yet polities have a knack for not following the best laid plans. Empires may ebb and flow but imperial patterns are never far from the surface of the international order. Arguably, the Cold War offered a post-colonial re-ordering around the confrontation of two modern empires, while the post–Cold War reawakened the mindset and practices of older empires, not least the universalizing impulse in Europe. In the process, and as discussed in this book, some of these old reflexes have come back to the fore on the European stage, at first incrementally, and then intensely with the Eurocrisis. If we are far from the 'spiritual unity' proclaimed behind the postwar drive to create 'Eurafrica' as a third geopolitical pole between U.S. and Soviet ambitions, we still must ask whether colonialism is not part of Europe's DNA (Behr, 2007; Nicolaidis et al., 2014).

To be sure, the relevance of the trope of 'empire' to the twenty-first century is not all or even mostly due to the old continent. Instead, and with 9/11, "Empires that once seemed to belong in one of history's many dustbins – an outmoded form of politics, to be studied only through traces left across the shattered landscapes of their former subject peoples," have come to seem contentious, interesting, highly topical, and perhaps, not all bad (Pagden 2006). From its policing of the free world during the Cold War, to the drive to combat militant Islamist terrorism, the United States resurrected the spectre of imperialism for some, rehabilitating the imperial promise of order for others.[1] Wherever one stands vis-à-vis the renewed salience of empire, it is clear that Europe has played the side-kick in this new version of imperialism through conquest and battle.

Yet the story of Europe's imperial leanings is also more than derivative of evolving Western interventionism. 'Empire,' for better or worse, has become a watchword in Europe's dealings with its close or far away neighbors, as well as in its relations with former colonies, from the resurrection of the lens of nineteenth-century standards of civilization to denunciations of 'neo-colonialism.[2] But the Eurocrisis also seems to have brought the colonial trope closer to home. Here then we find another meaning of 'post'-imperial – this time 'post' as reproduction of prior patterns recycled under a new discourse. Hence, the notion of 'post' when affixed to the 'imperial' or the 'colonial' (terms which we will use interchangeably) answers to two rather different definitions: the first 'post' as in dealing with and transcending Europe's colonial past; the second 'post' as in reproducing its imperial legacy whether or not the pattern is denied or celebrated.

We can perhaps better understand the relationship between these two readings by recalling Behr's contribution to this volume in which, via a genealogy of its Latin significations, we recognize that 'empire' itself is a site of polysemy. Starting with John Darwin's definition of imperialism "as the sustained effort to assimilate a country or region to the political, economic or cultural system of another power" we can posit that empires are always one way or another characterized by centre-periphery relations whereby through more or less coercive inducements, the centre seeks to govern the periphery 'at a distance' following Hartmut Behr's apt characterization. But in doing so, there is always a gradation between different expressions of the imperial from material to ideational. At one end of the spectrum, the imperial is a mode of governance, a description of manifest actions aimed at ensuring the security and prosperity of metropoles though some combination of co-option and coercion of their more or less loosely interconnected peripheries. At the other end of the spectrum, imperial is a state of mind, a sensibility inculcated by habits of imperial governance to be sure – and hence most often and most prominently encountered in conjunction with imperial might – but also often outlasting the very imperial machineries by which imperial mindsets were initially engendered.

This capacity of imperialistic sensibilities to outlive empire recalls the Gramscian notion of hegemony later appropriated by the likes of Foucault, Said, Babha, and Chakrabarty in their readings of the enduring power of dominant groups to "shape conceptions of the normal" as Manners has it, to the exclusion or detriment of others (Diez 2013, 194). Thus, while the imperial mindset is a function of colonialism, it can continue to reverberate long after the demise of empire. After all, imperial governance is about management of security, economic, and political affairs, whereas imperial sensitivities, though engendered by imperial management, become woven into the woof of individual and collective psychologies, memories, aspirations, and fears. These have a life of their own and can be affected by multiple factors that are dissonant with the 'real world' balance of power (e.g. denial, insecurity, egoism, and indeed concrete factors, like an insulated geography or full treasury). In the case of Europe, the enduring resonance of the imperial is of course also a function of the fact that European decline is relative not absolute. After all, and in no small measure due to capital accumulated as a result of colonialism, European countries enjoy levels of development and welfare as well as an embedded-ness in international institutions that ensure enduring if diminished influence in international affairs.

Crucially, this persistence of imperial capacities and logics is a result of the fact that Europeans' historical successes were enabled by resources and labor appropriated from the world 'without.' This is a basic historical fact documented in a flourishing body of interdisciplinary scholarship.[3] Yet, narratives of the EU's foundation and purpose have been remarkably resistant to acknowledging this co-constitution of the internal and the external. Our argument in this chapter is predicated on this recognition, for any understanding of Europe's post-imperial condition must grapple with the historical reality that imperialism – whether it is to be transcended or reproduced – was a two-way street. Thus, while one can analytically disaggregate between internal and external manifestations of the post-imperial condition, it is necessary to remain cognizant of their interconnection.

In this chapter, we start with the assumption that while the discussion as to whether or to what extent the EU ought to be characterized as 'empire' is a fruitful and productive one, we can take some of the axioms developed in this book as given (see also, inter alia, Zielonka 2006). We argue first that Europe as embodied in today's EU is best characterized by its post-imperial condition, that is, the tension between its aspiration to transcend or overcome its imperial legacies on one hand, and its propensity to reproduce and project these legacies on the other; and second that in doing so, scholars need to make more explicit the relationship between internal and external imperial patterns. On both these counts, our ambition is to propose a way of framing the question that occupies the editors and contributors to this volume rather than offer a satisfactory treatment thereof. We ask how the EU has dealt with its post-imperial condition over time, and what normative guidelines could help it do so better. Revisiting our recent argument on the analogy between the nineteenth-century standard of civilization and the EU's relations with the rest of the world, we suggest that the EU's narratives and modes of actions today have only partially succeeded in dealing with its hegemonic hangover (Nicolaidis 2014).[4] We do not know whether internal or external imperial patterns reinforce or mitigate each other. Thus, the definitive reconfiguration of international order away from Europe paradoxically may lead to the reassertion of imperial tendencies internally, as the great powers within Europe retrench and regroup. By the same token, its ability in a number of arenas to transcend imperial habits internally can have ramifications for the EU's engagement of its neighbors and the broader world.

We first defend the idea that the EU has long embarked on a post-imperial project that is indeed grounded on a commitment to non-domination internally as well as externally. Second, we show that this project has in part failed both within and without, because old habits die hard, and because of evolving internal and external conjectural factors. Finally, we ask how the EU may best deal with its post-imperial condition – namely pursue a 'decentring agenda' – by focusing on the cases of Turkey and Ukraine.

'Post' as transcendence: Non-domination and equality

In some ways, today's EU project can still be defined against an imperialism it sought to escape more than half a century ago. At one level, this has to do with the continent itself, a continent that has hovered for two millennia between various forms of fragmentation and (imperial) union from Rome to Byzantine, Holy Roman to Soviet, Habsburg to Ottoman and eventually to Nazi Europe. A second imperial strand is located 'beyond the seas', as some would say, with Europeans' 'compulsive colonialism' driven, as Juan Rossi pithily puts it, by the 'endemic illness' of a minuscule continent's pathological need to expand (Rossi 2015). Clearly, however, these two ancestral godparents were not represented equally at the side of the EU cradle: the former would be transcended, the latter all but denied. Faced with these various modes of remembering and forgetting, scholars can be forgiven when they disagree on the referent for 'Europe's Empires' (Marks, 2012 vs Hansen and Jonsson 2013). What matters for our purposes is how the two are related.

The mainstream reading of the birth of the EU is that of a continental anti-hegemonic project, a rejection of previous hegemonic attempts at unification which have characterized the aftermath of Europe's wars for a millennium (Lacroix and Nicolaidis, 2010). Yet, as Jan Zielonka, Gary Marks, and others have cogently argued, this would entail reproducing elements of former European Empires – including above all the Holy Roman variant from the late medieval to the late Baroque period when the *translatio imperii* had all but disappeared in favor of distributed sovereignty. In post-World War II Europe, peace would require not only the taming of nationalism in general, with Europe's peoples giving up on self-realization through 'othering' and sharing sovereignty instead, but also a more concrete set of mechanisms to contain the historical appetite for power on the part of the big states (Magnette and Nicolaidis, 2005). The people of France or Germany *qua states* would be constrained by the new institutional arrangements making it impossible to subjugate other countries or the continent as a whole. And EU institutions would ensure that even as of when the threat of war would recede, the norm of non-domination *among peoples* would remain.

The EU therefore can be seen as creating an institutionalized balance of power among states to ensure non-subordination between them. Coalitions and negotiations have replaced alliances and bandwagoning to entrench the balance in a web of institutionalized distribution of roles and rules of behaviour (e.g. rotating presidency of the Council, disproportionate representation and vote in the Commission, Parliament, and Council). And as the stakes for Europe changed from the survival of states to the autonomy of its peoples, shifting our analytical prism from the major key of IR to the minor key of democratic theory, the imperative of interstate non-domination is translated into its republican requisite to ban the exercise of arbitrary power of one person against another (Pettit 1997). The EU, with its referenda, elections and polls sets up a dynamic of peoples checking peoples as it were, predicated on the sense on the part of its citizens that the common project assumes their equality irrespective of the size and power of their member state of origin.

In theory then, as well as in juridical practice, the EC–EU project set into motion a fundamental transformation from an imperial to an federal genus, grounded on formal equality between states and the politics of emulation; this meant in turn trading in the imperial centre seeking to govern other Europeans 'at a distance' for federal shared governance or governing 'together'.

It is this transformation and its translation in political and democratic terms that the nascent literature on *demoi-cratic* theory seeks to capture building on the broader literature on European integration while emphasizing the technologies of pluralism embedded therein.[5] Accordingly, the EU is a flawed but nevertheless tentative demoi-cracy in the making, i.e. a union of peoples who govern together but not as one. These people have sought to refine what Joseph Weiler (2001) called 'constitutional tolerance', through the co-mingling of their democratic orders by choice, a choice that needs to be seen as ultimately reversible through permissible exit. Admittedly, we encounter here the elasticity of the notion of 'Empire'. With this version of the EU, we are far from classic Empires in a polity where the question of final authority is still left open and heterarchy reigns such that the EU is a 'networks of elements in which each element shares the same horizontal position of power and authority' (Halberstram 2009). In this regard, as noted above, we are very close to the kind of neo-medieval form of empire discussed by Jan Zielonka, with diffuse and overlapping authority. And yet, the analogy is incomplete at best simply because empires pre-dated the democratic age. The EU has had to develop a political form that combines that of multi-centric Empire (or empire without domination) with democratic anchoring in its separate and autonomous states. It may be no surprise that it has not quite succeeded in doing so – a point to which we come back.

The second part of the story of the EU's birth and growth under the shadow of its past is more invisible yet critical: the ways the 'outside,' namely the overseas colonial inheritance, contributed to the construction of the 'inside' and vice versa. Confronting the second legacy, we suggest, has been subordinated to the first, and yet the efficacy of EU agency in the world depends upon its recognition. The self-appointment of the EU as a 'credible force for good' in international relations, as Solana, its first foreign policy representative once declared, depends upon a core axiom: the need for consistency between the two sides of the coin. While the creation of the EC was in part about forgetting the colonial past of these member states and more generally abstaining from the global stage, this imperative for consistency must permeate its progressive return to this very stage since the 1970s and more forcefully with the end of the Cold War.

Indeed, the standard story of the reinvention of Europe as a normative project from the earliest days of the EC to its progressive assertion as a 'civilian' or 'normative' power in the last two decades, rested on what the EU was trying to do 'inside': sticking to its now localized ambition to civilize Europe rather than the world. After a civil war exported to the world, unilateral universalism could no longer be sold as benign whether as a justificatory discourse for colonialism or as a guide for external action after decolonization (Nicolaidis 2015). Instead, the EU dealt with mundane issues like trade liberalization, competition rule, and product standards. As a different kind of polity internally, it could be a different kind of actor externally: if it was to enlarge it would be 'by invitation,, if it was to export standards, it would be by persuasion. Subjugation of non-Europeans could not be part of the story.

This self-image and the practices by which it was accompanied were underwritten by both the structure and the spirit of the times. After all, the pursuit of inclusive practices was bolstered politically and economically by United States involvement in Europe's reconstruction and, above all, by its guarantee of a permissive security environment as part and parcel of deterrence of the Soviet Union in the wake of the Berlin crisis. This meant that nascent pan-European institutions did not even develop the capacity for post- or neo-imperial power projection in military terms. The US security vision for the region as part of its broader policy of containment also necessitated coalition-building in the fight against the Warsaw Pact. An outcome of this for European ability to internalize difference was the co-option of both Greece and Turkey – on an equal footing at the beginning – through the parallel evolution of Marshall Plan and NATO arrangements and European Economic Community Association Agreements. Tellingly, posters from the era promoting the Marshall plan, display the Greek and Turkish flags at the heart of a reconstructed European body politic – semiotics that are hard to imagine today.

If the Marshall Plan and NATO fed the dynamic of European integration and expansion by allowing inclusive enlargement (the very nexus of the 'within' and the 'without') to become the almost sole focus of Europe's foreign policy, they also directly enabled the EU (if not all its member states) to devote the lion's share of their budgets to non-security concerns. The ensuing economic surplus, in turn, served European southern enlargement towards the new Mediterranean democracies. If the enlargement process was reminiscent of imperial practices as some of us have argued (Behr 2007; Nicolaidis and Fisher Onar 2013), this would be redeemed by the equal status awaiting the members to be.

Meanwhile, as decolonization – the de jure transcendence of Europe's imperial legacy – unfolded across the 1960s and 1970s, a certain post-imperial sense of solidarity with the nascent nation-states of Africa and Asia infused youth and (left) intellectual cadres many of whom would go on to become national and EU-level leaders.[6] In this way, affective and intellectual bases for a 'decentred agenda' transcendent of the imperial past as opposed to hierarchical engagement of the extra-European world were in evidence early on in the European project, although they were by no means the dominant key.

By the 1990s–2000s the apparent transcendence of empire gained momentum as the EU took in a host of member states whose histories and sensitivities pluralized the post-imperial ambition. Indeed the sixteen new member states which have joined since the end of the Cold War, not only doubled the surface of the EU but turned it into a space of many former colonies. As Dimitar Bechev (2015) observes, the EU now includes Malta and Cyprus which were British colonial possessions as recently as the early 1960s, while for many of the new Eastern European members the memory of imperial satellite status vis-à-vis the Soviet Union is barely more than two decades old. Radical differences between dominant historical legacies of imperial rule not only distinguish 'Europe' from 'non-Europe' but Europeans among themselves. We are not even facing an East–West divergence within the EU echoing the Iron curtain, since member states like Ireland and Greece have had their own experience with foreign domination. But eastern and southeastern Europe might have a special role to play when it comes to the transcendence of Europe's imperial past in the eyes of the rest of the world (Davies 1996). For, as argued by Bechev, the 'return to Europe' of the 'lands between' is all the more powerful insofar as they still carry the seal of the continent's not-too-distant imperial identities and host the relics of the pre-Soviet empires as well form the Habsburgs to the Ottoman, Romanov, Holy Roman, Byzantine, and Venetian imperial projects, among others. Indeed, 'the region has also been the graveyard of the imperial idea as the original target of the Wilsonian principle of self-determination – the very principle which is so influential in the emergence of Third World independence movements challenging the dominance of European colonial powers' (Bechev 2015). Hence, and even though from the outside, the EU is often as little more than its big member states, part of the post-imperial promise lies with its own engagement with its internal diversity and its capacity to offer a more polyphonic sensitivity on the global stage (Macaj and Nicolaidis 2014).

'Post' as reproduction: Europe's colonial temptations

Yet, there was always an important twist to the mainstream story of the EU's birth and development. That is that the post-imperial challenge does not stop at eschewing direct horizontal domination between countries. With greater interdependence and increasingly centralized competences, the risk of domination has slowly reasserted itself in another guise, as vertical. For fear of dominance by a Napoleon, members have given up power to Brussels. And due to the congruence of functional and political pressures as European integration and enlargement unfolded over decades – and then dramatically with the Eurocrisis – the three safeguards against neo-imperialism which characterized integration at its beginnings have been progressively and partially eroded: namely, that the competences thus transferred be circumscribed; that the central authority be collectively owned and controlled by its many component states; and that the strongest countries be equally bound by collective constraints. Certainly, these are demanding safeguards: as pre-1865 U.S. federalists so passionately reminded their contemporaries, when power is transferred from the units to a new centre – however 'decentralized' this centre may be – it is always prone to capture by permanent majorities or otherwise tyrannical agents. And indeed, Europe today runs the risk – the old Kantian fear – of embracing classic federal state domination in order to escape classic imperial domination, drifting from the Charybdis of horizontal domination to the Scylla of vertical domination (Nicolaidis 2013).[7]

Crucially the risk is always that one country may capture the centre and thus conflate horizontal and vertical domination. This is what many believe has happened with Germany's role in Europe in the wake of the Eurozone crisis. But given Germany's own inclinations, we cannot and should not easily brandish the imperialist bogyman. To be sure, this is not a story where power disappears. If the normative ideal of European demoicracy is to transcend the *pathologies* of anarchy (as the core characteristic of the international realm) but not the *nature* of anarchy as a horizontal ordering of power, the ideal calls for taming the exercise of power without indulging the teleological belief that power asymmetries can be abolished or wished away. Demoicracy is an exercise in power mitigation not denial. As theorists of the English school like Bull and Wright would have it, international order, i.e. peace, demands that we put power to work, that collective expectations be built and institutionalized to entrench 'great power responsibility.' In an order characterized by the rule of law, be it domestic or international, it is the arbitrary use of power that needs to be curbed not power per se (Walker & Palombella 2009, Nicolaidis and Kleinfeld, 2012). This is all the more true in a proto-demoicratic EU, which encompasses countries with great asymmetries in their wealth and demographics. This is not a realm of absolutes and power cannot be wished away. The idea was simple and powerful:

with power comes responsibility rather than domination. The answer remains as always: *how* is this disproportionate power exercised?

One of the great lessons of the Eurocrisis is that national democracies interacting under conditions of interdependence tread a fine line between the legitimate forging of shared commitments to keep the common show on the road and the arbitrary use of centralized powers to impose duties and obligations and thus prescribe the rules of cooperation the critical difference is what we can term the *single standpoint* (Bohman 2007, 2008). That single standpoint can be national, ideological, technocratic or some combination thereof. Indeed it has long been clear that freedom as non-domination was far from embedded in the political culture of some of the larger Member States, often subject to a pervasive Gulliver syndrome (Magnette and Nicolaidis 2005). Many in France in particular never quite gave up on the neo-imperial dream of the EU as France-writ-large. But the Eurocrisis has magnified this pathology, creating new patterns of soft domination on the part not only of Germany but also of northern/creditor states in particular whereby 'governing at a distance' becomes entrenched in EU practices. Their 'governing at a distance' through the Troika for countries under bailout programmes, or through the European Semester for all others at risk, is shaped by a core belief: that there is a right way of governing irrespective of the local processes that this governing may affect.

Thus, the perceived return of imperialism as reproduction of hierarchical habits in the EU is simply due to the assertion of the will of one or a subset of member states in ways that preempt democratic contestation in the political arena of another. The ability to govern at a distance emanates from a conviction in the creditor-EU of superior economic understandings and technical acumen. But this in turn would not be possible without a decision-making architecture that allows for monolithic choice corresponding to the preferences of parties that do not bare the consequences of these choices. The question is not whether member states collectively and the Commission concurrently in writing their blueprint are legitimately entitled to suggest and design some of the disciplines that will make shared membership in EMU sustainable. The question is rather whether in doing so, they ought to act as if there could be one solution, one 'right approach' to macroeconomic policy. Institutionalised imperialism becomes possible when legitimized by the technocratic (*ordoliberal*) belief that economic policy can legitimately be subtracted from politics and the collective resolution of conflict in the democratic sphere where various forces interact.

Some may object that IMF-type conditionality imposed on countries that cannot pay increases the likelihood of their doing so provides a collective good, trust in the global financial system, that is in everyone interest. But however one gauges the conditionality story, the EU was predicated on doing away specific reciprocity or measures targeting specific member countries in favor of disciplines applied to all and agreed in common. The problem with the EU today is once removed. Namely, it is that this conditionality logic with its neo-imperial undertones of governing at a distance has captured EU institutions themselves, thus conflating two hitherto separate logics, namely that of conditionality and that of polity-building (Nicolaidis and Watson 2014). Arguably, governing at a distance might be legitimate in temporary states of exception created by unsustainable sovereign debt. But the merger in question has sought to make permanent some elements of conditionality that are highly intrusive, and were forged in the heat of the moment. Hard cases make bad law, unless great care is taken; and the stress of crisis resolution is not an easy setting in which to shape a new permanent architecture for EMU that does not impose a single country's will. Conditionality implies an intrusiveness – and fosters a divisiveness – that do not belong in the operating process of a post-imperial European polity over the long run: to confuse these short- and long-run disciplines, embedding conditionality mechanisms as part of EMU governance in normal times, is a kind of structural merger fraught with political risks.

This story is not only one about the standards that pertain to shared governance in Europe. It relates in fact to a more fundamental dimension that resides in the perceptions, frustrations and fears of European publics. To pick only one theatre, it may not have been surprising to have witnessed the many variations on accusations of German neo-imperialism (sic) in the Greek media (Nicolaidis et al. 2014). More troubling is the way in which the discourse has capitalized on the Greek collective memory of the Second World War, using images that the Greeks were *already* socialized with to compare Germany's current 'peculiar, economic hegemony'[8] with the traumatic wartime Nazi Occupation. The Greek posture at least in some quarters has been squarely framed as one of resistance against foreign domination, urging Germany, to 'respect those who sacrificed themselves for the liberation of Germany and humanity from the Nazi yoke.'[9] A typical headline spoke of a 'suffocating euro-tutelage,' declaring 'for the first time, the Commission and the ECB implement a model of perpetual co-government in a member state.'[10] Whatever the merit of these assertions, the question at the heart of Europe's future today is whether such practices and the sentiments they give rise to will become entrenched throughout all of debtor-Europe or whether the EU will be able to encourage truly democratically sustainable reforms.

It is indeed fascinating that this question be asked at the very historical moment when global power shifts and the obvious albeit relative 'provincialization' of the EU in the international system that this entails is putting enormous pressure on the member states individually and collectively to compete politically and economically in order to retain a place in the global pecking order. At a time when the German government appears, quite regally, to be ignoring accusations of neo-imperial governing at a distance within Europe, the implication is that creditor hegemony and/or hubris is what it takes if Europeans do not want, one day, to be governed at a distance by the likes of China.

What is to be done? The decentring agenda

Elsewhere, we have argued that in order to respond to the pragmatic challenges as well as anxieties engendered by the rise of the 'Rest' it is necessary for the EU and its members to 'decentre' habits of thinking and behaving that are post-imperial in the sense of reproduction: namely, attitudes emanating from the nineteenth-century era of European global hegemony which continue to situate Europe at the centre of the world's affairs and at the top of its hierarchy. This lingering post-imperial imagination, we contend, compromises EU engagement of the formerly dominated world, especially in its relations with rising actors on an increasingly multipolar global stage. For such players, the memory of European military and economic dominance and cultural hubris remains aggravating – invoked to potent populist effect in tropes like China's 'hundred years of humiliation' or Iran's exhortation against 'Westoxification' (Fisher Onar and Nicolaidis 2013). The hostilities, suspicions, and mutual recriminations that this engenders – evident in hawkish policies and the soaring of xenophobia in EU countries – in turn, impedes Europeans' ability to achieve a sense of the post-imperial as transcendence.

To overcome this, we argue for a three-step rubric for 'decentring' Europe's international relations and the analytical apparatus we use in its assessment. The three logics at play have both a sequential and a parallel structure such that each emanates from the former, while all three also can be pursued simultaneously. The first and best-known move as popularized by Chakrabarty is to seek to *provincialize* Europe. At one level, this entails questioning received wisdom about for instance, the uni-directional radiation of civilization on one hand and enlightened modernity on the other to less elevated corners of the world.[11] At another level, it requires recognizing the contribution of others to the flourishing of Europe since at least the early modern era, the legacy of which continues to tangibly empower the EU, its members, and its citizens, and materially disadvantage those who have inherited societies, polities, economies, and ecologies brutalized by European colonialism.[12]

As a second step toward decentering is *engagement*. This means striving to see the world as it looks to others. A seemingly straightforward task, in practice engaging others' priorities is always tricky. This is because the questions one asks and the interpretations one brings to bear to the answers one receives are always intertwined with one's own priorities and interests. Thus, while it is a natural starting point to engage by asking what others think of Europe and the EU, one must also be prepared to accept that Europe may figure rather negatively, if at all.

On these grounds, the third step in the decentering agenda is to work toward *reconstruction*. This refers to the need to infuse and invigorate EU policy engagement with knowledge and sensibilities that emanate from extra-European perspectives – as well as those voices of vulnerable groups, often second- or third-generation migrants, within the EU. This more inclusive framework is a functional imperative if one is to retain relevance in a non-European world pecking order, and a step toward achieving in normative terms the illustrious state that the likes of Solana and Baroso have long evoked as an aspirational ideal, namely alignment of the outside and the inside – what we see as the transcendence rather than the reproduction of Europe's 'post-imperial' condition. To be sure, this does not mean uncritically taking on board all practices and positions put forth by extra- or new-European interlocutors, but rather modulating the EU's tone and prescriptions toward more fruitful collaborative outcomes.

A tale of two civilizations? Turkey as Europe's post-imperial testing ground

The urgency of decentring is attested to by the bungling of Turkey's EU candidacy, arguably the case par excellence of the post-imperial condition-as-reproduction trumping – at least for the time being – the post-imperial condition as-transcendence. When Ankara's formal candidacy to the Union was declared in 1999, however, this did not seem a foregone conclusion (Fisher Onar 2009, 2015). On the contrary, Turkey's membership trajectory was widely seen as a litmus test for the inclusionary capacity of the EU project on equality grounds. Would it spur the Union to evolve in a cosmopolitan post-national direction reconciled not only to post-Christian secular difference, but also to Muslim difference however secularized? In other words, would the standards of civilization mind-set – what on the Turkish side was referred to half facetiously as the 'Capitulations syndrome,' referring to nineteenth century quasi-imperial usurpation of aspects of Ottoman sovereignty – be truly overcome? Many, especially within the EU's liberal and left-leaning political elite and intelligentsia, committed to and mobilized toward substantiating this aspiration. Negotiations toward opening accession negotiations and concomitant reforms in Turkey were embarked upon in apparent good faith along with a plethora of official and civil society exchanges. Budgets were allocated, institutions were established, laws were passed, relationships were forged and, for all appearances, Turkey underwent an EU-oriented transformation. But if this was congruent with a triumphal sense in the early 2000s that the EU was at the threshold of achieving its manifest destiny as an agent of post-imperial transcendence, in practice, relations became increasingly strained.

Resistance was discernible from the start in the reservations expressed by prominent Christian Democrats who nursed civilizational anxieties about Turkey's prospective membership. It was amplified by the 9/11 attacks and the new zeitgeist they ushered in along with centre-right governments in France and Germany whose leadership courted to some extent the far right that rose to prominence in this period in both national and EU parliamentary politics. Fuelled by the atrocities committed by Islamist extremists in London, Madrid, and Amsterdam, the far right saw Turkish accession as tantamount to handing over the keys of (post-) Christian Europe to an ineluctably expansive and barbaric Islamist bloc, lambasting, moreover, the EU-level accession process as just one more instance of anti-*demoi*cratic excess on the part of culturally deracinated EU political elites.

In time, if not necessarily as colorfully as in its far-right articulation, the view of Europe as a geo-cultural bloc prevailed, the 'post-imperial' condition as reproduction of exclusionary hierarchies by which we can characterize much European engagement of countries like Turkey or Egypt and the perceived impossibility of their meaningful integration with the West. To be sure, not all of Europe's geo-cultural 'Others' are Muslim: Russia and the United States also have served this role at various junctures (Neumann 1999; Morozov and Rumelili 2012). Nor are all Muslims perceived through the same prism. Muslim minority communities in European societies, for example, may be read through a somewhat less securitized optic than, for example, states and societies in Muslim-majority countries, and certainly more than Islamist-led governments of Muslim-majority states. Proximity, size, and level of development also matter. Hence, Albania is envisaged as – eventually – internalizable, while the mantra beloved of those sceptical of Turkey's EU trajectory has long been that the country was 'too large, too poor, and too Muslim' for inclusion. The appeal of the refrain (despite Turkey's rapid economic development in the interim) is suggestive of the interplay between the post-imperial and Western conditions, in that Turkey is deemed too alien to even be 'governed from afar.' That Turkey's detractors in Europe would rather forfeit enduring influence over and potentially alienate an important ally than work through the existential anxieties that the country's candidacy evokes suggests that the post-imperial vis-à-vis Europe's own neighborhood is at some operative level bound up in the memory not only of empire as the overseas colonial projects of the sixteenth through nineteenth centuries, but also earlier Holy Roman incarnations of European *imperium*.

The Turkish case also speaks to the fallout for European foreign policy of this mixed bag imperial heritage. For the opening and then de facto if not formal closing of the window of accession, accompanied and sometimes set off a series of developments in Turkey, from partial democratization in the mid-2000s driven by a party with political Islamist roots, to the capture of the state by that same party by the end of the decade (Öktem 2011). As the prospect of EU accession dimmed, and outreach to Turkey's own post-imperial neighborhood – the Ottoman successor states of the Balkans and Middle East – proved fruitful, Ankara began to position itself as a multiregional actor (Öktem, Kadıoğlu, Karli 2012). Increasingly, this entailed evocation of civilizational rationales wholly congruent with the tale of Turkey as Europe's Other being articulated within the EU but inversed, casting Turkey as the authentic and benign hegemon the region had been waiting for to rescue its denizens from European double standards and exploitation. While this claim has proved more aspirational than practicable in the aftermath of the Arab revolutions and the uncertainties they have unleashed, it does testify to the unintended consequences of failure to confront the tension between Europe's post-imperialism and Turkey's 'Western condition' or the unavoidable nature of its Western trope (Akkoyunlu et al. 2013). By not confronting its post-imperial condition in enlargement policy, and not withstanding the limits of its influence over a government with increasing authoritarian tendency, the EU has failed to enlist a crucial partner at a time of great flux in their shared neighborhood.

Neighborhood as the limes of empire: For a right not to choose?

If relations with Turkey have soured for the time being, the EU's post-colonial credentials could perhaps best be tested in what it has come to call its eastern neighborhood, where countries that are not candidates for accession belong to a shared neighborhood between Russia and the EU. Perhaps more accurately, these countries now constitute not a shared but a contested neighborhood in the full senses of the term, a grey zone made up by the limes (the outer limits of the empire as they were called by the Romans) between two powers with very different relations to their colonial legacies. Whatever their contradictory aspirations, this is a structural fact not a Russian ploy: countries in the contested neighborhood are culturally, ethnically and ideologically in between. Indeed while each in different ways, these countries are all divided between a 'pro-EU' (and not just Western) side, which hankers after the kind of rise in prosperity witnessed in Poland (Knaus, 2014), and the eastern pro-Russia side, often suspicious of what they see as European values as well as promises. Accordingly, countries like Azerbaijan, Byelorussia, or Armenia resist the EU's eastern partnership, seemingly perceiving it as an instance of post-imperial reproduction.

Should the EU and Russia confront each other in this region as classic imperial powers each vying to keep or expand its respective sphere of influence? The latest crisis in Ukraine is but one expression of this broader question due to a great extent to the combination between two gaps: the gap between the parts of the populations who want to join the EU and those drawn to Russia (and all those in between); and the gap between the aspiration of the former and the EU's propensity to deliver on these aspirations. As Borosz's account in this volume reminds us, Ukraine's membership in the European Union is off the table for the foreseeable future – but this has not kept the country from being torn apart.

We believe that a truly post-imperial approach for the EU needs to start by rejecting the old spheres of influence approach – something the EU has proclaimed it was doing all along while often acting as if it didn't. Is it enough to claim or even clumsily practice a 'transformative approach' in the region, committed to exporting all good things from democracy to rational economic governance and the rule of law that underpins it all, while ignoring both the colonial underpinnings of the approach and the geo-political context of such (desirable) transformation? As argued by Elena Korosteleva as well as contributors in this volume, the neighborhood policy may have had the right intentions but the means by which it has been conducted in the last decade have been overwhelmingly Eurocentric and paternalistic (Korosteleva 2015).[13] The EU's approach has often overlooked the deeply entrenched cleavages in most of these countries and assumed that an external power could simply empower pro-Western parties or certain actors within this camp without destabilizing effects. Pragmatically, the EU needs to truly shape a new and decentred approach to relations on its eastern front including by choosing instruments that empower actors for change who are most capable of mediating conflicts, from societal to military.

On the geopolitical front, Russia must be confronted in its claim that it alone respects the diverse make up of its former satellites. One way for the EU to do so is to visibly uphold a principle akin to a *right not to choose* for countries in the region. By this we mean not just a de facto right – as help by any sovereign country – but a proclaimed policy on the part of the EU, pro-actively pursued with all concerned. Such a right would likely be perceived as a stabilizing factor and serve the unity of Europe's divided neighbors.

Is such a right akin to a general call for neutrality in the contested neighborhood? No. But it would be reminiscent of the third word philosophy of non-alignment promulgated in the heydays of decolonization. As a post-imperial move, it would mean giving full agency to middle states so that they themselves determine the localized order which affects them. By explicitly maximizing their room for manoeuvre between their intrusive imperial neighbors, such a right not to choose would turn them from objects of hegemony to the shapers of a space within a dual hegemony with and overlapping realms. To be sure, competition between the two hegemons would not necessarily relent but these in-between states would be put in a position to design schemes for mutual accommodation rather than be forced to balance against either side.

Specifically, a right not to choose implies for the EU to abandon the enlargement model in dealing with its neighbors – at least while the prospect of enlargement is inexistent – a model that systematically connects access and convergence, rewarding the latter through access to market, visas and eventually membership. This is an approach based on a concentric circle vision of 'more or less members' with Brussels at its centre.

Perhaps counter-intuitively, a right not to choose would involve taking the full political import of trade negotiations, which appear as technical and are led by technical experts. Apparently, in discussions on the trade agreement with Ukraine, the EU did encourage Russia to consider adapting its approach so that its Eurasian customs union (or a version thereof) would allow individual members to negotiate their own separate trade deals. But while technically the EU was reassuring Russia that it could handle a deep free trade agreement between the EU and Ukraine, it failed to show how this was to happen or to frame it this way politically. Not before the spring of 2014, as the war on the eastern front was already raging, did EU institutions start examining seriously the possibility of amending their own approach in this regard. The technicality of EU trade policy and its character as trade lawyers' *domaine reservé* – as if the 'standards' were somehow a uniquely rationale and a-political matter of governance – constitutes a serious structural weakness for the EU when accords and political goals are increasingly at odds. In this case, it is indeed the content of the trade deal that ratcheted up the Russian threat.

This right not to choose is of course not incompatible with EU convergence and ultimately a right to choose their partners for these countries. Is it not better for the EU to frame the relationship as 'not choosing' and actually seeing support for reforms? To be sure, there will be questioning in the future as to whether the reforms that may occur in these countries are the product of external EU pressure under expectations of eventual accession or internally devised structural change with EU and other support. But a post-imperial EU still needs to pursue its interests as with any other 'normal' actor in the international system and remains in the business of exporting stability: be visible on the ground, cooperate on border control, humanitarian assistance and reconstruction as well as the creation of a common communication space. If and when the countries to Europe's east chose to converge and demonstrate that they are able to, their choice needs not be a choice *against* Russia. Indeed, Putin's Russia, like that of a purportedly 'neo-Ottoman' Turkey alienated from its EU prospects, has its own vision of the post-colonial, and that is harping back to an earlier era (the Concert of Vienna) in which Russia is again a key player. The EU needs to convey strongly that it itself has embraced a new era where the big players cannot tell smaller ones what to do and when the security of people as well as states is paramount. Only such a precept ought to underpin a new security pact from Lisbon to Vladivostok.

Conclusion

In this chapter, we have reflected on what we call Europe's post-imperial condition, which calls for Europeans to reflect on how deeply rooted in colonial patterns was the original project of European integration, and on why many chose to forget this. We also need to recognize the different and multiple meanings of the 'imperial past' which prevail in countries in east and central Europe, southern or northern Europe as well as in former European former colonies who see the EU through the lens of their own postcolonial status. It is the confrontation between these imperial legacies and the difficulty to transcend them by recognizing then and now the critical role of 'others' within and without in the constitution of the EU project which forge Europe's post-imperial condition. Our notion of the post-imperial as both transcendence and as reproduction, and the modalities, dangers, and promise of each on the internal and external playing fields, suggests that while the EU has made much formal and indeed existential progress toward confronting echoes of imperialism, imperial patterns die hard.

Post-colonial studies used to have their object squarely located in the world of the 'subaltern' along the paths opened by the likes of Edward Said, Homi Bhabha, Gayatri Spivak, and many others. Many of the symbolic and effective types of oppression which they unveiled and fought, still exist. But the echoes are fainter and more confusing than in their immediately postcolonial times. Power is more diffuse and hybridity more pervasive. Europe has moved on by denying, reproducing and atoning for its pasts in equal measure. We need to update talk of the postcolonial condition for a changing world and confront Europe's claims to post-imperialism. In the end, the EU may have become an empire in new clothes, but let us hope this may come to be a post-imperial empire.

Notes

1 For a masterful account of the modalities of (Anglo-)American imperial amnesia and memory as seen from the Indian Ocean, see Engseng Ho, 2004.
2 See, for example, seminal work on this of Behr (2007) and Stivachtis, (2008). See also Nicolaidis, Sebe, and Maas (2015).
3 In the field of international relations, the work of John Hobson (e.g. 2007; 2012) stands as perhaps the most cogent articulation of this 'mutual constitution' of Europe and its colonies and the indebtedness of the former to the latter.
4 In Nicolaidis et al. (2014) we discuss the analogy between nineteenth-century standards of civilization and today's EU along two dimensions. *Agency denial* or the tendency to deny agency to new members in different domains not only in determining the rules applicable to them but also in determining who was to have agency in the first place; and *Hierarchy* or the inequality that exists where some agents systematically have more power than others and are institutionally recognized to have higher worth.

While we find significant variation along these dimensions, we conclude that there is little doubt that the SoC mindset and practices are alive and well.

5 See, for example, Besson (2006); Bohman (2007); Cheneval, Lavenex, and Schimmelfennig (2014); Cheneval and Schimmelfennig (2013); (Nicolaidis and Kleinfeld 2012; Nicolaidis 2013).

6 This trend, exemplified by Sartre's engagement of Fanon, was about recognizing that the post-imperial condition involved the mutually constitutive role of internal and external dynamics. As Aimé Césaire put it at the heyday of mid-century decolonization, imperialism had 'worked to decivilize the colonizer, to brutalize him in the true sense of the world' (cited in Vergès, 2011).

7 There is a subtle difference between these two classic forms and their more EU-compatible cousins (federal union and neo-medieval empire).

8 Stuart Holland translated by Yannis Varoufakis, 'Schäuble Adds Insult to Injury.' 23 July 2013. Available at: http://yanisvaroufakis.eu/2013/07/26/debt-guilt-and-german-history-a-reply-to-wolfgang-schauble-by-stuart-holland/ (Accessed 10 May 2015).

9 *Avgi* 06/01/10, pp. 8–9, 'The German Economics Minister Appears "Provocative" and 'Insolent.'

10 *Avgi* 10/01/10, front page.

11 There is an expansive literature on what Blaut (2012) was among the first to call this diffusionist tendency. For a recent discussion, see Jan-Gorg Deutsch (2014).

12 For a literature review including the notable contributions of John Hobson to the IR variant of the argument, see Fisher Onar and Nicolaidis (2013).

13 See also Bechev and Nicolaidis (2010).

References

Akkoyunlu, Karabekir, Kalypso Nicolaidis, and Kerem Öktem. 2013. *The Western condition: Turkey, the US and the EU in the New Middle East*. Oxford: SEESOX Book Series on Current Affairs.

Bechev, Dimitar. 2015. From the Soviet bloc to the new middle age: East-central Europe's three imperial moments. In Kalypso Nicolaidis, Berny Sebe, and Gari Maas (eds.), *Echoes of empire: Identity, memory, and colonial legacies*. London: I. B. Tauris.

Bechev, Dimitar and Nicolaidis, Kalypso, 2010. From policy to polity: Can the EU's special relations with its neighbourhood be decentred? *Journal of Common Market Studies*, June.

Behr, Hartmut. 2007. The European Union in the legacies of imperial rule? EU accession politics viewed from a historical comparative perspective. *European Journal of International Relations* 13(2): 239–62.

Besson, Samantha. 2006. The European Union and human rights: Towards a post-national human rights institution? *Human Rights Law Review* 6(2): 323–60.

Blaut, James Morris. 2012. *The colonizer's model of the world: Geographical diffusionism and Eurocentric History*. New York: Guilford.

Bohman, James. 2007. *Democracy across borders*. Boston: MIT Press.

Bohman, James. 2008. Transnational democracy and nondomination. In C. Laborde and J. Maynor (eds.), 190–216. *Republicanism and political theory*. London: Blackwell.

Cheneval, Francis, and Frank Schimmelfennig. 2013. The case for democracy in the European Union. *JCMS: Journal of Common Market Studies* 51(2): 334–50.

Cheneval, Francis, Sandra Lavenex, and Frank Schimmelfennig. 2014. Demoi-cracy in the European Union: Principles, institutions, policies. *Journal of European Public Policy* ahead-of-print, 1–18.

Davies, Norman. 1996. *Europe: A history*. Oxford: Oxford University Press.

Deutsch, Jan-Gorg. 2014. Colonial modernities: A View from the imperial verandah, c. 1880–1960. In In Kalypso Nicolaidis, Berny Sebe, and Gari Maas (eds.), *Echoes of empire: Identity, memory, and colonial legacies*. London: I. B. Tauris.

Diez, Thomas 2013. Normative power as hegemony. *Cooperation and Conflict* 48(2): 194–210.

Fisher Onar, Nora. 2009. Echoes of a universalism lost: Rival representations of the Ottomans in today's Turkey. *Middle Eastern Studies* 45(2).

Fisher Onar, Nora. 2015. History, memory, and historiography: Contesting Ottoman legacies in Turkey, 1923–2012. In Kalypso Nicolaidis, Berny Sebe, and Gari Maas (eds.), *Echoes of empire: Identity, memory, and colonial legacies*. London: I. B. Tauris.

Fisher Onar, Nora, and Kalypso Nicolaidis. 2013. The decentering agenda: Europe as a post-colonial power. *Cooperation and Conflict* 48(2): 283–303.

Halberstam, Daniel. 2009. Constitutional heterarchy: The centrality of conflict in the European Union and the United States. In Jeffery Dunoff and Joel Trachtman (eds.), *Ruling the world? Constitutionalism, international law and global governance*, 326–355. Cambridge: Cambridge University Press.

Hansen, Peo and Stefan Jonsson. 2015. Building Eurafrica: Reviving colonialism through European integration, 1920–60. In In Kalypso Nicolaidis, Berny Sebe, and Gari Maas (eds.), *Echoes of empire: Identity, memory, and colonial legacies*. London: I. B. Tauris.

Hansen, Peo, and Stefan Jonsson. 2013. Imperial origins of European integration and the case of Eurafrica: A reply to Gary Marks' "Europe and Its Empires." *JCMS: Journal of Common Market Studies* 50: 1028–41.

Ho, Enseng. 2004. Empire through diasporic eyes: A view from the other boat. *Comparative Study of Society and History* 46(2), 210–246.

Hobson, John. 2007. Is critical theory always for the white West and for Western imperialism? Beyond Westphalian towards a post-racist critical IR. *Review of International Studies* 33(1): 91–116.

Hobson, John. 2012. *The Eurocentric conception of world politics: Western international theory, 1760–2010*. Cambridge: Cambridge University Press.

Knaus, Gerald. 2014. Why they look West – Ukraine, poverty and the EU. *European Stability Initiative Newsletter*, 21 March.

Korosteleva, Elena. 2015. The EU and its eastern neighbours: Why 'othering' matters. In In Kalypso Nicolaidis, Berny Sebe, and Gari Maas (eds.), *Echoes of empire: Identity, memory, and colonial legacies*. London: I. B. Tauris.

Lacroix, Justine, and Kalypso Nicolaidis. 2010. *European stories: Intellectual debates on Europe in national contexts*. Oxford: Oxford University Press.

Macaj, Gjovalin, and Kalypso Nicolaidis. 2014. Beyond 'one voice'? Global Europe's engagement with its own diversity. *Journal of European Public Policy* 21(7): 1067–1083.

Magnette, Paul, and Kalypso Nicolaidis,. 2005. Coping with the Lilliput syndrome: Large vs. small member states in the European Convention. *European Public Law* 11(1): 85–104.

Marks, Gary. 2012. Europe and its empires: From Rome to the European Union. *Journal of Common Market Studies* 50: 1–20.

Morozov, Viatcheslav, and Bahar Rumelili. 2012. The external constitution of European identity: Russia and Turkey as Europe-makers. *Cooperation and Conflict* 47(1): 28–48.

Neumann, Iver B. 1999. *Uses of the other: 'The East' in European identity formation*. Manchester: Manchester University Press.

Nicolaidis, Kalypso. 2013. European demoicracy and its crisis. *Journal of Common Market Studies* 51(2): 351–369

Nicolaidis, Kalypso. 2015. Southern barbarians? A post-colonial critic of EUniversalism. In In Kalypso Nicolaidis, Berny Sebe, and Gari Maas (eds.), *Echoes of empire: Identity, memory, and colonial legacies*. London: I. B. Tauris.

Nicolaidis, Kalypso, and Rachel Kleinfeld. 2012. *Rethinking Europe's 'rule of law' and enlargement agenda: The fundamental dilemma*. No. 49. OECD Publishing.

Nicolaidis, Kalypso, Berny Seby, and Gari Maas (eds.). 2015. *Echoes of empire: Identity, memory, and colonial legacies*. London: I. B. Tauris.

Nicolaidis, Kalypso, Claire Vergerio, Nora Onar Fisher, and Juri Viehoff. 2014. From metropolis to microcosmos: Europe's new standards of civilisation. *Millennium. Journal of International Studies* 42(3): 718–45.

Nicolaidis, Kalypso, and Max Watson 2014. Europe's democracy trilemma. *International Affairs*. 90(6): 1403–19.

Öktem, Kerem. 2011. *Angry nation: Turkey since 1989*. London: Zed Books.

Öktem, Kerem, Kadıoğlu, Ayşe, Mehmet Karlı (Eds.). 2012. *Another empire? Turkey's new foreign policy in the 2000s*. Istanbul: Bilgi University Press.

Pagden, Anthony. 2006. The empire's new clothes: From empire to federation, yesterday and today. *Common Knowledge* 12(1): 36–46.

Pettitm Philip. 1997. *Republicanism: A theory of freedom and government*. Oxford: Oxford University Press.

Rossi, Juan-Jose. 2015. The history, identity, crisis, and endemic submission of the American continent. In Kalypso Nicolaidis, Berny Sebe, and Gari Maas (eds.), *Echoes of empire: Identity, memory, and colonial legacies*. London: I. B. Tauris.

Stivachtis, Yannis. 2008. Civilization and international society: The case of European Union expansion. *Contemporary Politics* 14(1): 71–89.

Vergès, Francoise. 2011. Xenophobia and the Civilizing Mission. *opendemocracy*, 13 May 2011. Available at: www.opendemocracy.net/françoise-vergès/xenophobia-and-civilizing-mission.

Walker, Neil, and Gianluigi Palombella (eds.). 2009. *Relocating the rule of law*. Oxford: Hart.

Weiler, Joseph. 2001. Federalism and constitutionalism: Europe's Sonderweg. In Kalypso Nicolaidis and Robert Howse (eds.). *The federal vision*. Oxford: Oxford University Press.

Zielonka, Jan. 2006. Europe as empire: The nature of the enlarged European Union. *Central European Review of International Affairs*, *27*, 135.

8 Linguistic imperialism of and in the European Union

Robert Phillipson

Introduction

While addressing the House of Commons on 24 August 1941, Winston Churchill noted: "The British Empire and the United States who, fortunately for the progress of mankind, happen to speak the same language and very largely think the same thoughts."[1] When receiving an honorary degree at Harvard University on 6 September 1943, he also stated that "the power to control language offers far better prizes than taking away people's provinces or lands or grinding them down in exploitation. The empires of the future are the empires of the mind."[2] These statements reveal something of the complexity of analysing language policy in historical and current processes of greater European and transatlantic integration. There are many constituent elements and agendas. Teasing out causal factors and isolating the specific role played by language policy is a considerable challenge. It is an important issue, but one that few social scientists have engaged with, even in the study of European integration. In law and principle, all EU official languages have equal status, but in reality French was primus inter pares in the early years, whereas gradually over the past four decades English has become dominant. The Union's 'respect' for linguistic diversity is a noble principle but elusive. The article analyses the historical record of the British and American empires, and the interlocking of two projects, the formation of a European Union, and the globalisation of English. It explores whether English linguistic hegemony worldwide and within the EU institutional framework can be seen as linguistic imperialism and what the implications are for speakers of other languages.

The terms 'empire', 'imperialism', 'colonialism', and 'neo-colonialism' are tricky, because they overlap to some extent, but more importantly because the terms have 'a complicated history and many different, fiercely contested meanings. . . . Defining something as imperial or colonial today almost always implies hostility to it, viewing it as inherently immoral or illegitimate . . . the subject is so highly charged with political passions and emotion' (Howe 2002, 9, 34). The topics have also generated a vast industry of historical and political scholarship that is of direct relevance to the study of language policy in the modern world, though language issues seldom figure prominently in them. Harvey (2005) stresses the need to define the concept imperialism if it is to be used analytically rather than merely polemically. This principle guided my definition of linguistic imperialism as a variant of linguicism, operating through structures and ideologies, and entailing unequal treatment for groups identified by language (Phillipson 1992, 2009) in comparable ways to racism, sexism, and classism.

The article tracks the transition from the transportation of European peoples and languages to other continents to the establishment of a world order underpinned by US military and economic might and the popularization of US norms worldwide. These are disseminated through Hollywood products, media forms and technologies, business strategies, scientific and educational activities, and advertising that markets consumerist capitalism. English plays a central role in all of these.

There has been a transition from the occupation of land to the occupation and appropriation of cultural and linguistic mental spaces, as Churchill astutely anticipated. The ideology of *terra nullius*, the myth of 'empty' land, has been succeeded and supplemented by the dissemination of an American *cultura nullius*, cultural practices projected as universally valid, but fluid and adaptable in their interaction with other cultures. English is increasingly projected as a *lingua nullius*, a language not owned by anyone, as though it serves all equally well. English tends to be internalised as detached from the underlying imperialist forces, military, economic, and cultural that explain its capitalist dissemination. Exploration of the role currently played by English in the integration of Europe can illuminate these momentous, turbulent changes.

Global Americanisation entails processes of McDonaldisation (Hamelink 1994; Ritzer 2011), the standardisation of modern social life through processes of control and predictability, and through the subordination of progressively more aspects of life to the commodification engendered by neoliberal market forces. Europeanisation exemplifies this process. English is marketed as a lingua franca in processes that serve to sanitise linguistic imperialism. Linguistic imperialism has many parameters, with several supply and demand factors, but is primarily a question of inequality, of speakers or users of one language being unjustly privileged. The EU's language policies are facilitating the localisation of the 'global English' project, its products and processes (Phillipson 2012a), as will be exemplified in this chapter.

The historical background to the empire of English

Languages of empire – Greek, Latin, Persian, Arabic, Sanskrit, Chinese, and many others – have underpinned political and military control, commerce and the promotion of several major religions. In the Roman empire that covered much of Europe and North Africa, the strategy for co-opting a conquered people was insightfully analysed 2000 years ago by Tacitus (1948, 72), whose uncle, Agricola, was charged with converting the British to Roman norms:

> The sons of chiefs . . . in place of distaste for the Latin language came a passion to command it. In the same way, our national dress came into favour and

> the toga was everywhere to be seen. And so the Britons were gradually led on to the amenities that make vice agreeable – arcades, baths and sumptuous banquets. They spoke of such novelties as 'civilization' when really they were only a feature of enslavement.

The current position of several European languages – primarily French, Portuguese, Spanish, and Russian as well as English – on non-European continents is due to processes of global Europeanisation and linguistic imposition over the past five centuries. The countries that were defeated in 20th century wars, Germany, Italy, and Japan, had their imperial ambitions and their language empires aborted.

The *terra nullius* doctrine that has served as a fraudulent cover for the dispossession of the territories, cultures, and languages of the Americas and Australasia was a confirmation of policies promulgated by the Papacy prior to the Requerimento that Spanish conquistadores took with them to the 'New World',

> drawn up (in Castilian) at the behest of King Ferdinand of Castille in 1513 . . . extended the tradition of the Crusades, and Castille's own reconquest of Granada, a battle for Christ closer to home which became a model for Cortez's expedition to Mexico in 1519, and Pizzarro's to Peru, where he murdered King Atuahalpa in 1532.
>
> (Errington 2008, 25)

The locals who could not understand Spanish were considered 'subhuman, and so could be subjugated forthwith' (ibid.).

The English philosopher John Locke provided a rationalisation for Europeans arrogating to themselves a God-given right to occupy territory elsewhere. In the chapter on Property in *Two treatises of government*, 1690/1988, Locke argues that God commanded people to labour, as a result of which they can increase their possessions: 'God, by commanding to subdue, gave Authority so far to *appropriate*' (1690/1988, 292, emphasis in original). Since the indigenous peoples of America have failed to labour, 'they are rich in Land, and poor in all the Comforts of Life'. Nature has given them the same resources as people elsewhere, and productive territory, but they 'for want of improving it by labour, have not one hundredth part of the Conveniences we enjoy: And a King of a large and fruitful Territory there feeds, lodges, and is clad worse than a day Labourer in England' (ibid., 296–7). To which Locke adds that 'In the beginning, all the World was *America*, and more so than that is now; for no such thing as *Money* was any where known' (ibid., 301, emphasis in original). The fruits of labour can be converted into gold, silver, or money, which can then be used as a way of legitimating 'disproportionate and unequal Possession of the Earth', this inequality being, in Locke's claim, 'tacitly but voluntarily' agreed on by society (ibid., 302).

This argument was supposed to justify European colonisation and sanctify Christian proselytization. Land in what became named the Americas was *terra nullius*, land belonging to no-one, to which its benighted inhabitants had no claim or rights. The ideological foundation for this argument is the dichotomy between Us ('civilised') and Them ('barbarians') that has been deeply rooted in the thinking of the Western world since the time of the ancient Greeks. The same fraudulence applied when the British took over African land and dispossessed its occupants. Colonised Kenyans became exploited labour in the 'White Highlands' and 'learned in school that white people had discovered Mount Kenya and many of our lakes, including Lake Victoria' (Ngũgĩ 2010, 168). The sale of African land to Arabs and Asians in need of food supplies is a present-day variant of this dispossession.

In the Americas some Europeans were appalled by how barbarically the inhabitants of the 'new' world were treated. Bartolomé de Las Casas wrote a thesis *In defense of the Indians* in 1552–1553 in which he argued that indigenous peoples in the Americas should not be considered subhuman and therefore eliminated, since they shared all the basic characteristics of humans worldwide, the only difference being that they were not Christian. They were 'neither slaves nor barbarians in any morally relevant sense of these terms . . . the fact that they were ignorant of God is not a sufficient ground for denying them the basic rights of life and possession' (Bartelson 2009, 79, 80). This understanding did not prevail in the Americas.

US national identity was forged through the dispossession and near extermination of the indigenous peoples, their genocide (Ward Churchill 1997), the myth of unoccupied territory, the surplus value extorted from slave labour, and an active process of national imagination, one deeply permeated by religion. The USA is a warfare society rather than a welfare society, initially in North America, now globally (Hixson 2008; P. C. Roberts 2014; Petras 2014; www.tomdispatch.com). The nationalist revolt of 1776 and the ensuing state formation and constitution privileged white male slave-owning Euro-Americans. These founding fathers devised a constitution in which ' "We, the people" elided hierarchies of race, class, and gender' (Hixson 2008, 39). This legacy continues to this day, when Asiatics or Arabs with whom the West is at war are seen as so subhuman that they do not merit a body count.

From the time of the USA declaring its independence, it has seen itself as a model for the world, with a divine mission to impose its values. George Washington saw the United States as a 'rising empire' and in 1786 wrote that, 'However unimportant America may be considered at present . . . there will assuredly come a day when this country will have some weight in the scale of empires'. The address was read out in its entirety in Congress every February until the mid-1970s. (A. Roberts 2008, 68)

Roberts, a modern-day historian of the English-speaking peoples in the triumphalist tradition of Macaulay and Winston Churchill, also cites Rudyard Kipling (A. Roberts 2008, 144), who wrote in his autobiography that he 'never got over the wonder of a people who, having extirpated the aboriginals of their continent more completely than any other modern race had done, honestly believed they were a godly New England community, setting examples to brutal Mankind'.

Kipling could see through US falsity while himself seeing colonised Indians as 'half-savage, half-child' and legitimating the British empire to a vast readership in his own poetry and novels. He also proclaimed that a Christian God was behind British military success and empire.[3]

The Monroe Doctrine of 1823 articulated a policy of ensuring that the Americas would remain a sphere of interest determined by the USA rather than European powers. This was only partially successful before 1914 because of massive British investments in mining and railways throughout Latin America: Argentina was seen as late as 1920 as a necessary part of the British Empire, albeit the 'informal' Empire (Darwin 2009, 137, 373).

Global Americanization, which Locke appears to anticipate, was in full swing by the late 19th century, as noted in 1912 by George Bernard Shaw, born in 1856: 'What has been happening in my lifetime is the Americanisation of the world.'[4] In recent decades it has been in the guise of globalisation (Bourdieu 2001), one dimension of which is linguistic imperialism (Phillipson 1992, 2009, Skutnabb-Kangas and Phillipson 2010). The synergies between language and globalisation currently are being explored from several scholarly angles (Coupland 2010).

One of the most visible causal factors is cultural globalisation in the media:

> 70–80% of all TV fiction shown on European TV is American. [. . .] American movies, American TV and the American lifestyle for the populations of the world and Europe at large have become the lingua franca of globalization, the closest we get to a visual world culture'
>
> (Bondebjerg 2003, 79, 81)

By contrast, in the USA the market share of films of foreign origin is 1%. A second symptom of cultural insularity is that far fewer translations of foreign-language books are published in the USA and the UK as compared with the numbers in continental European countries.[5] There is therefore a massive asymmetry in how cultural globalisation impacts on the two sides of the Atlantic. The extended reach of American English also varies: in countries in northern Europe, visual media products are disseminated with the original English sound track. This is one factor accounting for greater proficiency in English in the Scandinavian countries and the Netherlands. These demographically small countries are more open to penetration by English in academia, business, and international relations. Elsewhere in Europe it is mainly in large corporations and finance that English figures prominently, while in higher education and research the use of English is accelerating.

Language policy in the USA has fluctuated over time, but the underlying principle has been to transform a diverse local and immigrant population into monolingual English users, as briskly articulated by President Theodore Roosevelt (1919): 'We have room for but one flag, the American flag . . . We have room for but one language here, and that is the English language'.

The USA became a colonial power in Asia in the 1890s. Imperial exploitation in the Philippines required that education should follow the same model as in the USA, with an insistence on an exclusive use of English from 1898 to 1940:

> Public education, specifically language and literature education during the American colonial period, was designed to directly support American colonialism. The combined power of the canon, curriculum, and pedagogy constituted the ideological strategies resulting in rationalising, naturalizing, and legitimizing myths about colonial relationships and realities.
>
> (Martin 2002, 210)

The pattern was comparable in the British empire, in Africa (Rodney 1972) and in India, though here a much larger elite was educated to serve British interests. English served the process of elite formation throughout the colonial empire, a process that has intensified after independence.

In today's India, English is the language of power, used as an indication of greater control over outcomes of social activities. 'Over the post-Independence years, English has become the single most important predictor of socio-economic mobility. [. . .] With the globalized economy, English education widens the discrepancy between the social classes' (Mohanty 2006, 268–9).

India's post-independence language policy entails inclusion for the few who have a dominant role nationally and international links, and marginalisation for the many (Drèze and Sen 2014). Nehru (1956[6]) wanted to prevent the emergence after independence of an English-knowing caste that was out of touch with the rest of the population, but this is exactly what has happened. To suggest that a similar stratificational process might be under way in Europe might seem improbable, but it is not inconceivable in processes of global financial capital mobility and the formation of a transnational capitalist class.

European integration

The conventional wisdom of recent decades has been that the French and Germans are the driving force behind greater integration in Europe. This is only part of the story. The role of the USA in shaping the post-1945 world (the creation of the UN, the World Bank, the IMF, NATO, WTO) is well known (Smith 2003; Pieterse 2004; Harvey 2005). What is less well known is the involvement of the US in shaping modern Europe, as highlighted in a study by a top Danish civil servant, an adviser to the Danish prime minister at the time of Danish entry to the EU in 1973, along with the UK and Ireland, and later employed in the EU system. His book (Holm 2001), prophetically entitled *The European Anarchy*, bewails the lack of vision of current European leaders, their petty national agendas and inability to think long-term.

The links between the pioneer European architects of what has become the EU, Jean Monnet in particular, and the US political elite, before and after World

War II, are described in detail in Pascaline Winand's (1993) *Eisenhower, Kennedy, and the United States of Europe*. Monnet had spent many years in the U.S. between the wars, and became personal friends with a large number of Americans in senior foreign policy positions in Washington, which gave him direct access to both Eisenhower and Kennedy. While Monnet and many key Europeans were quite open about their wish to create a federal Europe on the model of the USA, the Americans were shrewd enough to influence policies decisively but to remain discreetly in the background.

The planning process had started in the Council on Foreign Relations, founded in 1921, which drew on 'the elite of the American business, academic, law, media and government communities' (ibid., 2). The COFR, with the editor of *Foreign Affairs,* saw the need in September 1939 for policy papers: 682 memoranda were transmitted to the Department of State, mainly funded by the Rockefeller foundation (ibid., 3).

John Foster Dulles, a Republican who later became Eisenhower's Secretary of State (Foreign Secretary), proposed Western Europe as a single economic unit in 1947. This was the agenda underlying the Marshall Plan that ensured massive economic progress in non-communist Europe. Sixteen European countries formed the Committee for European Economic Cooperation on 15 July 1947. The French government 'Schuman Plan', 9 May 1950, was essentially written by Monnet, with assistance from Americans based in France (ibid., 22). There were many competing views on both sides of the Atlantic (Atlanticists, internationalists, pragmatists, and Europeanists in the US; Gaullists, the British, Europeanists in Europe), but those in favour of a unification that would be economic, political and military were able to influence matters decisively. General Eisenhower, when Supreme Allied Commander, Europe, 'made a strong plea for European economic and political integration before the English-Speaking Union' in London on 3 July 1951 (ibid., 28).

A draft treaty prepared in 1952, essentially by Monnet, envisaged a directly elected People's Chamber, a European Executive Council, a Council of National Ministers, and a European Court. Monnet formed an Action Committee for a United States of Europe on 13 October 1955 (ibid., 77). Monnet became the director of the first transnational institution, the European Coal and Steel Community, and was the architect behind the institutions of the European Economic Community, later the European Community, later still the European Union. The free flow of goods, services, capital, and people was a founding principle of European integration in plans from 1956, and was ultimately achieved with the common market in the 1990s (ibid., 129). Americans had ambassadors at each of the key European institutions and treated their principals as heads of state when they visited Washington. American frustration with the limitations of the EEC (and the risk of it competing with the US economy) led to the creation of the Organization for Economic Cooperation and Development (OECD), a looser federation with larger membership, including Canada and the US. In the longer term the goal of the Europeanists was – and still is – an economic union between the US and Europe.

There are annual EU–US summit meetings. At the 2007 meeting, a Transatlantic Economic Integration Plan was endorsed, as well as coordination of foreign policy globally. In effect this means that the EU accepts corporate America's global agenda, as loyal but junior partners. This fits well with the New American Century project, the Cheney–Wolfowitz–Rumsfeld doctrine that was implemented under Bush II. The instruments for achieving integration have been the European Round Table of Industrialists, the Transatlantic Business Dialogue, and the Transatlantic Economic Partnership (Monbiot 2000), culminating in the negotiations in 2014 of the Transatlantic Trade and Investment Partnership (TTIP; also known as the Transatlantic Free Trade Area). The UK has spearheaded the adoption of this model in Europe, with its key role in global finance and strong military involvement as visible symptoms of commitment to US strategic interests. British half-hearted commitment to EU ideals is one complication.

The six founding member states agreed to accord equal rights to four languages, after blocking an attempt by the French to grant a superordinate status to French. Eurolaw and all major documents have equal validity in all official languages, currently 24. The market forces behind English have progressively made it the dominant language in conducting EU affairs de facto but not de jure. In theory other languages than English should be used in the external relations of the EU[7], but the European Commission privileges English. It conducts negotiations with applicant states in English, a procedure that restricts the capacity of ordinary citizens, including well-qualified ones, to follow the negotiation process (Phillipson 2003, 123–4). The legal status of documents translated into Polish or Czech, when Poland and the Czech Republic were applying, had no juridical 'authenticity', unlike the English text. EU–US negotiations take place in just one language – no prize for guessing which.

It is an important principle that legal acts, texts with legal effect in member states, should be accessible in a national language. There is however the serious fact of variation between languages, each with their semantic and grammatical baggage evolved in different historical trajectories and legal systems. As a result there are serious interpretation problems for lawyers and judges in both national courts (Kjær and Adamo 2011) and at the European Court of Justice (ECJ; Neergaard and Nielsen 2013). Semantic 'unity in diversity' is elusive when texts in different languages are supposed to have the same meaning.

ECJ legal method, the Community method, is in constant evolution (Neergaard and Nielsen 2013). The role of the ECJ is to adjudicate in the light of Eurolaw, including the principles enshrined in treaties that are designed to promote peace, security, and a neoliberal market economy. Analysis of litigation over many years in the ECJ reveals that the court does more than merely clarify Eurolaw.[8] The Court has based judgements on five sets of variables (natural law, legal positivism, common law, legal realism, fundamental rights): its approach can be literal, historical, contextual, or comparative (contrasting different national traditions), and teleological. This means that cases are determined in relation to the overall goals of European unification, including a rigid commitment to market forces.

The Court's conclusions are therefore controversial, since they entail an expansion of what is decreed in EU treaties and the exclusion of alternative economic thinking. ECJ judgements not only *interpret* what the law is understood to be but are also *constitutionalising* it. They are 'constructing' Europe in a never-ending project of European unification. ECJ judgements take this project forward, despite widespread disagreement about where the EU is heading, and without the accountability to citizens that a parliament has, or the participation of the governments of member states. Input is potentially from many languages and cultures. The outcome is formulated in French, the working language of the ECJ, with the unanimous backing of a judge from each member state, for promulgation in all official languages.

This is a novel form of supranational governance, one that constitutional and international lawyers who are evolving a more critical approach to legal aspects of global governance are analysing (de Búrca et al. 2014).[9] The integration of EU member states into a union has required an innovative evolution of legal practice: 'Integration through Law' means that treaties and Eurolaw enshrine how activity in member states should be conducted and coordinated across the union. Governance principles are determined at the supranational inter-governmental level, following which the Commission attempts to ensure that measures are implemented in member states, a mechanism of authoritarian executive managerialism (Joerges and Weimer 2014) that did not exist before membership of the EU. Languages are the instrument for achieving this.

No EU decrees on language, education, or culture have legal force, since these fields have always been seen as a national prerogative. On the other hand many EU funding schemes do impact on these aspects of social life, just as the conduct of EU affairs in its institutions entails the use of particular languages for a wide range of functions. Since language policy is left to market forces, to overt and covert principles, and to decisions and compromises at national, institutional and local levels, it inevitably functions inequitably. The market forces behind English strengthen its hegemony.

Projects in symbiosis: A European Union and global English

> I like to think of British and Americans moving about freely over each other's wide estates with hardly a sense of being foreigners to one another. But I do not see why we should not try to spread our common language even more widely throughout the globe and, without seeking selfish advantage over any, possess ourselves of this invaluable amenity and birthright.
>
> Winston Churchill, 1943[10]

In 1943 the British Empire was seriously weakened, British success in the Second World War was dependent on the American war machine, and massive financial loans from the USA. Transatlantic partnership builds on the cultural origins of millions of Europeans who emigrated to the USA, Britain as the dominant colonising power, supplanting the Dutch, Spanish and French, and English as a link language. Churchill's first major point in his talk at Harvard is support for USA global dominance, camouflaged as 'world responsibility'.

Second, Churchill sees the UK and USA as linked by 'blood and history'. Links between the two countries remained close even after the US Declaration of Independence. Churchill sees the two nations as united by 'law, language, and literature', exemplified by morality, justice, fair play, and support for the weak – norms that both countries are better at articulating than implementing.

Third, he stresses that in the war effort, American, British and Canadian forces have a joint command. He proposes that this should continue after the war, and only cease once a global system for peace maintenance has been established. The United Nations was soon established for this purpose, in a form that maintained the principle of the permanent members of the Security Council, including the USA and UK, playing a decisive role, which they still do.

Fourth, a key issue in Churchill's speech is his articulation of a plan for English as a globally dominant language worldwide, this task pretentiously claimed to be the 'birth right' of the British and Americans.

These four dimensions, globalization, consanguinity, military unification, and linguistic expansion form a complete package. The aims of global American dominance, with the UK in full support, included the integration of the economies of Europe – a condition for Marshall aid – and the establishment of English as the dominant international language.

Churchill also articulates a vision of potential UK and USA 'common citizenship'. Here he echoes Cecil Rhodes, who envisaged the USA rejoining the United Kingdom that it broke away from in 1776. He bequeathed the vast fortune made in the gold mines of South Africa to fund activities to cement links between the USA and UK and to promote Anglo-American dominance worldwide. His legacy funds the Rhodes scholarships at Oxford University, with Bill Clinton as a typical beneficiary.

Churchill's total faith in the USA has been shared by all subsequent British prime ministers. The Margaret Thatcher Center for Freedom at the Heritage Foundation in Washington, DC,[11] has as its goal the promotion of US/UK dominance worldwide, as does its British counterpart.[12] The ubiquitous activities of Tony Blair are in the same spirit, while enabling him to accumulate prodigious personal wealth.

Churchill's plan to spread the English language throughout the world is packaged as being disinterested, which all evidence of British and American colonisation worldwide contradicts. Plans for English to function as a 'world language' under UK and US leadership had already emerged in the 1930s, with funding from the Carnegie Foundation (Phillipson 2009, 112–5). They were intensively pursued from the 1950s (Phillipson 1992, 137–72). The promotion of English became a key dimension of the policies of the UK and the United States of America. The English language industry has expanded massively and is of major importance for the British economy. Its key constituents are publishers, university departments of applied linguistics and English teaching, language schools, BBC multi-media English teaching, and educational consultancies worldwide.

'The English language teaching sector directly earns nearly £1.3 billion for the UK in invisible exports and our other education related exports earn up to

£10 billion a year more', writes Lord Neil Kinnock in a Foreword to *English next* (Graddol 2006), a report commissioned by the British Council, 'the United Kingdom's international organisation for educational opportunities and cultural relations', a central conduit for British cultural and economic diplomacy. It is committed to expanding the learning and use of English worldwide. The teaching and examining of English are a major source of this parastatal's revenue. A country that is notoriously monolingual intriguingly markets itself as having an infinite supply of 'experts' who are capable of solving the language learning problems of educational systems in multilingual countries worldwide.

The British Council ought, according to a policy survey conducted by a pro-government NGO to be more energetic: the students it teaches and 'the 800,000 people who take exams administered by the Council every year . . . would make good targets for public diplomacy activity', as part of

> Diplomacy by Stealth: Working with others to achieve our goals. . . . The general lesson is . . . make sure it appears to be coming from a foreign government as little as possible. Increasingly . . . it must work through organisations and networks that are separate from, independent of, and even culturally suspicious toward government itself.
>
> (Leonard, Stead and Smewing 2002, 81)

Thus the activities of English teachers, some of whom may disapprove of their own government, can stealthily serve whatever the government sees as a national cause – local English for the global purposes of Britain, and indirectly for American empire within the emerging European empire, in which English linguistic capital is accumulating.

In Europe the use of English has expanded rapidly in recent decades. Its extensive visibility serves to make the learning of English more attractive than learning other languages. The UK has a vested interest in promoting this trend, and the increased influence that follows with it, as well as economic benefits. Other European countries are subsidising this process, to the detriment of the learning of languages such as French, German and Russian. A report prepared for a French language education policy body has calculated the effects on the economy of the UK and Ireland of the investment in the market for English learning (Grin 2005). Favouring English results in five types of quantifiable effect: a privileged market, communication savings, language learning savings, alternative human capital investment, and legitimacy and rhetorical effects. Grin concludes that a conservative estimate is that continental European countries are transferring to the UK and Ireland at least €10 billion per year, more probably about €16 to 17 billion a year. This figure substantially exceeds the British budget rebate of €5 billion annually.

English is at the summit of a linguistic hierarchy. English linguistic hegemony is reinforced structurally (material investment) and ideologically. The practice of learning English in ways that marginalise other languages and hinder or prevent their learning – through linguistic policies that amount to linguistic imperialism – was established in colonising contexts in the British Isles (the imposition of

English in Wales, Ireland, and Scotland) and the Americas (the destruction of local languages, gradual elimination of other immigrant languages). Linguistic capital was invested in the dominant language (time in schools, university departments, publications) and not in other languages. In colonial empires European languages were invariably the languages of power. The system has largely been maintained in former colonies, the term 'postcolonial' occluding a linguistic hegemony that has remained in place.

Empirical study of the factors determining language policies can elucidate in any given context whether linguistic imperialism is in force. With the learning and use of English expanding in continental Europe, the issue of whether or not it impacts negatively on other languages is of increasing concern. Perception of English as a threat to the continued vitality of national languages has been analysed in Germany (Oberreuter et al. 2012), the four Scandinavian countries, and Finland (Hultgren et al. in press), and in continental Europe (Harder 2009; Gregersen 2014; Hultgren & Jensen in press; Phillipson in press). A Nordic intergovernmental Declaration on Language Policy aims at maintaining the vitality of national languages while also ensuring that international languages, mainly English, are learned.[13] The position is dynamically evolving, and unpredictable: linguistic capital accumulation may be exclusively beneficial, through the addition of English to linguistic repertoires, with national languages remaining as the unifying language in all areas of life. By contrast if the linguistic capital is accumulated by processes of dispossession, as in classic colonialism, and a national language is no longer used in key societal functions – in higher education, government business, major commercial enterprises, the media – then there is evidence of linguistic imperialism.[14]

Language policy in the EU system

The management of multilingualism in EU affairs is demanding. Language policy is intrinsically complex because of the interlocking of languages with national interests – with politics, commerce, the media, education, and culture. Analysis of EU language policy often suffers from a failure to distinguish between the use of languages in different institutions, between different needs and practices in writing (sometimes via translation) and in speech (via interpretation), and different principles applying in work at an EU institution as opposed to communications from the EU to citizens or member state governments. The cost of the language services is often described as excessive, but according to the EU itself 'the cost of all language services in all EU institutions amounts to *less than 1% of the annual general budget of the EU*. Divided by the population of the EU, this comes to *around €2 per person per year*'[15] (emphasis in the original). This is a modest price to pay for the right of all EU citizens to speak or write in the language that they feel most comfortable in.

Language policy in the EU is politically sensitive. It touches existential national nerves, as frankly conceded by a German Head of Mission at the EU: there is 'no more emotional topic in the EU than the language issue.'[16] Or in the words of a

French Member of the European Parliament, 'the topic can be considered explosive in Europe.'[17] At the intergovernmental level therefore language policy has tended to be politically untouchable, apart from the endorsement of bland proclamations in favour of multilingualism and foreign language learning, and schemes to encourage states to act to achieve these goals. There is a lot of rhetoric advocating diversity, but English occupies more and more space, both in EU institutions and in the corporate world, the media, and many kinds of international activity.

The Maastricht Treaty authorised the EU to fund activities in the field of language and education, since which time many programmes ('actions') have been initiated, directly in school education, higher education and research, and indirectly in countless other ways. However, the rhetoric of multilingualism as a defining European characteristic ignores the fact that for the past two centuries, most European states have aimed at making their citizens monolingual. Principles of linguistic equality and multilingual diversity have thus only fragile foundations to build on in virtually all member states. Finland, with the equal status of Finnish and Swedish, is an exception to this rule, whereas the management of linguistic diversity in Belgium and Ireland is more problematic. Major change in the status of regional languages has taken place in Spain and Wales, whereas elsewhere minority languages remain marginal.

Language policy issues were ignored by the Convention on the Future of Europe (2002–2003), despite pleas from NGOs from several countries for language rights to be strengthened in a European constitutional treaty. There is a mismatch between the broad sweep of Article 22 of *The Charter of Fundamental Rights of the European Union* – 'The Union shall respect cultural, religious and linguistic diversity' (now incorporated in the Lisbon Treaty) – and everyday realities. The formulation creates no obligations on states nor any legally enforceable rights for individuals or groups. The most extreme form of declaring that the Charter's commitment is merely hot air was given voice by a senior French civil servant in a conference paper in the USA. Yves Marek, counsellor to Jacques Toubon[18] when Minister of Culture and Francophonie, claims blandly that 'in the field of linguistic rights, like in other fields of human rights, there is no right but only . . . politics'. This shows a national civil servant following the precepts of Machiavelli (*The Prince*, 1514), whereas the EU system attempts to ensure equilibrium between the interests of all member states and their languages, and requires states to make compromises. Marek also claimed that it is the French understanding of national languages that underlies how the EU handles multilingualism. This is a disturbing claim, since Marek also falsely states that in France there are no linguistic minorities, hence 'no discrimination between so-called minorities'.[19]

It is unusual for a government representative to be so openly cynical about how the EU should operate, and to reveal that he thinks that universal human rights principles can be ignored. These revelations exemplify why it is so difficult to form supranational language policies on the basis of a mutual understanding of what is at stake, and what criteria and principles should be in force.

EU institutions can be considered as in effect practising linguistic apartheid, even if Eurolaw is promulgated in all official languages. Minority languages have no place. Full interpretation between all EU languages is only provided for in certain contexts. The Commission's website typically has all texts in English, fewer in French, and even fewer in other languages. Documents for consideration in member states are often dispatched from Brussels in English, and possibly French, rather than in the relevant national language.[20] Draft texts are nearly all in English. These developments led the *Délégation nationale à la langue française et aux langues de France*, in its Annual Report of 2006 to conclude 'le français tend à devenir une langue de traduction et non plus de conception'. In other words a monolingual culture and mindset within EU institutions affects both content and form.

The websites of EU presidencies have been criticised by the European ombudsman for using an excessively limited choice of languages.[21] The rotating Presidency's websites are generally only in English, French and the relevant country's language. When some German speakers complained to the ombudsman about this inequality of access, he determined that presidencies were at fault in using such a small set of languages, and that the practice should be changed. A follow-up vote in the European Parliament on 20 November 2008 specifying that 'the information on the Council Presidency website should ideally be available in all official Community languages' was endorsed by an overwhelming majority. However, from the Swedish presidency in 2009 to the Greek presidency of 2014 the ombudsman's recommendations have been ignored. The EU system fails to live up to the ideals of 'respecting' multilingualism that the EU in principle is committed to.

These examples show that EU linguistic governance is undemocratic, whether administered by the Commission or the governments of member states. The language policies in place erect barriers between a technocratic elite and citizens of diverse linguistic backgrounds.

The government of Slovakia used the 'reflection' period after the rejection of the draft constitutional treaty by France, Ireland, and the Netherlands to convene a National Convention on the EU with broad participation. One topic that Slovakia chose to focus on was language policy. The deputy Prime Minister, Dušan Čaplovič, wrote on 26 March 2007 to the foreign ministers of all member and candidate states, and to EU commissioners, arguing for an intergovernmental study of language policy issues in the EU system to be established. A detailed case was made, including information that new member states were convinced that their languages were not being treated fairly. Translators and interpreters from 'small' states like Denmark and Sweden share this concern. The letter referred to a feasibility study concerning the creation of a European Agency for Linguistic Diversity and Language Learning of 25 May 2005 (see below). It cited several EU initiatives to strengthen multilingualism. It noted that despite the unanimous recommendations of the European Parliament's Committee on Culture and Education (A6–0372/2006, of 23 October 2006) aimed at strengthening language policy activity and structure, the plenary session of the Parliament rejected them. It concludes with the hope that despite the cultural and linguistic heterogeneity of EU member states, progress towards the goal of linguistic democracy can be achieved.

The Slovaks received encouraging replies from Austria, Croatia, the Czech Republic, Greece, Italy, the Netherlands, Portugal, and Spain, but no reply at all from other member states or the Commission. As my informant wryly comments, language problems are taboo, and 'non-reactions/replies are evidence of a poor level of current political culture and politeness of national and EU politicians.'[22]

The feasibility study referred to by the Slovaks is a rare instance of the EU commissioning a professional evaluation of some language policy issues, at the request of the European Parliament, and commissioned by the Directorate-General for Education and Culture. The task was given to a consultancy with wide experience of servicing EU institutions. Their mandate excluded attention to the internal workings of EU institutions and migrant languages. Their detailed, 118-page study of 18 May 2005, made available on the DG's website, drew on extensive consultation with a wide range of people concerned with many aspects of language policy. It analyses needs, conditions, and modalities, and confirms that a wealth of professional expertise exists that decision-makers ought to draw on. It makes a strong case for either a Linguistic Agency, like other high-prestige EU agencies (dealing, for instance, with the environment in Copenhagen and racism in Vienna), or alternatively a network of Language Diversity Centres to strengthen policy formation and implementation, particularly for regional minority languages. The study reveals a widespread perception that there is a serious need for policy advice and information for national and EU decision-makers. This was overwhelmingly the case in new member states, whereas the established ones considered such functions 'not useful'. There was also near unanimity in responses in rejecting English as a sole *lingua franca*. The study concludes that 'A no-action scenario would seriously undermine the credibility of the EU in this field.'

In fact the Linguistic Agency proposal was rejected unilaterally by the Commission. It is impossible to know on what grounds, but if an agency had been established, there would necessarily have been a reduction of the freedom of manoeuvre of the Commission and its ability to determine language policy overtly in 'actions', and covertly through *laissez faire*.

There have been funds for language research, two projects on multilingualism under Framework Programme 6,[23] and one completed project under Framework Programme 7.[24] The DG for Education and Culture has coordinated various schemes for strengthening language learning. Some strengthen a wide range of European languages; many strengthen English. Relatively speaking the funds involved are small as compared with what national governments spend on education.

Whatever credibility the EU might have gained by nominating a Commissioner for Multilingualism, Leonard Orban from Romania, 2007–2010, was seriously undermined by no-action on an Academy, reduced action on minority languages, and a general failure to influence language policy decisions at the national or supranational levels. Most of the Commissioner's speeches consisted of platitudinous generalities about support for diversity and language learning, and it is probably in the nature of his role that they have to be. Language issues were downgraded in 2010 by being returned to the DG for Education and Culture. It is also a major problem that there is virtually no expertise in the Commission in fields such as multilingualism, bilingual education, and language policy. As in the civil service of member states, Eurocrats are as mobile as politicians, and as soon as experience may have been attained, either they move elsewhere in the system, or a short-term contract ends their employment.

The rhetoric of strengthening linguistic diversity and multilingualism has been totally ignored in the management of the Bologna process. Its objectives as formulated in 1999 were: 'within the framework of our institutional competences and taking full respect of the diversity of cultures, languages, national education systems and of University autonomy – to consolidate a European Higher Education Area at the latest by 2010'. The process is a Council of Europe initiative, though currently it is the European Commission that is the principal driving force behind it, with universities and national ministries of higher education more or less committed to it. It brings together the Ministers for Education of 47 European countries. The European Commission funds studies that figure prominently at the bi-annual meeting of Ministers. The communiqués from these report on practicalities, and the successes and failures of the synchronization of a uniform cycle of higher education degrees, but they never refer to language policy. Implicitly this means that 'internationalisation' equates with 'English-medium higher education', although this is in conflict with the declared goals of the process. (Phillipson 2006, Meyer 2011). The European higher education 'area' is in effect a market.

This is not surprising because this European process is a direct result of education being increasingly considered a service that can be traded, under the aegis of the World Trade Organisation, and more specifically of the General Agreement on Trade in Services. Member states have been legally committed to this 'liberalization' process since 1995, but there is a fundamental unresolved tension between education as a human right, a public good, and trading in educational services. The pressures to reduce what are seen as national trading barriers are intense. Higher education is more vulnerable to international commercialisation than is basic education, though this is also increasingly seen as a market rather than a public service. It used to be assumed that EU law on the common market and the free movement of services did not apply to education or health care, but cases determined by the European Court of Justice on higher education and other social services such as residential care have overturned this principle (Hervey 2014a, 355). National higher education is now a 'free' market, part of the global export trade of universities, with universities in English-speaking countries in the lead. They export the same content as back home, and the same language, expanding the empire of English.

A former German Minister of culture, Hans Joachim Meyer, is convinced that the Bologna process builds on fundamental ignorance of the strengths and weaknesses of universities in the USA and the UK, and is a crude attempt to americanise European universities. He is appalled that German academia has distanced itself from its own rich traditions and is in effect substituting English for German as the medium of instruction and publication: 'Contrary to the wording affirmed in the Bologna Declaration, the reform of higher education serves the purpose of replacing the linguistic and cultural diversity of Europe by an English linguistic monopoly'[25] (Meyer 2011, 61). If this is in fact happening, and this is an empirical question that cannot be firmly answered at present, it is very clear evidence of the European empire being a very junior partner in American empire.

The website of the Bologna process is exclusively in English.[26] It is no surprise that when international interest in the Bologna process is referred to on this website, the countries concerned are Australia, Canada, New Zealand and the United States, all of whom are competitors with Europe in attracting fee-paying foreign students – and offer English-medium instruction. The website for the European Research Area, an extension from the Bologna process, is in English, French, and German,[27] though its Progress report for 2013 is only in English. The website is surprisingly frank in equating the research 'area' with a market: 'The 2014 ERA survey will be crucial for identifying areas where progress in the implementation of actions required to complete a single market for researchers, knowledge and technology has been made'.

Many continental European countries have also moved into English-medium degrees, mainly to attract foreign students, but the statistics on this activity are unreliable. Data from Germany, as reported by Sabine Kunst, Minister of Science, Research and Culture in Brandenburg, and President of the Deutscher Akademischer Austauschdienst, show that the number of English-medium degrees in Germany tends to be grossly inflated: 'The actual number of English-medium degrees represents no more that 4% of the totality of 15,134 degrees currently offered in higher education – at the Bachelor level we are even down to just under 1%' (Kunst 2012, 73). Proficiency in English is increasingly needed in many scholarly fields in Germany,[28] but that is a different issue.

The same failure to tackle the language policy issue applies to evaluations of the Erasmus programme. The report *The Impact of Erasmus on European Higher Education: Quality, Openness and Internationalisation* (IP/09/301, Brussels, 20 February 2009) fails to refer to languages. When the research institution responsible for the study was asked to explain this, the reply stated (personal communication): 'Unfortunately neither the research team nor the commissioner (DG EAC) did put language education and language of instruction on the strategic agenda of our study.' This is another symptom of the myopia of Eurocrats and the experts that they commission studies from. There is a great deal of rhetoric about quality and internationalisation – and language is irrelevant, provided English is used!

The Commission has global ambitions for the Bologna process. EU Commissioner Jan Figel stated on 10 May 2007:

> Bologna reforms are important but Europe should now go beyond them, as universities should also modernise the content of their curricula, create virtual campuses and reform their governance. They should also professionalize their management, diversify their funding and open up to new types of learners, businesses and society at large, in Europe and beyond. [. . .] The Commission supports the global strategy in concrete terms through its policies and programmes.

In other words, universities should follow a neoliberal agenda, should be run like businesses, in partnership with industry, and privatise. This is academic and linguistic McDonaldisation, the creation of global uniformity and predictability, marketed with the fashionable buzzwords, 'accountability, employability, degree certification'.

While EU policies are influential, member states and their institutions share responsibility for the neglect of language policy issues. The website of the European University Association[29] fails to mention language policy in connection with its priorities, the most important of which is 'building the European Higher Education Area through the Bologna process.' No mention is made of European doctorates (Doctor Europaeus/ Europaea). These originated from an initiative in 1991 of the former Confederation of European Union Rectors' Conferences. The doctoral schemes exist in cross-national partnerships in a number of natural and social science fields. The key criteria for obtaining such a doctorate include the use of minimally two languages, research activity in two countries, and assessment by professors from minimally two countries.[30]

A further example of how a hegemonic status for English is being established, strengthening its position both within the Commission and in member states, can be seen in the way the DG for Research operates. Over the past six years I have been involved as an expert assessing applications for research funding in the language policy area and reports of the progress of EU funded research. The procedures in Brussels and the research itself provide evidence of the complexity of European integration, which is seldom optimally effective.

In the 'Guide for applicants' for funding from the Seventh Framework Programme there is the following advice: 'Proposals may be prepared in any official language of the European Union. If your proposal is not in English, a translation of the full proposal would be of assistance to the experts'[31], i.e. to those assessing the quality of the proposal for funding. The rhetoric of all EU languages being valid is formally acknowledged, but it is clear that applications have to be written in English. Applicants for whom English is not the primary professional language – many in southern and eastern Europe and elsewhere – are at a significant structural disadvantage when the application has to be in English. The expert evaluators are drawn from all EU countries, for many of whom English is not the primary working language, even if they are professional researchers. Even if they can 'manage' in English, their facility in being able to express themselves optimally in English may be limited, both in speech and when formulating the written response in English that all applicants are entitled to, when every word counts. This example of how the EU conducts its affairs reveals clearly that efficiency and linguistic equality are seriously constrained. This discrimination on grounds of language is in conflict with the EU's commitment to 'respecting' language diversity. While there is some strength in the argument that this way of conducting affairs is necessary for pragmatic or practical reasons, it ignores the reality of those with high-level proficiency in English being favoured.

These examples show how the hegemony of English is being consolidated, through processes of linguistic imperialism and McDonaldisation. Several of the examples reported on confirm a pattern of European Commission 'authoritarian executive managerialism', with policies overriding informed scientific input[32] and recommendations by the ombudsman or European parliament. Laissez faire language policies, and the assumption that globalization and European unification require proficiency in English, are symptomatic of the way the global English project has been internalised. The EU is an eager handmaiden facilitating the expansion of English and leaving it up to member states to take responsibility for other languages if they choose to. This is a re-run of what Tacitus described as taking place with Roman interests and Latin 2000 years ago, and which theorists of colonial liberation refer to as a colonised consciousness. Mental colonisation, uncritically embracing the language of the imperial power, facilitates empire-building and maintenance. Monolingualism at the highest administrative level is a characteristic of all empires, with other languages tolerated, marginalised, or obliterated. Native speakers of the dominant language play a key role in legitimating this process, examples of which are provided in the concluding section.

Lingua franca discourse

> Some people imagine that English is likely to become the lingua franca of India. That seems to me a fantastic conception, except in respect of a handful of upper-class intelligentsia. It has no relation to the problem of mass education and culture (. . .) even the most rabid of our nationalists hardly realize how much they are cribbed and confined by the British outlook in relation to India.
>
> *Jawaharlal Nehru*, 1936[33]

Is it possible that the future Prime Minister of India's worry[34] can bear comparison with what we are currently experiencing in Europe? Could the European upper echelon of decision-makers (I hesitate to refer to them as an intelligentsia) be so cribbed (confined to a small space) and confined by their admiration for things American that incorporation into a 21st century American empire is already well established? American ambitions have for centuries been explicitly imperial: 'The whole world should adopt the American system. The American system can survive in America only if it becomes a world system' (President Harry Truman 1947, cited in Pieterse 2004, 131). Any such world system or empire will have English as the dominant language, to the dismay of French presidents and to many European intellectuals as well as nationalists. How could adoption of English as an imperial European language be justified or legitimated?

English is often described as a lingua franca. This generally seems to imply that the language is a neutral instrument for 'international' communication between speakers who do not share a mother tongue. This understanding of the term may mislead one into believing that lingua franca English is disconnected from the many purposes it serves in key societal domains. English might be more accurately related to distinct contexts of use. It can and does function as a pre-eminent international *lingua economica* (in business and advertising, the main language of corporate neoliberalism), a *lingua emotiva* (the imaginary of Hollywood, popular music, consumerism and hedonism), a *lingua academica* (in research publications, at international conferences, and as a medium for content learning in higher education), and a *lingua cultura* (rooted in the literary texts of English-speaking nations that school foreign language education traditionally aims at, and integrates with language learning as one element of general education). English is a major *lingua bellica* in NATO, which is not only active in Europe but worldwide (Nazemroaya 2012). Also, English has become a major *lingua bellica* worldwide as the U.S. has 350 bases and 800 military facilities in 130 countries (Pieterse 2004, 58). Moreover, US armed forces are [now] involved in 49 out of 54 African states, along with the former colonial powers of France and Britain, in what's becoming a new carve-up of the continent' (Milne 2014, 20). English is also a major *lingua politica* in international organizations such as the United Nations and the European Union. The worldwide presence of English as a *lingua Americana* is due to the massive economic, cultural and military impact of the USA, English functioning in each of the categories adumbrated here.

In the EU system, English, French and German are described as procedural languages for select purposes in the Commission. This term is used because these languages, now mainly English, serve as a *lingua executiva* for very specific functions in EU administration, and in political negotiations for reaching consensus on policies. Effectiveness in such interaction requires an extremely high level of linguistic proficiency.

There is an ironic historical continuity in the use of a term lingua franca to refer to contemporary English since it was first used to describe the language of Christian crusaders from western Europe in the Middle Ages (1095–1300), who travelled to drive out Islam from Jerusalem and Palestine. The crusaders were understood as speaking lingua franca, the term deriving from the Arabic *lisan alfiranj*,[35] when crusading Europeans of various origins were seen by Arabs as Franks. These were a tribe from Germany who settled in France, hence the name of the country France. The continent that bears the name Europe now was then generally referred to as Christendom.

The term lingua franca became established in later centuries in the eastern Mediterranean to describe the simplified language that was used between people from different linguistic backgrounds for commercial trading purposes. It was a restricted form of language, mixing elements from several European languages that had evolved from Latin (French, Italian, Catalan), Greek, and Arabic. A lingua franca in this sense of the term is limited, shrunken, incomplete language. It is comparable to pidgin languages used for commercial transactions in other regions of the world. There is therefore a logical inconsistency in applying it to a rich national language that also has international functions.

Among the many orchestrating a rhetoric that uncritically promotes global English, Churchill's descendants, are uninformed and uncritical native speakers. Advocacy of global English is at its most aggressive when the Director of the British Council in Germany claims that 'English should be the sole official language of the European Union'[36]. Glyn Morgan (2005), a Welshman now in the

USA, in *The Idea of a European Super-State. Public Justification and European Integration*, writes that

> The spread of English as the European lingua franca, the emergence of a common transnational youth culture, the convergence of business practices, and – most important of all – widespread adoption of European constitutional practices (and perhaps even a Constitution) can be seen as steps along the road to a European nation-state.

He may be right about such steps, but he seems unaware that his possible scenario builds on biased presuppositions:

- it assumes that English is a neutral lingua franca, serving all equally well, whereas high-level proficiency in English is rare in much of Europe, and in any case, many languages serve lingua franca purposes in Europe,
- it fails to reveal that 'a common transnational youth culture' is essentially American, promoting a Hollywood consumerist ideology,
- it ignores the fact that 'business practices' derive from the US corporate world, and the conceptual universe it embodies, and that is taught at business schools, in asymmetrical symbiosis with national traditions,
- EU constitutional practices and legislation have hybrid origins, and equal force in 24 languages, so that a possible European nation-state could never be monolingual.

Morgan exemplifies the tendency of many native speakers of English to consider Anglo-American linguistic norms and practices as universally valid and archetypically human (Wierzbicka 2006, 11 ff.). I would add that he also takes Americanisation as a universal norm.

The Belgian political scientist Philippe van Parijs states in an EU publication: 'English will gradually replace multilingualism not only in the huge posters that hang from the Berlaymont building, but also in highly sensitive contexts such as directly-applicable legislation or plenary session interventions by members of the European Parliament' (European Commission 2010, 90). This was in a study of lingua franca, written by staff of the European Commission, and published by it anonymously, which gives it a semblance of representing the institution's position on the role of English. (On fallacies in a book by van Parijs that argues for English becoming universal, see Phillipson 2012b.) Scholars who focus exclusively on the instrumental use of a language ignore its connection to power, class, and the interests behind use of the language. By advocating English for everyone, their work unintentionally 'becomes a crucial element of an international business class structure. It facilitates the growth and spread of multinational corporations and trade' (Ives 2006, 136–7)[37]. This of course is a primary goal of the EU. This strengthens the global 1%, the transnational capitalist class (Phillips, Huff, and Higdon 2014).

The EU lingua franca study fits squarely into the mould of biased special pleading for English. It covers some historical and contemporary ground, but selectively, and without ever clarifying in what way the term 'lingua franca' is understood or used in EU contexts. The study fails to address the issue of the actual use made of English in the EU system, which was a prime goal of the study[38]. It assumes English functions in a neutral egalitarian way, and while noting that there can be an element of hierarchy involved, it ignores the political and economic factors that account for the way English has expanded worldwide and in continental Europe. The study includes transcripts of interviews with three individuals, without their status or role being described. Two of those interviewed are passionately committed to promoting a greater use of English. It is disturbing that an institution that works to maintain multilingualism can publish such an unscholarly text, one that simply equates lingua franca with English.

Labelling English as a lingua franca, if this is understood as a culturally neutral medium that puts everyone on an equal footing, is simply incorrect. It is a pernicious term if the communicative interaction in question relates to what is a first language for some, but for others a foreign language. It is a false term for a language that is taught as a subject in general education, which presupposes study of the cultural contexts in which the language has evolved and is used.

It can also be considered an invalid term when used to describe English as a *lingua academica*, a language of scientific activity. A German scholar considers that

> the English used as an international scientific language is not a lingua franca, a non-language. English is a completely normal language with its specific monolingual semantics, like all other languages. [. . .] It is the bearer, like all other natural languages, of a particular vision of the world. As such it is not universal and purely objective, which is what real lingua francas were.
>
> (Trabant 2012, 108; see also Wierzbicka 2014)

Scientific activity does not merely refer to objectively verifiable objects. Scholars from the 'English-speaking world' draw on the entire English-using conceptual universe. English therefore cannot be universally valid or correspond to general human traits. Its expansion is imperialist:

> In as much as these monolingual, specific textual worlds are replacing and suppressing other scientific languages, a particular semantic world is being expanded to the entire world. They are therefore not universal but imperial and colonial, in the same way as political empires destroy and degrade other particular (scholarly) cultures. A gigantic destruction of knowledge has taken hold.
>
> (Trabant 2012, 108)

A related point is made by another German scholar. Scientific communication in English is not neutral, not a lingua franca, when native speakers of English act as gatekeepers in the field of publications, since stylistic quality differs in

German, Chinese, Polish etc. (Fiedler 2011). Scientific productivity benefits from different models of thinking in different languages: (ibid: 5–6). It is common for the French to argue on similar lines, rejecting '*la pensée unique*', when insisting that English should not replace other languages.

Loose reference to English as a lingua franca runs the risk of political disconnection and obfuscation. It can obscure the reality of particular interests being promoted through an increased use of English. It dovetails with the interest of the British and Americans in their language being consolidated as the current language of power and influence. Flagging English as 'the world's lingua franca', or 'the lingua franca of the European Union' represents banal linguicism. Such claims are eminently falsifiable, but the claims create the impression that Churchill's vision of English being used worldwide is coming to life, and strengthening American and British influence.

In conclusion

It is a fundamental error to take language policy for granted, as though market forces and the use of particular languages do not have structural and ideological causes and consequences. Seeing English as being neutral, as a *lingua nullius*, is as deluded as the colonising concept *terra nullius*, which it has largely come to replace in processes of colonisation of the mind. It is a truism that any language can serve good or evil purposes, to consolidate or combat imperialism. Users of English as a primary language, whether native speakers of English (many of whom are monolingual) or people for whom English has become an important professional language, need to be alert to the implications of language policy and its interlocking with social injustice.

There are historical reasons for English as the language of people in the dominant English-speaking countries becoming a key medium of international finance and corporate activity that now integrates owners of capital worldwide. The institutions that service this system, including the EU, are not promoting British, American, or EU empire in the traditional sense but rather a neo-imperial system which strengthens the hold of the transnational capital class. The current crises in the economies of many EU member states indicate that the system is fundamentally dysfunctional for the government of these states and for individuals who do not hold and cannot accumulate capital, one dimension of which is linguistic capital.

'Global English' is a project rather than a reality. The discourse of global English or of English as a unifying language in Europe serves to substantiate processes of language hierarchisation. It can serve to displace and dispossess speakers of other languages. Global English and European integration are projects that there are powerful Anglo-American and corporate forces behind, forces that now occupy space in EU institutions and have uncritical advocates in academia. Many of the activities of the EU that aim at strengthening a common market dovetail with the marketisation of English as universally relevant, despite its origins and the reality that the increased use of English serves some interests better than others. English can be seen as a neo-imperial language that strengthens the capital interests that thrive worldwide.

Hardt and Negri's (2000, 32–33) controversial book on empire sees power in de-territorialised networks, and elucidates why it has been so important for the corporate world to dominate not only the media but also education, which is increasingly run to service the economy, and produce consumers rather than critical citizens. English contributes to the imperial production of subjectivities, through communicative networks, creating a synergy that integrates structural and ideological elements in the new world 'order'. Among the key networks are the language policies administered in the EU system of 'authoritarian executive managerialism'. These privilege English and dovetail with the role of English in many international organisations. This symbolic violence is invariably contested but is widely, uncritically internalised, although 'friends and enemies' may refuse to accept dominance. It is therefore perfectly possible that the global linguistic map may change violently in the coming decades.

In order to assess whether English can be considered a neo-imperial language, what is needed is to identify the purposes to which English is being put in particular contexts, and by whom. Is English serving the interests of the global 1% domestically and internationally, and neglecting the issue of 'mass education and culture', as Nehru feared? Capitalist neoliberalism is intensifying the gap between haves and have-nots in the USA, the UK, and in their former colonies – countries where English is the dominant language – and English has an increasing presence in decision-making in continental Europe. The causal factors facilitating this development are identifiable, the pull and push variables (resources, ideologies) that are invariably involved in linguistic imperialism.

I have elaborated a theoretical foundation for analysing English as a neo-imperial language at greater length elsewhere (Phillipson 2009, 123–38). I build on Harvey's analysis of capitalist imperialism as shifting from a territorially-derived state and empire towards 'imperialism as a diffuse political-economic process in space and time in which command over and use of capital takes primacy' (Harvey 2005, 26), and the importance of the American military machine for empire. One can analyse what a state, or combination of states, or an institution such as a corporation or a university, does to achieve its goals, including the way it manages linguistic capital. One can track practices of 'production, trade, commerce, capital flows, money transfers, labour migration, technology transfer, currency speculation, flows of information, cultural impulses, and the like' (ibid.) and the role played by English and other languages in facilitating and constituting these interactions.

The evidence presented in this article documents how English is promoted as a neo-imperial language, with linguistic capital accumulation and dispossession as a major constituent of contemporary empire. Those in the global 1% are either proficient in English or able to fund services that function in English and which enable them to augment personal and corporate financial capital accumulation. The European Union is a key player in this business, not an autonomous empire but integrated into the global networks of corporate and banking interests in the

USA and Europe, not least in the UK (the City of London, with its links to Hong Kong and Singapore as well as Frankfurt) and the tax havens that deprive states of the funding necessary for managing societies equitably. There is an intensification of military activities by the USA, NATO, and the EU (notably the UK and France, but other 'willing' states like Denmark). There are clear signs of military overreach, especially in the Middle East and Afghanistan. There is massive evidence of corruption in political systems, and in the leading banks. These trends correlate with greater use of English.

Political disaffection, disillusionment and apathy are widespread in a large proportion of citizens on both sides of the Atlantic. This signifies more than a mere democratic deficit. Empires that rely increasingly on military force, and on physical and electronic control of their citizens, are fundamentally repressive and unstable.

> An empire has a unified center, a state in control of its subjects and private enterprises, a productive capacity that leads the societies within its imperial reach, an historical civilization of architecture, art, and culture, and most of all enduring public infrastructures and great works across its domains of command.
>
> (McMurtry 2014, 254)

This does not match up with American empire in any narrow political sense, nor with the EU with its complex mix of sovereignty at the national and supranational levels, and the interlocking of politics with corporate and military interests. On the other hand the EU now does have a relatively 'unified centre', where a great deal of power is concentrated in the Council, Commission, and ECJ. English plays a significant role here, as it does in the corporate world, and, of course, in US and UK government.

In Europe the parameters determining hierarchies of language nationally and supra-nationally are multiple and mobile, but the presence of English cannot be ignored. There is an unresolved tension between the maintenance of the autonomy of national languages and the hegemonic consolidation of English in the supranational EU institutions and potentially within each member state. How the linguistic mosaic of Europe will evolve in the coming decades is unpredictable, but if cultural and linguistic diversity are to be maintained, there is manifestly a need for explicit language policy formation and implementation. This should be grounded on ethical principles that value diversity and that contribute to groups and individuals enjoying linguistic human rights.

Notes

1 In House of Commons, 24 August 1941.

2 When receiving an honorary degree at Harvard University, 6 September 1943. www.winstonchurchill.org/learn/speeches/speeches-of-winston-churchill/118-the-price-of-greatness.

3 'For the Lord our God Most High/He hath made the deep as dry,/He hath smote for us a pathway/to the ends of all the earth!' (Kipling 1913, p. 1, first published 1896). On Kipling's psychology see Nandy (1983).
4 Cited in Holroyd (1997, 660).
5 Extensive data on translations is compiled by UNESCO and International PEN.
6 Cited in Gopal (1980, 507).
7 See 'Linguistic diversity and multilingualism in the European Union', Council Conclusions 1995, approved by member states' foreign ministers, cited in Phillipson 2003, 193–4.
8 I am indebted to Hervey (2014b) for points in this and the following paragraph.
9 The Council of Europe was acting in a similar spirit in its Democracy through Law activities; see Skutnabb-Kangas and Phillipson (1994, 107).
10 See endnote 2.
11 www.thatchercenter.org
12 www.margaretthatcher.org
13 A declaration on a Nordic language policy: www.norden.org
14 The term in use in Nordic political discourse about consequences of the increased use of English is 'domain loss', but this is a vague concept that conceals agency. Agents of linguistic capital accumulation and dispossession need to be identified and can be.
15 http://ec.europa.eu/dgs/translation/faq/index_en.htm, accessed 3 May 2014.
16 'Es gibt in der EU kein emotionaleres Thema als Sprachen.' Wilhelm Schönfelder, cited in *Süddeutsche Zeitung*, 1 April 2005.
17 'Un sujet qui peut être qualifié d'explosif en Europe'. Pierre Lequiller, Président, réunion ouverte à l'ensemble des membres français du Parlement Européen, le 11 juin 2003, pour débattre le *Rapport sur la diversité linguistique au sein de l'Union européenne*, préparé par Michel Herbillon, auprès de la Délégation pour l'Union Européenne.
18 Toubon later became Minister of Justice, so that the name given to the legislation in France aimed at stemming the tide of the invasion of English in France in 1994 is popularly known as the *Loi Toubon*.
19 For analysis, see Phillipson (2003, 45–7).
20 There is a shortage of empirical documentation of this reality. The issue is explored in articles in Berthoud et al. (2013).
21 See the European Ombudsman's press release No. 6/2006, and Draft Recommendation to the Council of the EU in complaint 1487/2005,GG-
22 I am grateful to Josef Reinvart of the Slovak Ministry of Foreign Affairs, personal communication, 8 November 2007, for the information reported here.
23 LINEE produced banal results. DYLAN achieved more; see Berthoud et al. (2013), but also demonstrated the limitations of research collaboration across national borders, research traditions, and incompatible subprojects.
24 See www.eldia-project.org. Others are in a start-up phase.
25 Entgegen dem Wortlaut der Bologna-Erklärung dient also die Studienreform dem Ziel, die dort beschworene sprachliche und kulturelle Vielfalt Europas durch ein englisches Sprachmonopol zu ersetzen (Meyer 2011, 61).
26 www.ehea.info
27 http://ec.europa.eu/research/era/index_en.htm
28 The German Rectors' Conference passed a resolution on *Language policy at German universities* at its 11th General Meeting of 22 November 2011. This diagnoses challenges and makes recommendations for promoting 'multilingualism and ensuring that German remains a language of science and scholarship'; in English, at www.hrk.de.
29 www.eua.be/Home.aspx
30 For an example, see www.campus.manchester.ac.uk/medialibrary/researchoffice/graduate education/g-eurodoc.pdf
31 http://cordis.europa.eu

32 The EU's Chief Scientific Advisor, Ann Glover, stated that her experience is that facts are subordinated to the EU's political agenda, www.euractiv.com/(27 May 2014). Her own advice to the Commission president is not made public.
33 Cited in Gopal (1980, 525).
34 Whatever Nehru may have wished, the policies he implemented served to strengthen the hold of English in India.
35 For a history of the term 'lingua franca', and some examples of different uses of the term, see Phillipson (2009, 165–7).
36 Cited in *Frankfurter Allgemeine Zeitung*, 26 February 2002.
37 For a related criticism of the work of Abram de Swaan, see Phillipson (2009, 251–7).
38 The unscholarly crudity of the study can be seen in its 'conclusion', which fails to sum up ideas presented earlier and introduces completely new ones.

References

Bartelson, Jens. 2009. *Visions of world community*. Cambridge: Cambridge University Press.

Berthoud, Anne-Claude, François Grin and Georges Lüdi, eds. 2013. *Exploring the dynamics of multilingualism: The DYLAN project*. Amsterdam: John Benjamins.

Bondebjerg, Ib. 2003. Culture, media and globalization. In *Humanities – Essential research for Europe* 71–88. Copenhagen: Danish Research Council for the Humanities.

Bourdieu, Pierre. 2001. *Contre-feux 2. Pour un mouvement social européen*. Paris: Raisons d'agir.

Churchill, Ward. 1997. *A little matter of genocide: Holocaust and denial in the Americas 1492 to the present*. San Francisco: City Lights Books.

Coupland, Nikolas, ed. 2010. *The handbook of language and globalization*. Malden, MA: Wiley-Blackwell.

Darwin, John. 2009. *The empire project: The rise and fall of the British world-system 1830–1970*. Cambridge: Cambridge University Press.

De Búrca, Gráinne, Claire Kilpatrick and Joanne Scott, eds. 2014. *Critical legal perspectives on global governance*. Oxford: Hart.

Dimova, Slobodanka, Anna Kristina Hultgren and Christian Jensen. In press. *English-medium instruction in higher education in Europe*. Berlin: Mouton de Gruyter.

Drèze, Jean and Amartya Sen. 2014. *An uncertain glory. India and its contradictions*. London: Penguin.

Errington, Joseph. 2008. *Linguistics in a colonial world: A story of language, meaning, and power*. Malden, MA: Blackwell.

European Commission 2010. *Lingua franca: Chimera or reality?* Brussels: DG Translation.

Fiedler, Sabine, 2011. Scientific communication in a lingua franca. Unpublished paper presented at the Internacia Ligo de Esperantistaj Instruistoj conference, Copenhagen, 22–23 July 2011.

Gopal, Sarvepalli, ed. 1980. *Jawaharlal Nehru: An anthology*. Delhi: Oxford University Press.

Graddol, David. 2006. *English next*. London: British Council.

Gregersen, Frans (ed.). 2014. *Hvor parallelt. Om parallelspråkighet på Nordens universiteter*. København: Nordisk Ministerråd (TemaNord: 535; www.norden.org).

Grin, François. 2005. L'enseignement des langues étrangères comme politique publique. Rapport au Haut Conseil de l'évaluation de l'école, Paris, n° 19.

Hamelink, Cees. 1994. *Trends in world communication: on disempowerment and self-empowerment*. Penang: Southbound and Third World Network.

Harder, Peter, ed. 2009. *English in Denmark: Language policy, internationalization and university teaching*. Copenhagen: Museum Tusculanum Press.
Hardt, Michael and Antonio Negri. 2000. *Empire*. Cambridge, MA: Harvard University Press.
Harvey, David. 2005 [2003]. *The new imperialism*. Oxford: Oxford University Press.
Hervey, Tamara. 2014a. Re-judging social rights in the EU. In de Búrca, Kilpatrick and Scott, 345–368.
Hervey, Tamara. 2014b. *Judicial methods in EU law.* Lecture at the Law Faculty, University of Lund, Sweden, 20 March 2014.
Hixson, Walter L. 2008. *The myth of American diplomacy. National identity and U.S. foreign policy*. New Haven: Yale University Press.
Holm, Erik. 2001. *The European anarchy. Europe's hard road into high politics*. Copenhagen: Copenhagen Business School Press.
Holroyd, Michael. 1997. *Bernard Shaw: The one-volume definitive edition.* London: Chatto and Windus.
Howe, Stephen. 2002. *Empire. A very short introduction.* Oxford: Oxford University Press.
Hultgren, Anna Kristina and Jacob Thøgersen, eds. In press. *Language policy in the Nordic countries, ideology and practice*. Amsterdam: John Benjamins.
Ives, Peter. 2006. 'Global English': linguistic imperialism or practical lingua franca? *Studies in Language & Capitalism* 1: 121–141.
Joerges, Christian and Maria Weimer. 2014. A crisis of executive managerialism in the EU: No alternative? In Gráinne De Búrca, Claire Kilpatrick, and Joanne Scott (eds.), 295–322. *Critical legal perspectives on global governance*. Oxford: Hart.
Kipling, Rudyard. 1913. (1896). *The seven seas*. London: Methuen.
Kjær, Anne Lise and Silvia Adamo, eds. 2011. *Linguistic diversity and European democracy*. Farnham: Ashgate.
Kunst, Sabine. 2012. Podiumsgespräch 'Bildings- und wissenschaftspolitische Aspekte'. In Oberreuter *et al.*, eds., 73–75.
Leonard, Mark, Catherine Stead and Conrad Smewing. 2002. *Public diplomacy*. London: Foreign Policy Centre, http://fpc.org.uk/fsblob/35.pdf
Locke, John. 1988 (1690). *Two treatises of government.* Cambridge: Cambridge University Press.
Martin, Isabel Pefianco. 2002. Canon and pedagogy: The role of American colonial education in defining standards for Philippine literature. In *Englishes in Asia: Communication, identity, power & education*, ed. Andy Kirkpatrick, 201–211. Melbourne: Language Australia.
McMurtry, John. 2014. The Ukraine crisis: decoding its deep structural meaning. In *Flashpoint in Ukraine: How the US drive for hegemony risks World War III*, ed. Stephen Lendman, 244–261. Atlanta, GA: Clarity Press.
Meyer, Hans Joachim. 2011. Bologna eller Harvard? Realität und Ideologie bei der deutschen Studienreform. *Zeitschrift für Politik*, Sonderband 4: 51–62.
Milne, Seamus. 2014. Terror is the fruit of NATO's war with Libya. *The Guardian Weekly* 30.05.2014, 20.
Mohanty, Ajit. 2006. Multilingualism and predicaments of education in India. In *Imagining multilingual schools: Languages in education and globalization*, ed. Ofelia García, Tove Skutnabb-Kangas and María E. Torres-Guzmán, 262–83. Clevedon: Multilingual Matters.
Monbiot, George. 2000. *Captive state: The corporate takeover of Britain.* London: Macmillan.

Morgan, Glyn. 2005. *The idea of a European super-state: Public justification and European integration*. Princeton, NJ: Princeton University Press.

Nandy, Ashis. 1983. *The intimate enemy. Loss and recovery of self under colonialism*. New Delhi: Oxford University Press.

Nazemroaya, Mahdi Darius. 2012. *The globalization of NATO*. Atlanta, GA: Clarity Press.

Neergaard, Ulla and Ruth Nielsen, eds. 2013. *European legal method – Towards a new European legal realism?* Copenhagen: DJØF.

Ngũgĩ wa Thiong'o. 2010. *Dreams in a time of war. A childhood memoir*. London: Harvill Secker.

Oberreuter, Heinrich, Wilhelm Krull, Hans Joachim Meyer und Konrad Ehlich, hg. 2012. *Deutsch in der Wissenschaft. Ein politischer und wissenschaftlicher Diskurs*. München: Olzog Verlag.

Petras, James 2014. *The politics of empire: The US, Israel and the Middle East*. Atlanta, GA: Clarity Press.

Phillips, Peter, Mickey Huff and Nolan Higdon. 2014. Ukraine: another step in capitalism's global dominance strategies and power inside the transnational global corporate class and US-NATO global empire. In *Flashpoint in Ukraine. How the US drive for hegemony risks World War III*, ed. Stephen Lendman, 54–63. Atlanta, GA: Clarity Press.

Phillipson, Robert. 1992. *Linguistic imperialism*. Oxford: Oxford University Press.

Phillipson, Robert. 2003. *English-only Europe? Challenging language policy*. London: Routledge.

Phillipson, Robert. 2006. English, a cuckoo in the European higher education nest of languages? *European Journal of English Studies* 10(1): 13–32.

Phillipson, Robert. 2009. *Linguistic imperialism continued*. New York: Routledge.

Phillipson, Robert. 2012a. One area, one market, one language: Linguistic McDonaldisation and EU rhetoric. In *Sprache(n) als europäisches Kulturgut* (Languages as European cultural asset), ed. Claudia Schmidt-Hahn, 115–126. Innsbruck: Studienverlag.

Phillipson, Robert. 2012b. Languages, genocide, and justice in the European integration process. Review article on "Indigenous Children's Education as Linguistic Genocide and a Crime against Humanity? A Global View" (Skutnabb-Kangas and Dunbar) and "Linguistic Justice for Europe and for the World" (van Parijs). *Journal of Contemporary European Studies* 20(3): 377–381.

Phillipson, Robert. In press. English as threat or opportunity in European higher education. In Slobodanka Dimova, Anna Kristina Hultgren and Christian Jensen (eds.), *English-medium instruction in higher education in Europe*. Berlin: Mouton de Gruyter.

Pieterse, Jan N. 2004. *Globalization or empire*. New York: Routledge.

Ritzer, George. 2011. *The McDonaldization of society 6*. Thousand Oaks, CA: Sage.

Roberts, Andrew. 2008 (2006). *A history of the English-speaking peoples since 1900*. New York: Harper Perennial.

Roberts, Paul Craig. 2014. *How America was lost: From 9/11 to the police/warfare state*. Atlanta, GA: Clarity Press.

Rodney, Walter. 1972. *How Europe underdeveloped Africa*. London: Bogle-l'Ouverture.

Roosevelt, Theodore. 1919. Letter to R. K. Hurd, January 3. www.truthorfiction.com/roosevelt-immigration/

Skutnabb-Kangas, Tove and Robert Phillipson. 1994. Linguistic human rights, past and present. In *Linguistic Human Rights: Overcoming Linguistic Discrimination*, ed. Tove Skutnabb-Kangas and Robert Phillipson, 71–110. Berlin: Mouton de Gruyter.

Skutnabb-Kangas, Tove and Robert Phillipson. 2010. The global politics of language: markets, maintenance, marginalization or murder. In *The Handbook of Language and Globalization*, ed. Nikolas Coupland, 77–100. Malden, MA: Wiley-Blackwell.

Smith, Neil. 2003. *American empire. Roosevelt's geographer and the prelude to globalization*. Berkeley: University of California Press.
Tacitus 1948 [97–98]. *Tacitus on Britain and Germany*, translated by H. Mattingley. West Drayton: Penguin.
Trabant, Jürgen. 2012. Über die Lingua Franca der Wissenschaft. In Heinrich Oberreuter, Wilhelm Krull, Hans Joachim Meyer und Konrad Ehlich (eds.), *Deutsch in der Wissenschaft. Ein politischer und wissenschaftlicher Diskurs,* 101–107. München: Olzog Verlag.
Wierzbicka, Anna. 2006. *English: meaning and culture*. New York: Oxford University Press.
Wierzbicka, Anna 2014. *Imprisoned in English: The hazards of English as a default language*. New York: Oxford University Press.
Winand, Pascaline. 1993. *Eisenhower, Kennedy, and the United States of Europe*. New York: St. Martin's Press.

9 Through a glass, darkly

The symbols of European Empire

Russell Foster

For now we see through a glass, darkly;
but then face to face: now I know in part,
but then shall I know even as also I am known
1 Corinthians 13:12 (KJV)

Introduction

In his first letter to the Corinthians, Saint Paul illustrates a theological point with a convenient metaphor. Of course, Paul is not speaking about politics, but his words shed light on a key characteristic of visual representations and symbolic communication. In his metaphor, Paul uses the analogy of an Iron Age mirror to imply that we can never see the *reflection* of God, but only a poor *representation* through the texts and speeches of human representatives.[1] Our human eyes cannot see a metaphysical abstraction, such as *God*. Such concepts, asserts Paul, are beyond the ken of mere mortals, and the closest we can come is a crude representation which must not be confused with a reflection of the face of God.

Taking Paul's analogy, it is arguable that we also cannot see a *political* abstraction. Consider "Europe". We can see the topological, geological entity we call Europe – all that is required is a brief trip into orbit, and we can peer down at the jumbled mass of land and seas that forms the western part of Earth's largest continent, which we historically term "Europe". But while we can see *topological* Europe, we cannot see *political* Europe. The best we can do, like peering into Paul's looking-glass, is to communicate this metaphysical abstraction through symbols. Yet one drawback of visual symbols is that we look and see but through the glass, darkly. We see not a reflection but a representation of Europe. And in the case of EU symbolism, this is a representation not of what the EU *is* but what it *should be*. Not European Union, but European Empire.

In recent years, scholars and policymakers have increasingly questioned the nature of the EU (McCormick 2013; McCormick 2007; Liddle 2009; Foster 2013). As emphasised prominently by Jürgen Habermas (2013, 122), 'the European Union is at a crossroads.' The EU certainly faces various challenges, and the response of elites is to seek salvation in the emergence of an EU identity. This quest among EU elites cannot be understated. Indeed for former Dutch Prime

Minister Jan Peter Balkenende (in Poettering et al. 2006, 31), 'Europe cannot be built without people who feel European.'

It has long been recognised (Haas 1963) that a European *community* relies upon the emergence of a European *identity*. For an EU struggling to legitimise and explain its existence, and attempting to integrate 506 million people after rapid eastwards expansion and the continuing aftershocks of financial and macro-political crises, European-ness is of vital significance. Yet what does it mean to 'feel European', and how is such an identity encouraged?

Notwithstanding the debate on the extent to which a European identity exists,[2] it would be difficult to deny that there is a common "cultural heritage" to European societies. Even if there is not, and there is absolutely nothing connecting Portuguese to Poles, EU policymakers behave according to the firm conviction that there *is* such a connection (Poettering et al. 2006). Indeed the 1973 Copenhagen Declaration stressed this point emphatically; that Europe is defined by *sameness* (Beck and Grande 2008, 51). The EU seeks to build upon this "sameness" to engender a "European" identity (EPP-ED 2004) expressed through symbolism. Previous research has demonstrated the crucial importance of EU visual images and artefacts in political discourses (Wintle 2009; Sparke 2005; Thrift 2004; Walters 2002). This chapter will examine how symbols express the discourse of empire through *synecdoche* – 'images that . . . can condense the meaning of a whole narrative without linguistic mediation' (Bottici and Challand 2013, 6). This is what lends symbols their supreme power – their ability to condense vast narratives into recognisable, digestible images; a form of 'visual shortcut to the part of our minds that understands them' (Nozedar 2010, 13).

The symbols of the EU are, in the early twenty-first century, well-established (Fornäs 2012). The flag, anthem, holiday, and other markers of EU identity were created in the mid-twentieth century, and have become sufficiently entrenched in EU myth as to be inextricable (Bottici and Challand 2013, 1–14). Thus an investigation of symbols reveals the imperial imagination at the heart of the European Union. As the EU believes its various crises can be ended by *economic* means (Liddle 2009; EPP-ED 2004), this chapter examines the most visible and most emotive connection between the EU and its citizens – currency and its symbols. This link between the state and the emotions of its citizens is arguably the foundation of political life in the Union, as 'an active policy that calls . . . for a common will on the part of the member states is dependent on the motives and convictions of the citizens themselves' (Derrida and Habermas 2006, 15; in Beck and Grande 2008, 45–6).

In their impassioned speech, Derrida and Habermas highlighted that 'a European identity is no longer linked to a political identity created by constitutional norms; rather it is connoted *with common cultural norms and values.*' Grande stresses Derrida's and Habermas' proposed solution: 'European identity ought to be "thickened" by reanimating the common "cultural heritage" of Europe' (Beck and Grande 2008, 46). Since the signing of the Maastricht Treaty in 1993, the EU has increasingly transformed from a distant collection of financiers and industrialists (Haas 1963, 459–64) to an entity which has an impact on the everyday lives of its citizens – not always with positive reception. The gap between EU elites and citizens is still very large, and hence this chapter examines one of the few connections between elite visions and everyday actions. This is currency, the everyday manifestation of this elite vision. Euro currency symbols are much more recent – and change more rapidly. This iconography is still in the process of forming, and it is in currency that we see most visibly the expression of empire. Currency encapsulates the shift from a distant EEC to a mundane EU which is challenged, taken for granted, or actively applauded; from *Zollverein* to *Vaterland* (Sonntag 2011, 115–30) – at least in the hopes of EU elites. By examining the iconography on euro currency, this chapter argues that the most frequently-encountered link between EU and citizen is saturated with an imagination which suggests that the EU is nothing less than empire.

European empire

Despite being one of the apparent cornerstones of International Relations theory, there is little to no consensus on what "empire" actually *is* – as demonstrated by the manifold interpretations of empire in relation to the EU (Foster and Johnson 2014; Stivachtis 2013; Behr 2007; Böröcz 2001; Zielonka 2006). But as the proverb urges us, we need to identify a working definition. For the purposes of this chapter, "empire" is not a taxonomy of state but rather a discourse; an expression of power and ambition which is used to endow an artificial political project with *sovereignty, legitimacy, superiority, exclusivity*, and, most importantly, *destiny*.

The original Latin legal term *imperium* had, to the Romans, many meanings which need not delay us here.[3] What is significant for us is that whatever *imperium* meant to the ancient Romans, these meanings became completely irrelevant when, at a precise moment, *imperium* changed. This moment was shortly before noon on Christmas Day AD 800, when Pope Leo III proclaimed Charlemagne King of the Franks and eventual icon for twentieth-century European unification (Wilson 2005, 205–6; Latowsky 2013), as *'Imperator gubernans imperium Romanorum'*; *Emperor governing the Imperium of the Romans* (Davies 1998, 149). Again, the details of the complex international relations which led to this decision need not concern us; all that is necessary to know is that Leo and Charlemagne were grudging allies in a somewhat petty, but monumentally significant, game of political one-upmanship with the Byzantines in the East, with each side claiming to be the sole and rightful continuation of the classical Roman Empire. Pope Leo's invocation of the word *imperium* on Christmas Day was a political performance intended to claim that Charlemagne, and *only* Charlemagne, was the successor of Rome and the Romans' apparent God-given mission (in medieval minds) to unite Mankind (Le Goff 1988, 67–77). The Byzantines, convinced that *they* were the embodiment of Roman *imperium* (Gibbon 1998, 416) objected, and thus began a millennium-long diplomatic contest which spread to all European powers; a struggle for prestige in which the word *imperium* (along with its linguistic successors *empire, impero,* etc. and its vague Germanic equivalent, *Reich*) was adopted with varying degrees of success to validate the existence and ambitions of various rulers. Thus, *imperium* changed from a specific Roman legal term into a vague discourse, as societies adopted the word simply as a marker of prestige, a way to 'puff up' (Smith 2005, 274) their political projects by claiming that they alone had inherited Rome's divine mandate to unify all others, creating their own paternalistic vision of humanity as children to be brought together beneath the parental guidance of their *imperium*. It was this medieval discourse which influenced the philosophies of Early Modern and Modern Europeans, who carried this political baggage with them as they sailed around the world and encountered new societies; using the notion of *imperium* to justify planting flags on beaches, trading slaves, converting and conquering, and otherwise subordinating non-European peoples under a succession of Europeans and their emigrant offspring, all genuinely convinced that they were right because they were the inheritors of *imperium*.[4]

In this discourse we can identify a number of characteristics. First is *sovereignty* – the adopted state has sovereign power. In addition, there is *superiority* – the adopted state is not only different to others, it is better than them as it is the inheritor of a divine mission (Folz 1969). Also, *legitimacy* – the state's sovereignty is just, as it is the continuation of Rome and her mandate (Holland 2008). Connected to this is *exclusivity* – the state is not merely the inheritor of Rome, it is the *only* inheritor of Rome (Norwich 1998). And finally, *destiny* – not only does the chosen society have the sole *right* to rule, it has the *responsibility* to unite. Justifying this is a *manufactured history* which connects the present to an imagined past. This is the essence of empire: the self-righteous proclamation not only that *We are different from Them* but that *We are better than Them*, and, indeed, *We have the right and the responsibility to unite Them under Our benevolent protection, and mould Them in Our own image.*

"Empire" is best thought of as the geopolitical manifestation of *imperium*. Specific "empires" decline and fall, but the mantle of *imperium* is taken up by the new societies which emerge from the old, triumphantly proclaiming that they are the descendants of Rome. In the twenty-first century the language of empire is somewhat unpalatable (Cox 2003), but while the word might not be said out loud the discourse itself remains alive and well. Indeed, it is a discourse which can be identified, as the contributors to this volume so aptly demonstrate, in today's European Union.

Claims of European Empire vary significantly, and the essence of empire can be sought in various aspects of the EU. In this chapter, I argue not only that empire is a discourse but that the most powerful arena in which the discourse manifests, is in visual communication and the language of symbols. For it is via symbols that the visions of EU elites, and the imaginations of EU citizens, intersect. The result is the promotion – perhaps unwitting – of something which EU elites desperately desire: an identity as "European".

'Feeling European'

The EU is an unusual political project, of a kind not seen since the end of the Holy Roman Empire. This unusual entity has many of the trappings of an established nation-state, including the emotional paraphernalia of flag, anthem, motto, and "national" holiday. But, despite all of these attempts to manufacture a mythic identity for the Union, the EU lacks an identity to which citizens can affiliate. Before going further, it must be acknowledged that EU elites are not in the habit of simply making up an identity out of thin air. Albrecht Sonntag (2011, 115–30) opines, arguably correctly, that this is because the European Union has nothing capable of making an identity with which people *can* affiliate. The EU's lack of an emotional dimension is crucial, as it illustrates how the highly prized "European" identity is fundamentally imperial.

Sonntag argues that the Union suffers from a serious 'emotional deficit' (Sonntag 2011, 124), as EU citizens simply do not have the same emotional attachment to the Union that they do to their nation-states. It is difficult to have a dual identity, and as we are far more emotionally attached to the nation in whose culture we grew up, our emotional connection to a distant trade and customs union is rather meagre. This is not a trivial issue; in fact, the exact opposite. Emotional affiliation with a political project is of supreme importance. As Sonntag (2011, 124) points out, 'public opinion – and ultimately, people's political decisions – are framed to a large extent by emotions.' This has been increasingly visible in manifestations of public will – pro- or anti-EU – since the introduction of the Euro, the Eastern enlargements, and the Union's austere reactions to financial crises. Moreover, EU policymakers are keenly aware of the importance of emotion. It is not out of boredom that EU statisticians take opinion polls and laboriously toil over their Eurobarometer findings to discern peoples' opinions of the Union (Eurobarometer 2013a). This was recently made very visible in the 2014 elections to the European Parliament, which returned a substantial Eurosceptic body reflective of EU citizens' dissatisfaction and disassociation with the Union. As a result, we must consider three points. The first is that the EU's future is now, more than ever, reliant on a public sense of the Union's legitimacy. The second is that this legitimacy is reliant on citizens' affiliation with an EU identity. The third is that EU citizens' main interaction with the Union is via visual symbols, and thus an EU identity is dependent on an emotional connection with a plausible and visible manifestation of political identity via symbolic and visual language.

The relationship between legitimacy and identity has long been an issue for the EU (Haas 1958; Cafruny and Lankowski 1997). Prior to the Eastern enlargements and financial crisis, the EU enjoyed mainly *procedural legitimacy* resulting from member-states' 'superior governing performance' (Beetham and Lord 1998, 93). However the EU continues to be plagued by a 'democratic deficit' (McCormick 1986, 282) which raises challenging citizen questions about the Union's legitimacy due to a 'gap between popular will and the goals of elites who have made most of the key decisions' (McCormick 1986, 283). With Europeans' trust in the legitimacy of the Union shaken by crises of governability in the realms of finance, expansion, and migration (Liddle 2009), the EU increasingly depends upon the emergence of a coherent European identity (EPP-ED 2004). Since the signing of the Treaty of Rome, the drive for European unity has been predicated in *neo-functionalist theory*, stressing economic co-operation and assuming that a 'supranational' European identity would be formed from the 'spillover' of this integration (McCormick 2007; Sparke 2005, 239–312; Haas 1963). In the present day, this 'Gospel of Jean Monnet' (José Barroso, in Poettering et al. 2006) continues to form the basis of EU policy. Yet in recent years we have witnessed the emergence of a two-pronged strategy regarding identity.

To a significant extent, EU policymakers still assume that neo-functionalist economic integration and its spillover into civil society is *necessary* and *inevitable*. This may have been an astute stance during the early decades of a unified Europe, but since the Maastricht Treaty (1993), and particularly since the introduction of a common currency alongside rapid expansion, Europe has developed from an economic *community* dominated by elite markets and policies, to a political *union* whose socio-political impact is increasingly felt and critically perceived among European populations. Indeed this economic transformation has provided the EU with the most visible marker of collective identity – hard currency. The euro has transformed European economic integration from abstract and complicated financial deals between chief executives in bank boardrooms to a series of mundane, quotidian performances (Painter 2006) between ordinary citizens on the street. This provides the focus of our investigation – the symbols of the EU as manifest on the currency handled every day by three hundred and thirty million EU citizens. But in addition to this assumption of a spillover from economic integration, is a second aspect of European identity.

Clearly, an EU identity is actively sought by EU elites. But waiting for one to emerge organically is tedious. Meanwhile, the EU faces continuing economic woes and mounting political resistance from national groups whose dissatisfaction is increasingly audible. An identity must be encouraged. This is precisely what EU elites have done – and are continuing to do – through channels of political communication. With the rapid expansion of communications technologies and the subsequent 'ocularisation' (Rose 2012) of European society, the most powerful mechanism of promoting such an identity is the language of symbols.

Politics and symbols

> *Signs and symbols rule the world – not words nor laws.* (Foley 1993, 7)
>
> Confucius

For a polity as legalistic as the Union, Confucius' words are particularly applicable. To understand the EU as empire, we need to understand its symbols. Our word *symbol* comes through Latin from the Greek *sumbolon*, "sign of recognition". In a happy coincidence with the bringing-together that is empire, *sumbolon* comes ultimately from *σύμβολον*, or *sumballein*, "to bring together" (Whittick 1960, 4; Foley 1993, 9; Nozedar 2010, 11). Crucially, symbols act as a 'visual shortcut' (Nozedar 2010, 14) between our minds and an abstract concept. There are few polities harder to identify with than the *zollverein* that is the EU, thus its symbols are particularly important and especially illustrative of just how EU elites envision the Union. But first an important question must be asked. Why study symbols?

The easy answer is that political life *is* symbols. 'All social and economic activities are carried on by means of symbols . . . society is held together by acceptance of, and reverence for, its symbols' (Whittick 1960, 3). Previous research has demonstrated how EU artefacts and visual images communicate discourses (Ganster and Lorey 2005; Sparke 2005; Walters 2002; Foster 2013). As discourses are both language *and* practice, EU citizens' viewing of symbols continually remakes European-ness. The EU's visual images are 'spectacular expressions of state power' (Painter 2006, 752), but European-ness is made not in policies. It is made in mundane performances of the everyday: from euro cash transactions to choosing the correct queue at passport control – all of which are bound within the 'prosaic geographies of stateness' (Painter 2006), their power veiled by the sheer banality of the quotidian contexts in which they are used (Billig 1995; Anderson 1991).

Symbols are extremely powerful, connecting the citizen to elite ideals and ideologies, and are inherently imbued with political imaginations and ambitions (Foster 2013). Visual language is the first and most frequently encountered connection between citizen and state, particularly in newcomer and neighbouring states (Wintle 2009). Visual identity is a cornerstone of EU institutions' charters, encouraging European-ness through cultural technologies of rule. This contributes to an imagined community according to which *only* the EU holds legitimacy in Europe. The functionalist approach to integrating Europe relies upon the dismantling of formal borders, yet the desire to create European-ness anticipates and necessitates a new identity. This is a European identity located in citizens' interactions with symbols, and is visible in the mundane manifestations of the EU: in currency, documents, flags, and similar banal paraphernalia which simultaneously transcends frontiers while constructing a boundary between Europeans and non-Europeans.

Visual expressions of statehood persuasively express political power (Ganster and Lorey 2005) by constructing, institutionalising, and normalising European-ness through mundane symbols – whose power stems not from explicit proclamations but from their very banality and omnipresence which masks embedded discourses (Billig 1995; Foster 2013). Symbolic identity construction is therefore no longer a spillover of functionalism but an independent phenomenon whereby the banality of EU symbols causes the Union to seep into uninvolved areas of life – the EU's visual presence on currency and banal media (Billig 1995; Anderson 1991; Painter 2006, 752–55) – which contribute of the 'mundane omnipresence' (Fornäs 2012) of the EU in everyday life. Symbols constitute the initial and most frequently encountered connection between citizen and the EU, particularly in newcomer and neighbouring states (Wintle 2009; Walters 2002).

Symbols, then, are clearly of importance to citizens in the everyday context. Yet the power of symbols is not only manifest in civil society and everyday practices but also acknowledged in EU institutions' visual charters. They, too, express political power by constructing, institutionalising, and homogenising political imaginations. As their power stems from the very mundanity and omnipresence of these artefacts, visual symbols and visual rhetoric are saturated with embedded affective discourses (Billig 1995; Thrift 2004; Rose 2012). Visual symbols are fundamental to understanding political imaginations, as 'the force and effect of these mediating signs would remain a mystery if they were not ultimately rooted in . . . the very essence of consciousness' (Cassirer 1953, 105–6). In the case of the EU, these symbols express who does and does not, and who *should* and *should not*, belong in the EU, as well as claims of legitimate rule in Europe.

Of course, the EU is not the first to manufacture symbols. Those European conquerors in history who have sought to encourage a group identity have been only too aware of the power of symbols to act as rallying-points. Unfortunately Hegel's prediction was right, as European conquerors rarely heed history and end up repeating tragedies as farce. Julius Caesar, Charlemagne, Louis the Pious, Charles V, Napoleon, and even Hitler have attempted to manufacture a visual identity through symbols – and all have failed. Premodern potentates pillaged the iconography of ancient Rome, from eagles to garish coronations, to suggest that they were leading civilisation as the inheritors of Rome, encouraging a 'civilised' identity to which their disparate peoples would rally. More recently, Fascists (Klemperer 2006, 63–5) and Communists (Piercy 2013, 83–8) bombarded their European subjects with abstract icons symbolising their ideologies and the subsequent supremacy of those who emotionally affiliated with the swastika (Quinn 1994, 108–39) or the hammer and sickle (Figes and Kolonitskii 1999, 30–6). This is by no means a claim that the EU is following in the footsteps of Napoleon or Hitler by creating symbols; no more so than any multi-national megacorporation or local supermarket which encourages loyalty by creating a visual identity and expressing it in appropriate places (Napoles 1988; Chajet and Shachtman 1991). Indeed the EU is distinct from previous efforts to create a group identity as it does not shamelessly steal symbols from history, nor does it risk 'fatigue and reduce[d] receptiveness' (Sonntag 2011, 119) by plastering every available space with abstract symbols. Instead the EU has created its own symbols, solicited from Europe-wide competitions (Fornäs 2012), in order to express an imagined identity. And for multiple reasons, an EU identity can be nothing less than imagined – and imperial.

First is its lack of history. The European Union, technically, has only existed since 1992. Even if we lazily conflate it with the European Community, European Economic Community, and the European Coal and Steel Community, the lifespan of the current EU is still only a little more than half a century in age. For the majority of that lifespan, a united Europe was a distant political project only cared about by bankers, industrialists, and a handful of Franco-German statesmen (Haas 1963). It is quite a stretch to imagine that the EU, as a young polity, can have the same emotional appeal to its population(s) as a nation-state. Even if they are also largely artificial (Hobsbawm and Ranger 1983; Sonntag 2011), they are at least significantly old enough to be plausible fictions. It is even *more* of a stretch to imagine that people will politically identify with a distant, complicated, and somewhat dull network of finance treaties and fishing quotas. Exacerbating this lack of history are other factors.

Second is the lack of an effective Other against which the Self can be defined. In the absence of the Soviets, there is not a powerful enough rival to help shape

"EU-ropean-ness" (Bottici and Challand 2013, 113–44). Not even Turkey can serve as an effective *alter-Europa* to the same degree (EPP-ED 2004; Challand 2009).

Third, the raison d'être of the EU, peace, is no longer a novelty but for the new generations is simply a *fait accompli*. In effect, EU citizens embody what Norman Elias (cited in Sonntag 2011, 125–26) terms the 'fossilization of social habitus'. For those EU citizens who did not grow up amid the ashes of world war, or are too young to remember the threat of brigades of T-54s punching westwards through the Iron Curtain (Palacio in EPP-ED 2004; Bottici and Challand 2013, 113–44), the EU is no longer a peacekeeper but simply a banal entity, competing against older, far more visible, nation-states for the emotional loyalty and affective affiliation of their citizens (Sonntag 2011).

A *European* identity would therefore not be primordial but unashamedly constructivist. In the many centuries which have passed since the myth of Europa and the bull (Wintle 2009), endless investigations have sought to understand just what, if anything, separates *Europe* and *Europeans* from the rest of the Eurasian/North African landmasses and their inhabitants. The EU may triumphantly proclaim that *Europe* is defined by descent from the traditions of Ancient Greek civilisation, but there are many other versions of what defines "Europe"; religion, race, and retrospective historiography being contenders. But there is an even more vexing issue to deal with: if defining a *European* identity is tricky, defining a *European Union* identity is virtually impossible.

One thing is clear: *European* identity is elusive in the extreme, and *European Union* identity is more akin to a very weak 'brand loyalty' (Packard 1957, 171–213) than patriotism. Yet despite this, EU elites rigorously assert the need for a *European* identity. In the absence of such an identity emerging organically, there is only one option. Manufacture it. And what better medium in which to manufacture an identity, than in the banknotes and coins which slip, half-noticed, through three and a half million pairs of hands each day. Two core aspects of symbolic language (Piercy 2013, 13–16) to be examined are: the symbols themselves and the story embedded within them.

Symbols

Strictly speaking, the emblems of the EU are *associational symbols* (Whittick 1960, 5–8), their meaning elucidated through connection to "real world" entities. The first example is the name of the currency itself, in which synecdoche is embedded (Fornäs 2012). In legislation and literature we see continuous references to "the European flag" or "the European anthem"; not "the *European Union* flag". The same subtle synecdoche occurs with the name *"Euro"*. By appropriating such a word, the name suggests that it is a currency not merely for the *European Union* but for *Europe*. This leads us to a key question.

Just what *is* Europe? This seems an odd question, but it is one as old as "Europe" itself. *Where* does "Europe" begin and end? *When* did a collective European history begin? *Who* is "European" and who is not? Who *should* be "European", and who should not? For a generation who grew up with 'the mental map of Europe divided by a dotted line . . . on one side the forces of the Warsaw Pact, on the other the forces of NATO' (Palacio, in EPP-ED 2004, 181), does Russia – or an increasingly divided Ukraine – count as 'European'? What about Turkey, with whom Europeans have had a love-hate relationship since the Fall of Constantinople (Mansel 2005)? What about those countries in Western Europe – Norway, Switzerland, and microstates such as Monaco and the Holy See – who do not want to be part of the Union? Euro currency answers all of these questions with symbols.

Crucial to these questions is the issue of the frontier. In the words of Jacques Barrot, vice president of the European Commission, 'a definition of Europe's borders is essential for any reflection on European identity' (EPP-ED 2004, 41). The EU's currency skirts around these tricky questions by avoiding words, instead providing a graphic answer using convenient map.

In the modern world we are saturated with maps. We use them on a daily basis and we trust maps to be accurate, even though they are fundamentally incapable of showing the world as it is (Foster and Johnson 2014). Like St. Paul in this chapter's epigraph, we look at a map and see through a glass, darkly; for we see not a faithful *reflection* but a simplistic *representation*.

By using maps, the EU has unwittingly stumbled on the most powerful of tools with which to harness the affective, emotional bond upon which the legitimacy of the state depends (Sonntag 2011; Bernays 1952; Tye 1998). Yet, the maps which appear on euro currency are not merely representations; they are supreme expressions of empire.

According to the symbolism of the Euro, "Europe" is easily defined. Not least because the European Union and the continent of Europe are indistinguishable. Firstly, there is no distinction between EU states within the Eurozone, and those beyond. Sweden, Hungary, the United Kingdom, Denmark – these are portrayed by the maps as being part of the same currency area as those countries which do use the Euro. This does not merely result in confusion for travellers; this visual synecdoche implies that the Eurozone and the EU are the same entity. The synecdoche does not stop here. As is visible, EU currency maps go one step further by suggesting that the Eurozone, the EU, and the *entirety of the European landmass* are the same. According to these maps, not only is the euro legal tender in Copenhagen or Andorra, but the Union itself includes all of Europe and its inhabitants from the Atlantic to the Urals. This visual synecdoche is apparent, yet there is one further element of these maps which provides the 'visual shorthand' (Nozedar 2010, 13) which EU elites desire – they show not only who *is* European and who *should* be European, but who is *not*. The coins conveniently cut off Turkey from their maps, and while Turkey appears on the banknotes, it is clearly excluded from Europe. Alongside the states of North Africa, it appears in a pale shade which stands in sharp contrast to the heavy hue used to denote the main landmass of Europe, which cuts off at one traditional frontier of "Europe": the Urals. These maps are extraordinarily revealing.

It is essential to note that, prior to 2007, euro coin maps were slightly more accurate in that they included the outlines of European countries (although, inexplicably, non-Eurozone countries were shown, too). Such maps effectively portrayed the Union as *United in Diversity*: an assembly of countries sharing a common bond. Yet, in 2007 the maps were changed by the European Central Bank to denote the whole of Europe without internal borders, yet still cutting North Africa and Turkey out of the picture. The message proclaimed via these maps is clear – the message that this is what Europe *is*, and this is what the European Union *should be*. This is the nature of the Euro currency map – a political part representing a continental whole, and vice-versa – an emblem sufficiently similar to a specific image for its viewers to recognise it, yet sufficiently abstract to convey political unrealities. Indeed, the icon must be vaguely recognisable, for currency iconography functions according to 'mimetic verisimilitude' (Strassler 2009, 89); the public's ability to recognise symbols and icons in state-affiliated media as expressions of authority and assurance.

These maps not only facilitate synecdoche, they justify it, publically proclaiming a vision of European identity which offers an immediate border. For these maps, the European Union's border is not between the European Union and its non-EU neighbours, but instead between *all* Europeans on one side and *everyone else* on the other. They are imperial maps *per excellence*, and their imperial synecdoche is only further strengthened by the iconography's narrative – symbolic stories which spell out a completely imaginative history of Europe not as it was, but as it ought to have been.

Symbolic stories

Grande (Beck and Grande, 2008, 53) suggests that 'Europe's borders . . . cannot be found in a "common" history, culture or geography. Europe's borders must be defined politically'. The Euro's currency maps would suggest quite the opposite; that Europe's borders *can* be defined geographically. Yet, the maps are not alone on euro currency. appearing alongside them are symbols which suggests that 'a "common" history', one which EU policymakers so strongly desire (EPP-ED 2004), does indeed exist. These symbols are pictures of architecture. They are *symbols* as the bridges and gateways depicted on Euro currency are not representations of real-world buildings, but are imaginary constructs which enhance an imperial imagination.

On the reverse of Euro banknotes we see a triumphalist history of a united Europe – a history which is quintessentially imperial as it never existed and instead has been manufactured to suggest a legitimacy for the EU as the apex of a historical 'sameness'. On the reverse of the €5 we see a bridge and gateway in classical Graeco-Roman architecture. This establishes a historical theme which is developed in other banknotes. On the €10, we see a bridge and gateway in Romanesque style; on the €20 Gothic style; on the €50 Renaissance style; on the €100 Baroque; on the €200 Victorian architecture; and finally, on the €500, a modern industrial style. According to the European Central Bank (2015), the notes 'feature architectural styles from different periods in Europe's history'. But they are not a depiction of Europe's history. Instead, they correspond to an imaginary teleological development of Europe as a single community which has experienced a single (and suspiciously bloodless) history; a progressive march towards destiny with the accompanying suggestion that *all* Europe experienced the same neat path of development at the same time. It is no coincidence that the bridges and gateways adorning these notes and intersecting with the maps of Europe are a chronological account stretching back to an imagined beginning – Rome. They express the mantra of EU elites that Europeans can be defined by a shared history and shared cultural norms.

It is notable that these icons are completely fictional. Their designer, Robert Kalina, expressed (Fishman and Messina 2006, 28) that 'the idea was to create a feeling of commonality, of belonging. I worked hard so that either an Italian or a Frenchman could look at the Gothic windows on the €20 and say "That could be here in France" or "That could be here in Italy".' But this expresses a discourse of superiority which excludes those 'Other Europes' (Bottici and Challand 2013) which do not fit into this manufactured linear descent. This iconography 'deliberately constructs a common European historical memory' (Kaelberer 2004, 170) by appealing to a mythical Europe which can be traced back to Graeco-Roman civilisation. But this is simply not true. It is quite a stretch to claim that Sweden or Latvia were part of the same Classical world as Greece and Rome, equally problematic to visually proclaim that the eras depicted were single, homogenous affairs. Yet the discourse remains – the proclamation that *all* Europe has experienced the same history, that *all* Europe is the same, that *all* Europe stands in contrast to those beyond the collective – the Russians, the Turks, the North Africans – who did not share in this version of a communal continental history which never existed, but nevertheless is propagated to give the illusion of sovereign legitimacy. It is 'Europe . . . all around us, yet nowhere in particular' (Helleiner 2006, 1). Entwined with the map, the discourse suggested by these icons is ultimately imperial.

Euro currency maps convey the ideology that all EU citizens are part of the same Union, but the images entwined with the map exclude those areas of the Union which were not part of this imagined descent from Graeco-Roman civilisation and did not experience the same historical epochs as Western and Southern Europe. At the same time as they exclude rival versions of history and those who do not fit in its narrative, these symbols corral together Europeans who are not part of the Union. They depict not what the European Union *is* but what it *should be*, they express who is and who is not "European", and they conflate the EU with Europe to symbolically declare that there is only one legitimate sovereign on the European landmass – justified by its manufactured, unreal history – whose duty and destiny it is to unite the European peoples. This is a symbolic vision which would be recognisable to Napoleon and Charlemagne; a vision not of European *Union*, but of European *Empire.*

So far we have examined the content of EU currency symbols. But content itself is meaningless without an understanding of context. Abstract symbols are incapable of expressing a newly-formed concept, including the European Union. The circle of stars, for example, has absolutely no meaning unless it is explained either directly of associatively (Lock and Peters 1996, 615–53). Instead, association must be enabled by equating an abstract symbol (in this case the EU's flag) with a more immediately recognisable icon; a form of visual determinative whereby the recognisable symbol explains the abstract symbol. EU iconography is more than the sum of its parts, for it is through iconography as a whole that political ambitions are communicated from elites to citizens (Bernays 1952).

However, the process is not quite so easy. Attempts to construct a top-down European identity have historically been met with skepticism (McCormick 2007; McCormick 2013; Maas 2007); yet, following sixty years of successful European integration, the existence of a degree of European-ness cannot be denied (Barroso in Poettering et al. 2006). The discourse exists. Yet this discourse itself is not merely theoretical – it is both language *and* practice (Müller 2008), being continually re-formed and reinforced through everyday actions (Thrift 2004).

Despite the desire to create this European identity, one cannot be built out of thin air, and no amount of treaties or decrees will create the affective, emotive bond which Europeans have with their nation-states (Sonntag 2011). This is especially so as the mountains of paperwork on identity formation generated by the European Commission and Parliament are not actually *read* by European citizens (Eurobarometer 2013b, 1). European citizens' relationship with the Union is not in its dry and complicated publications but in the visual symbols we encounter on a daily basis. These symbols form a visual discourse and a 'mundane omnipresence' (Fornäs 2012) that is saturated with the normative goal of producing a visual discourse of what it means to be "European". This visual discourse is itself theory, language, *and* practice, and is continually reformed and reinforced through everyday actions of citizens encountering the EU through symbols (Wintle 2009; Thrift 2004). This triumphalist symbolic narrative is omnipresent but only half-noticed. Blue and gold flags flap half-heartedly outside civic centres and council chambers. The EU emblem lurks in the corner of our eyes as we shuffle into lines at passport control, or quietly nestles in our peripheral vision on the 'co-financed infrastructure construction site, on euro banknotes, on our car number plates, or even integrated into corporate logos' (Sonntag 2011, 116). Symbols clearly do not exist in isolation: they demarcate and define the physical manifestations of the Union and connect citizen to state. These symbols are ultimately rendered far more powerful than the sum of their parts by their prosaic existence.

The EU's visual images have been described as 'spectacular expressions of state power' (Painter 2006, 752). Of vital significance is the affective power of these images which is difficult to identify because this emotive quality is masked by the quotidian, or "daily", contexts in which they are used (Lüdtke 1995; Billig 1995; Anderson 1991). Maps of the Union (or what the Union *should be*) do not gather dust in untouched atlases – they make grandiose appearances every time a European buys a sandwich or queues up at the cash machine. Symbols of the EU's destiny to unite Europe are not restricted to elevators and hallways in the office-blocks of Brussels: they proclaim their bold, bright message each time an EU child receives their pocket money or an EU pedestrian tosses loose change to a saxophonist in the subway. Visions of who is a "European" and who is not – and the synecdochal blurring of EU and Europe – are not closeted away in desk drawers at the European Commission but are continually circulating between purses, hands, and cash registers. Thus currency colonises what Alf Lüdtke (1995) terms "*Alltagsgeschichte*", or "everyday narratives": the prosaic banalities of everyday existence which do not merely reflect political imaginations but which *create* the emotions that are the foundations of political actions (Sonntag 2011; Thrift 2004; Anderson 1991). Integral to this process are the symbols on currency which connect the citizen with the state. It is in these symbols and the half-acknowledged performances (Thrift 2004) in which they are deployed that the phenomenal power of EU visual symbols lies – not in their explicit acknowledgement but in their very mundanity.

The desired European identity is produced not only by EU policies, but far more significantly by routine performances which are bound within the 'prosaic geographies of stateness' (Painter 2006), becoming increasingly proliferate – as noticed by EU policymakers (Barroso, in Poettering et al. 2006).

This 'ethno-symbolism' (Wintle 2009) of the EU is achieved by appropriating 'the anthem, national colours, and images of historic events' (Jakubowska 1990, 10) to unify the population. What renders this act *imperial* is that the imagined community is unequal. It is unequal spatially between the established core and the parvenu peripheries. It is unequal temporally, between those who are already in the Union and those whose destiny is that they are yet to be absorbed. It is unequal ideologically, between those who may be deemed civilised, and those whose savagery is swept aside by synecdochal symbols which represent not only the Union but *all* Europe. The fact that not all Europeans are citizens of the Union is irrelevant – the map makes it clear that it is the Union's destiny to unite them all.

The discourse embedded within is clear. Europe and the Union are synonymous, a synecdoche, and it is the destiny of the Union to spread its borders and embrace the peoples of Europe into the imagined community they have constructed; a community which declares that only *Our* way is legitimate, that only *We* are sovereign, and that the duty to unite is taken up by *Us*. There is no room for alternatives. There is only the Union, and those whose ultimate destiny is to take their rightful place as members of one imagined community.

As Grande (2005, 45) identifies, 'one commonality that runs through all of the definitions [of "European identity"] is that by emphasising a European "we", the concept is based on constructions of some kind of "sameness". This is precisely the theme that we see in the prosaic iconography of the Union. We only need to glance at the banknotes to see this – bridges and gateways, symbols of progress and unity, which themselves are modelled in a chronological and teleological sequence dating back to Graeco-Roman civilisation. These express "our" Europeanness. But just who belongs in this vision, and who does not belong? Where do the Swedes, the Irish, or the Latvians fit into Graeco-Roman culture? Where is the Slavic, Byzantine, or Khrushchevian architecture of Eastern Europe? Why does the Circle of Stars encompass non-Eurozone peoples like the Danes and the British, or indeed why are the Norwegians and the Swiss, who are not in the

EU, included? And where, outside of an iconographer's imagination, did history progress in a neat, uninterrupted sequence from Roman to Carolingian, Gothic, Guelph, Baroque, fin de siècle, and art nouveau?

There is an easy answer to all of these questions – *empire*. Who belongs and who does not belong is irrelevant; instead these iconographies show who *should* and who *should not* belong in the European project. What happened in history, regardless of historians' debates, is less significant in these iconographies than what *should have happened* – a neat, sanitised, remarkably dull visual record of Europe progressing triumphantly through the ages towards a bright future defined by bridges and portals. And, ultimately, what the European Union *is* is far less relevant than what, according to these maps, the European Union *should be*. The actual past, present, and future of the Union; borders and membership statuses and accession negotiations; the actual cultural dynamics and spatial relationships of European populations, do not matter. What matters is what Europe's past *should have been*, what its present *should be*, and what the future *should become*. This normative triumphalism is the heart of *empire*.

Through cartography and iconography, a synecdoche appears wherein the Union and the European peoples become conflated. There is only *one* legitimate sovereign in Europe, these artefacts proclaim, its legitimacy assured by a manufactured memory cementing an imagined community (Anderson 1991), its presence guaranteed through prosaic political symbolism so ubiquitous as to be almost invisible. They function as 'memory theatre' (Atkinson and Cosgrove 1998, 28): those public displays of iconography and symbolism designed to convey 'official rhetoric' to the people. This is evident in two ways – synecdoche, and a manufactured history. They proclaim that the European Union is the *exclusive, legitimate sovereign* of Europe. It *does* rule and it *should* rule. And, like empires past, this political ambition is justified through a manufactured history which claims that the EU is the continuation of a united past. Crucially, these symbols provide what the EU lacks.

It was argued earlier that EU elites' desire to manufacture an EU identity is hampered by the absence of three keystones – a collective history to which they can appeal, an effective Other to help define the Self, and public sympathy for the peace provided by a unified Europe since 1945. The symbols adorning EU currency provide these three aspects. They offer a historical narrative which claims that the EU *should* rule, because Europe has always been united. They visually identify a handy Other, in the form of those who may border Europe but who are not, and never will be, European. And finally they symbolically state a new raison d'être for the Union – not the passive preservation of peace, but the active accumulation of all Europe. Indeed, this is presented as a fait accompli; the embodiment of manifest destiny. It is perhaps ironic that the pioneers of European integration in the 1950s looked to Charlemagne for inspiration, as the EU's current visual symbols express a form of political mission which would be familiar to the *Imperator*. For these humdrum symbols, ultimately, express *empire*.

Conclusions

The European Union is ultimately beneficial (McCormick 2013), yet it is arguable that Mitrany's 1963 prediction has manifested: 'the regional concept is not the triumph of the new internationalism but only an extension of the old nationalism' (Haas 1968, 46). Certainly, the EU is reliant on the same mechanisms of the old nation-states – symbolic language designed to appeal to citizens' emotions and foster the affective, emotional identification with the Union on which statehood and legitimacy rely.

The post–Berlin Wall era of EU expansion is drawing to a close. In May 2014 the governments of Russia, Belarus, and Kazakhstan formed a trading bloc in direct, explicit competition to the European Union – effectively preventing the EU from expanding any farther into Eurasia. Europe's *geopolitical* identity is perhaps soon to be finalised. Yet, while expansion may be slowing, the *social* identity of the Union, through its presence in the everyday lives of its citizens, is growing rapidly. The Union's leaders continue to seek a "European" identity to unite all Europeans within and without the Union, and pursue this goal through symbolic language. Yet, despite growing citizen hostility to the Union's presence in daily life, the Union's policymakers continue to base political practices on an increasingly obsolete functionalist foundation, assuming that national identity will become subordinate to supra-nationality. What we are seeing is the *recreation* of exclusionary discourses of empire in the imagined community of the European Union.

If the Union is to continue to develop or even exist in the face of growing dissatisfaction among European peoples, policies must reflect an awareness of the crucial importance of citizen participation and affiliation (Thrift 2004). People who '*feel* European' increasingly form their emotional connections (or lack thereof) to the Union not through the explicit politics of the polling station, but in response to EU symbols and icons permeating and producing the mundanity of everyday life. Ultimately European-ness is being made not by politicians in Brussels and Strasbourg, but by citizens queuing at passport control or exchanging euro cash, being continually reaffirmed in those prosaic, banal interactions which cement the concept of European-ness in everyday life (Ganster and Lorey 2005; Sparke 2005; Walters 2002; Painter 2006).

Perhaps Edgar Grande (Beck and Grande, 2008, 46) is right to claim that 'the debate on "European identity" must be considered as a "dangerous obsession" which could seriously obstruct the integration project as a whole'. Sonntag's recommendation that the EU abandon its attempt to propagate a pseudonational identity argues from a similar standpoint; namely that a distant, complicated, elite-driven technocracy such as the EU cannot have the same emotional and affective appeal as a nation-state (at least not yet), and any attempt to foster such a sentiment is misguided. Grande is right to call for citizen participation on forming a political identity, supported by Sonntag's demonstration that identity cannot be formed from top-down processes. To create such an identity requires *symbols*. As a community, the European Union is too complicated, too distant, too new, and frankly too boring (Sonntag 2011) to have the affective, emotional appeal of the nation-state which preceded each of us, within which each of us grew up, and whose symbols each of us has lived with on a daily basis for the whole of our lives. *Zollverein* is not *vaterland*. In its effort to make the EU seem more than a customs union, the Union has unleashed a visual bombardment of symbols, expressing an identity that is not *European Union* but *European*. But the consequence of this is that the identity in formation is imperial, for the Union symbolically and synecdochally annexes *all* Europe to a Union which has symbolically emerged as the apex of an illusory history, while visually pointing out those who will *never* be welcome.

In these symbols we can identify the exact same characteristics which signify the discourse of empire. We see sovereignty – the *zollverein* of the EU has, according to these symbols, greater sovereign power than the *vaterland*. In addition, there is superiority – Europe is not only different to non-Europe, it is better than them as it is the inheritor of a collective history. The Union has legitimacy – the EU's sovereignty is just, as it is the continuation of a mission and mandate to unite the Europeans. The EU's rule is exclusive – it is not merely the continuation of a false history, it is the *only* inheritor this history. And finally, the EU is an expression of manifest destiny – not only does the Union have the sole right to rule Europe, it has the responsibility to unite as the Union brings peace and progress as expressed through its symbols. Justifying all this is a manufactured history which connects the EU present to an imagined European past (Foster: in press). This is the essence of European Empire: the symbolic story not only that Europe is different from Them but that Europe is better than Them, and indeed Europe has the right and the responsibility to unite Them under Europe's benevolent protection, and mould Them in Europe's own image.

The maps and the iconography of the EU are a permanent celebration of a progressive march of history, an imagined community, a clear visual statement of who is welcome and who is not, and a whitewashed version of how European history ought to be imagined. These ideals are expressed not in one-off speeches or dense tomes of treaties and ratifications, but in prosaic, banal, everyday visions. The use of EU symbols in formal political settings is rather rare. Even the European Commission was obliged to drop efforts to legalise the familiar symbols of the Union in the 2007 Lisbon Treaty. Yet these formal uses are comparatively insignificant next to the everyday appearances which we barely notice. Looking at the symbols circulating in our everyday lives, we see not a true depiction of the Union but rather a conflated image; not a *reflection* of Europe but a *representation*, and a representation not of what Europe *is* but what it *should be*. In St. Paul's words, we see through a glass, darkly. And what we see is not European Union – it is European Empire.

Notes

1 More modern versions of the Bible offer more comprehensible, if somewhat less dramatic, versions. The NIV uses 'Now we see but a poor reflection in a mirror'.
2 On this issue, see, among others, Maas (2007); Dunkerley et al. (2002); Hansen and Weil (2001); Sonntag (2011).
3 For a fuller discussion of the meanings of *imperium*, see (Richardson 2008).
4 A narrative known to medieval Europeans as *translatio imperii*. See (Folz 1969, 228).

References

Anderson, B. 1991. *Imagined Communities: Reflections on the Origin and Spread of Nationalism*. London: Verso.

Atkinson, D. and D. Cosgrove. 1998. Urban Rhetoric and Embodied Identities: City, Nation, and Empire at the Vittorio Emanuele II Monument in Rome, 1870–1945. *Annals of the Association of American Geographers* 88(1): 28–49.

Beck, U. and E. Grande. 2008. *Cosmopolitan Europe* [trans. Ciaran Cronin]. Malden, MA: Polity.

Beetham, D. and C. Lord. 1998. *Legitimacy and the European Union*. London: Longman.

Behr, H. 2007. The European Union in the Legacies of Imperial Rule? EU Accession Politics Viewed from a Historical Comparative Perspective. *European Journal of International Relations* 13(2): 239–262.

Bernays, E. 1952. *Public Relations*. Norman: Oklahoma University Press.

Billig, M. 1995. *Banal Nationalism*. London: Sage.

Böröcz, J. 2001. Empire and Coloniality in the 'Eastern Enlargement' of the European Union. In Josef Böröcz and Melinda Kovács (eds.), 'Empire's New Clothes: Unveiling EU Enlargement', 1–305, *Central Europe Review*. http://aei.pitt.edu/144/01/Empire.pdf.

Bottici, C. and B. Challand. 2013. *Imagining Europe: Myth, Memory, and Identity*. Cambridge: Cambridge University Press.

Cafruny, A. and C Lankowski. 1997. *Europe's Ambiguous Unity: Conflict and Consensus in the Post-Maastricht Era*. Boulder, CO: Lynne Rienner.

Cassirer, E. 1953. *The Philosophy of Symbolic Forms Vol. I: Language*. New Haven: Yale University Press.

Chajet, C. and T. Shachtman. 1991. *Image by Design: From Corporate Vision to Business Reality*. Reading, MA: Addison-Wesley.

Challand, B. 2009. From Hammer and Sickle to Star and Crescent: The Question of Religion for European Identity and a Political Europe. *Religion, State and Society* 37/1: 65–80.

Cox, M. (2003). The Empire's Back in Town: or America's Imperial Temptation – Again. *Millennium* 32(1): 1–28.

Davies, R. 1988. *A History of Medieval Europe: From Constantine to Saint Louis*. Harlow: Longman.

Dunkerley, D., L. Hodgson, S. Konopacki, T. Spybey and A. Thompson. 2002. *Changing Europe: Identities, Nations and Citizens*. London: Routledge.

Eurobarometer. 2013a. *European Citizenship: Report*. Brussels: European Commission.

Eurobarometer. 2013b. *Media Use in the European Union*. Brussels: European Commission.

European Central Bank. 2015. www.ecb.europa.eu/euro/banknotes/html/index.en.html. Accessed 3 April 2015.

Figes, O. and B. Kolonitskii. 1999. *Interpreting the Russian Revolution: The Language and Symbols of 1917*. New Haven: Yale University Press.

Fishman, R. and A. Messina, eds. 2006. *The Year of the Euro: The Cultural, Social, and Political Import of Europe's Common Currency*. Notre Dame, IN: University of Notre Dame Press.

Foley, J. 1993. *The Guinness Encyclopaedia of Signs and Symbols*. London: Guinness Publishing.

Folz, R. 1969. *The Concept of Empire in Western Europe: From the Fifth to the Fourteenth Century*. Frome: Edward Arnold.

Fornäs, J. 2012. *Signifying €urope*. Chicago: University of Chicago Press.

Foster, R. 2013. *Tabula Imperii Europae*: A Cartographic Approach to the Current Debate on the European Union as Empire. *Geopolitics* 18(2): 371–402.

Foster, R. In press. *Tabulae Imperii Europaei: Mapping European Empire*. London: Routledge.
Foster, R., M. Edward, and M. Johnson. 2014. *The Crisis of the Twenty-First Century: Empire in the Age of Austerity*. Abingdon: Taylor and Francis.
Ganster, P. and D. Lorey, eds. 2005. *Borders and Border Politics in the Globalizing World*. Lanham, MD: Rowman and Littlefield.
Gibbon, E. 1998. *The Decline and Fall of the Roman Empire* [abridged by Antony Lentin and Brian Norman]. London: Wordsworth.
Grande, E. 2005. *Complex Sovereignty. Reconstituting Political Authority in the 21st Century*. Toronto University Press, Toronto.
Haas, E. 1963. *Beyond the Nation-State*. Berkeley, CA: Stanford Press.
Haas, E. 1968. *The Uniting of Europe*. Berkeley, CA: Stanford Press.
Habermas, J. 2013. *The Crisis of the European Union: A Response* [trans. Ciaran Cronin]. Cambridge, MA: Polity.
Hansen, R. and P. Weil, eds. 2001. *Towards a European Nationality*. Basingstoke: Palgrave.
Haas, E. 1958. *The Uniting of Europe*. Stanford: Stanford University Press.
Helleiner, E. 2006. One Money, One People? Political Identity and the Euro. *TIPEC Working Paper* 1(6): 1–31.
Hobsbawm, E. and T. Ranger (eds.). 1983. *The Invention of Tradition*. Cambridge: Cambridge University Press.
Holland, T. 2008. *Millennium*. London: Abacus.
Holy Bible: Authorized King James Version. 1988. Oxford: Oxford University Press.
Jakubowska, L. (1990). Political drama in Poland: The use of national symbols. *Anthropology Today* 6(4): 10–13.
Kaelberer, M. 2004. The euro and European identity: symbols, power and the politics of the European monetary union. *Review of International Studies* 30: 161–178.
Klemperer, V. 2006. *Lingua Terti Imperii: The Language of the Third Reich*. London: Bloomsbury.
Latowsky, A. 2013. *Emperor of the World: Charlemagne and the Construction of Imperial Authority, 800–1229*. Ithaca, NY: Cornell University Press.
Le Goff, J. 1988. *The Medieval Imagination*. Chicago: University of Chicago Press.
Liddle, R., ed. 2009. *After the Crisis: A New Socio-Economic Settlement for the EU*. London: Policy Network.
Lock, A. and C. Peters. 1996. *Handbook of Human Symbolic Evolution*. Oxford: Clarendon Press.
Lüdtke, A. 1995. *Histoire du Quotidien*. Paris: Maison des Sciences de l'Homme.
Maas, W. 2007. *Creating European Citizens*. Lanham, MA: Rowman and Littlefield.
Mansel, P. 2005. *Constantinople: City of the World's Desire, 1453–1924*. New York: St. Martin's.
McCormick, M. 1986. *Eternal Victory: Triumphal Rulership in Late Antiquity, Byzantium, and the Early Medieval West*. Cambridge: Cambridge University Press.
McCormick, J. 2007. *The European Superpower*. Basingstoke: Palgrave.
McCormick, J. 2013. *Why Europe Matters*. Basingstoke: Palgrave.
Müller, M. 2008. Reconsidering the concept of discourse for the field of critical geopolitics: Towards discourse as language *and* practice. *Political Geography* 27: 322–338.
Napoles, V. 1988. *Corporate Identity Design*. New York: Wiley.
Norwich, J. J. 1998. *A Short History of Byzantium*. London: Penguin.
Nozedar, A. 2010. *The Illustrated Signs & Symbols Sourcebook*. London: HarperCollins.
Packard, V. 1957. *The Hidden Persuaders*. New York: Ig Publishing.
Painter, J. 2006. Prosaic Geographies of Stateness. *Political Geography* 25: 752–774.

Piercy, J. 2013. *Symbols: A Universal Language*. London: Michael O'Mara Books.
Poettering, H., et al., eds. 2006. *Our Vision of Europe in 2020*. Brussels: European Parliament.
Quinn, M. 1994. *The Swastika: Constructing the Symbol*. London: Routledge.
Richardson, J. 2008. *The Language of Empire: Rome and the Idea of Empire from the Third Century BC to the Second Century AD*. Cambridge: Cambridge University Press.
Rose, G. 2012. *Visual Methodologies: An Introduction to Researching with Visual Materials* [3rd Ed.]. London: Sage.
Smith, J. 2005. *Europe after Rome: A New Cultural History, 500–1000*. Oxford: Oxford University Press.
Sonntag, A. 2011. False Expectations: The Counterproductive Side Effects of the EU's Use of Political Symbols. In S. Lucarelli, F. Cerutti and V. Schmidt, eds. *Debating Political Identity and Legitimacy in the European Union*. London: Routledge.
Sparke, M. 2005. *In the Space of Theory: Postfoundational Geographies of the Nation-State*. Minneapolis: University of Minnesota Press.
Stivachtis, Y. 2013. The English School and the Concept of "Empire": Theoretical and Practical/Political Implications. *Global Discourse* 3(1): 1–17.
Strassler, K. 2009. The Face of Money: Currency, Crisis, and Remediation in Post-Suharto Indonesia. *Cultural Anthropology* 24(1): 68–103.
Thrift, N. 2004. Intensities of Feeling: Towards a Spatial Politics of Affect. *Geografiska Annaler* 86: 57–78.
Tye, L. 1998. *The Father of Spin: Edward L. Bernays and the Birth of Public Relations*. New York: Henry Holt.
Walters, W. 2002. Mapping Schengenland: Depoliticising the Border. *Environment and Planning D* 20: 561–580.
Whittick, A. 1960. *Symbols, Signs, and their meaning*. London: Hill.
Wilson, D. 2005. *Charlemagne: The Great Adventure*. London: Hutchinson.
Wintle, M. 2009. *The Image of Europe: Visualizing Europe in Cartography and Iconography Throughout the Ages*. Cambridge: Cambridge University Press.
Zielonka, J. 2006. *Europe as Empire: The Nature of the Enlarged European Union*. Oxford: Oxford University Press.

Index

FSC
www.fsc.org
MIX
Papier | Fördert gute Waldnutzung
FSC® C083411

Kolibri 360 GmbH
Ferdinand-Jühlke-Straße 7
99095 Erfurt, Deutschland
produktsicherheit@kolibri360.de